LAUS DEO

Selections From My Articles In Canada Free Press

by Jim O'Neill

Laus Deo

ISBN 978-1-4700-6899-8

Acknowledgments

First of all I would like to thank Judi McLeod, editor of "Canada Free Press," for welcoming me there and keeping my stay as easy and rewarding as it has been. A tip of the hat is also in order for Brian Thompson who has done a yeoman's job of formatting and adding graphics to my articles (I saved the one of me looking like a hobbit).

Thanks are in order to Arlen Williams at "Gulag Bound" where I have also submitted my articles. I have no idea where Arlen gets the time and energy to do all he does.

I would like to thank the men and women of our armed services, who have sacrificed, are sacrificing, and will sacrifice so much for America. In addition I would like to extend a heartfelt and hearty hooyah! to members past and present of the UDT/SEAL community

I wish to thank my lengthy list of faithful email correspondents: Tom, Kelleigh, Ernest, Wanda, Vic, Van, Dave, Duke, JB, Sarge, Molly, Joan, Jan, Bob, Rob, John, Linda, Diane, Pat, Carmel, Carlos, Carmen, Mary, Joyce, Scotty, Michael, Robert, Tony, Vonda, Barb, Butch, Holly, and the many others too numerous to name — you know who you are (I just *know* I have forgotten one or two that I should have mentioned). Your input and feed-back are always valued and much appreciated.

Thank you to my fellow writers on the Internet (especially the ones on CFP) who have kept me informed and inspired.

My thanks go out to Lucianne Goldberg who pointed me in the right direction toward a literary agent, and her sons Jonah for writing "Liberal Fascism," and Joshua for his help with "Lucianne.com." The memory of the righteous will be a blessing.

Special thanks and love go to my mother — my best friend and most avid supporter. I have been blessed with her comforting, encouraging, and inspiring presence for many years. Thank you God.

Thanks and love goes to my step-father Bob for being a solid rock, a loving anchor for us all for so many years. To my siblings: Clark, Kate, and Mike — you have each in your own way made my life fuller, happier, and more interesting then it would have otherwise been — I love you all. My love to their families as well, especially Susan, Xana and Becky. And I send a prayer out in loving memory for my father Michael J. O'Neill.

My love to my daughter Shaner — I have considered her to be a blessing since the day of her birth. My love also to her husband, Pastor Britt Johnson.

Love and thanks to Jayne and her family, especially her mother Martha. Jayne is a blessing in my life that came, as Bonnie Raitt sang, in the "nick of time." I love you sweetheart.

I wish to give special thanks to my spiritual mentors. Especially Pir Vilayat Inayat Khan with whom I was privileged to share dashan in 1975, and the writings and teachings of Alan Watts, Dr. David R. Hawkins, Don Miguel Ruiz, Jelaludin Rumi, Ekhart Tolle, Paramahansa Yogananda, Roy Eugene Davis, Ram Dass, Brother Lawrence, Thich Nhat Hanh, Sogyal Rinpoche, Henry Drummond, Ken Willber, D. T. Suzuki, Eric Butterworth, Emmet Fox, and the many others who have had such a profound and positive impact on my spiritual growth over the years.

Last, but certainly not least, I wish to express gratitude to my Creator — especially for the balm of power, peace, and love poured upon me by Jesus my savior. May God bless America.

Laus Deo!

Contents

Preface

One of the benefits of writing for the Internet is the luxury of linking to other related material. I once asked a friend how long it took him to read one of my articles and he replied "about 5-6 hours." I was somewhat taken aback but realized "of course, if you read all of the links it could easily take that long."

Researching the links for my articles often takes about as long as writing the article itself — and that is saying something, for like Nathaniel Hawthorne I find that "easy reading is damn hard writing."

In any event, since this publication is for profit I decided to dispense with the links included in the original articles lest I inadvertently stray into legally treacherous territory. (Not to mention the "difficulties" involved in trying to link on hard-copy). :)

A few words on my habit of ending my articles with "Laus Deo:" I first read about the words "Laus Deo" (Praise God) being inscribed on the top of the Washington Monument in Newt Gingrich's little book "Rediscovering God in America: Reflections on the Role of Faith in Our Nation's History and Future."

I was struck by how the words, and where they were placed, tied together God and country; faith and the Founding Fathers in a beautifully succinct and understated way. Shortly after reading Gingrich's book in 2009 I wrote an article and ended it with "Laus Deo." I consider the return of America to the Constitution and its spiritual roots to be of such importance that I have made a habit of ending most of my articles with "Laus Deo" ever since.

Introduction

I have been told by those who know about such things that "books of articles don't sell" and that "you need to write a *real* book, not a compilation."

Nonetheless, I have chosen to publish a book consisting of some of my past articles because (1) although some of the references that they contain are dated, they are by and large still quite topical (and in any event of historical interest), and (2) I see no need to reinvent the wheel just so I can put my thoughts into a more marketable format. The articles work fine together as either stand-alone chapters or as an overview of a crucial period in America's history.

If it will help the reader the articles can be viewed as comprising the chapters in a non-fiction account of the ongoing destruction of the United States and Western civilization — and how that destruction was resisted. They can also act as a primer for those not up to speed regarding some of the more glaring problems we face today.

I have arranged the "chapters" in chronological order with the dates given when they were first published. I have revised each of the articles that appear here and taken the opportunity to fix any typos, and polish sentences and paragraphs.

Perhaps the main problem with self-editing for me is that I tend to see what I *meant* to type instead of what I *did* type. Consequently, I as often as not find a few typos and such in my articles after they are posted. To be afforded the opportunity to revise them once more is something I value.

Any changes that I have made have been largely stylistic ones. I have added a brief introduction to each article.

Godspeed and Laus Deo, Jim O'Neill — January, 2012

1

Heather Mallick is a Poo-Poo Head

September 25, 2008

This was the first article that I wrote for CFP, which makes it my first article period. I was researching a vicious hit piece that Heather Mallick wrote about Sarah Palin and I came across an article written by Judi McLeod, the editor of "Canada Free Press."

I wrote to Judi complimenting her on the article she wrote, and to make a long story short, ended up submitting my own article to her on the subject. The title is by way of underlining the immaturity inherent in ad hominem attacks. Not my finest article by any means, but not bad for a first attempt, IMHO. Feel free to skip ahead to the next "chapter" if you would prefer a topic with more gravitas.

As is now well known, Heather Mallick posted a childishly malicious attack against Sarah Palin on Mallick's CBC (Canadian Broadcasting Corporation) sponsored blog-site. I generally don't like *ad hominem* attacks at all – whether they come from the left or the right of the political spectrum, but I found Mallick's comments about Governor Palin to be especially mean and distasteful.

Ad hominem attacks are nothing new – especially in political circles, and they will be with us for the foreseeable future. That being the case, it behooves us to better understand what they are. *Ad hominem* means "against the person" and is a type of fallacious (illogical) argument that attacks a *person* instead of the *issues*. It is a type of reasoning that says,

"I can't attack your *logic*, so I'll attack the way you look, sound, and live – I'll attack *you*."

A few of Mallick's *ad hominem* comments will suffice to show the tenor of her article: "...she [Palin] isn't even female really." "Palin has a toned-down version of the porn actress look..." "Palin [is] vicious and profoundly dishonest." "[Palin adds] nothing to the ticket that the Republicans didn't already have sewn up, the white trash vote." And so on, *ad nauseum*.

Mallick's rant against Governor Palin is close to being a parody of an *ad hominem* attack, and is almost funny in its excess. Almost. If Mallick's article had appeared in some extreme left-wing blog-site I'd have said, "Everyone's entitled to their opinion," and let it go. But her article was not relegated to some fringe-element website – it was published under the auspices of the Canadian Broadcasting Corporation, and that is disturbing.

That the publicly funded (your tax dollars at work) CBC would publish trash like Mallick's article is indefensible. It does not matter which political candidate we endorse, we should find mean-spirited, vulgar, vitriolic slander to be objectionable, if not repulsive. The CBC should be fostering a national consciousness of fair play and tolerance, instead of propagating such venomous propaganda.

No doubt the CBC explains away Mallick's comments under the banners of "thought provoking" and "controversial." The CBC might as well call Nazi Joseph Goebbels' efforts "thought provoking" and "controversial." That the CBC has chosen to infect others with this type of inflammatory soul-sickness is troubling indeed.

I watched Canadian journalist David Warren offer his comments about Mallick's article, when he appeared on Fox News. Mr. Warren straddled the fence so adroitly that by the end of the interview I was not sure if he was condemning or condoning Mallick's article. One point he made, however, I found very especially interesting. He said that Mallick's article merely put into print what everyone says around the water-cooler at work.

I would suggest that Mr. Warren start frequenting a different water-cooler. I find it hard to believe that *all* Canadians spend every free moment gossiping about how horrid and tacky Governor Palin is. Good God, what a myopic viewpoint!

As we all know, the left-wing media (read that as almost all media) is startlingly blind to opinions that differ from their own. Their condescendingly antagonistic idea of "fair reporting" is laughable. If your opinion differs from theirs, then obviously "You just don't get it"—either because of mental deficiency, bad genes, or a poor education. That a conservative person might actually have important, valid, and sensible things to say "does not compute" with them.

So it does not come as a shock to me that the CBC would pander to the extreme left-wing. But it should bother Canadians on both sides of the political fence. Using tax dollars to promote hate-mongering is not something most Canadians would condone – I suspect. Then again, maybe I'm hanging around the wrong water-cooler.

2

A Well Groomed and Polished Trojan Horse

October 7, 2008

This article written before the Presidential election of 2008 begins with the question "Who is Barack Obama—really?" It is several years later, and I am still asking that question. Who is he — really?

Who is Barack Obama—really? He appeared on the national scene, seemingly out of nowhere, and became the Democratic Party's candidate for President. He has a laughably thin political track record. His major accomplishment while in office has been running for another office. We know he's an uncommonly slick snake-oil salesman, who's adept at writing disingenuous, self-promoting books. What else do we know? The Presidential Election is fast approaching, and time's running out. So, who is this guy?

In regard to his higher education; we know when and where he went to school—Occidental College, Columbia, Harvard—but that is about it. Obama's school records are kept under lock and key. Is there something in these records that Obama wants kept hidden?

How about the elusive thesis Obama wrote while at Columbia? His thesis would give the electorate some insight into his ideology during that formative period in his life. Obama is silent on the subject and, golly-gee, Columbia says it can't find any copies of the thesis – if it they ever existed. Obama's professor at the time claims that Obama spent a year writing this nonexistent thesis. Curiouser and curiouser.

What about Obama's religious values? What sort of faith guides his decisions, and acts as his moral compass? Let's take a look at reverend "God damn America" Wright—(I use reverend with a lower case "r" because Wright does not deserve the honorific "Reverend."

Anyone who has heard Wright's inflammatory, venom-filled rants knows that the "reverend" is about as spiritual as an anti-personnel mine. The warped and twisted logic that spews forth from this bigoted and treasonous demagogue would be laughable, if it were not for the fact that his "flock" buys into his garbage.

This is the reverend who claims that the U.S. government invented AIDS as a means of waging genocide against Afro-Americans. This is the reverend who is on record and video saying, "Not, God bless America—God damn America!"

This is Obama's spiritual mentor. This is the reverend that married him and Michelle. This is the reverend that baptized their two children. This is the reverend that was Obama's religious teacher for twenty years.

When reverend Wright's hate filled propaganda became public knowledge, Obama tried to downplay it. He compared Wright to "an old uncle who says things I don't always agree with." The public didn't buy Obama's ploy—so, for politically expedient reasons Obama cut Wright loose and disavowed him.

After twenty years of close association Obama "discovered" that reverend Wright was wrong? At the best, Obama does not appear to be a very astute judge of character.

What about Bill Ayers—unrepentant homegrown terrorist? In the 1960s and 70s Ayers was a prominent member of a group of violent radicals called the Weathermen. Ayers summed up his philosophy as: "Kill all the rich people. Break up their cars and apartments. Bring the revolution home; kill your parents."

A notable quote from Ayers: "There's something about a good bomb..." Something indeed. Most people would consider the term "good bomb" to be an oxymoron – but not Ayers.

Ayers is now a professor at the University of Illinois; he served with Obama on the board of the Woods Fund of Chicago for three years, and hosted a dinner at his home to help launch Obama's political career in 1995.

Obama says that he hardly knows Ayers. Listening to Obama one would think that he and Ayers only have met briefly, while waiting in line at a grocery store long ago, in a galaxy far, far away. There's more if you like fairy-tales.

Why does Obama deny being associated with so many of his associates? Why do Middle East terrorist groups support him? What about Obama's close ties with ACORN, Freddie Mac and Fannie Mae? What about his relationship with the racist Louis Farrakhan? What about his associations with Rashid Khalidi , Rezco, and Nadhmi Auchi? Why do we know so little about this man? What is he hiding? What is his real agenda?

In an article he wrote about Obama, Ed Lasky pointed out the dangers of an uninformed electorate being lead by an unexamined candidate. Time is running out people. We need to know the truth about Obama before it is too late.

I do not believe that Obama is merely an under-qualified and opportunistic politico. If only it were that simple. I have come to believe that Obama is a well-groomed and polished Trojan Horse poised to enter the White House. If Obama is elected President it will not be "God bless America," it will be "God help America." Don't say you weren't warned.

3

A Clear and Present Danger

October 14, 2008

As you can see, I was still "playing nice" with Democrats at the time I wrote this article. My attitude in that regard has undergone a sea change since then — as has my attitude toward the GOP.

Strange days indeed.

Merriam Webster's Dictionary of Law defines a "clear and present danger" as being "a risk or threat to safety or other public interests that is serious and imminent." You may be sure that Barack Obama's agenda poses a serious and imminent threat to the United States.

Before I explain that charge, let me make a couple of facts very clear: I am not a right-wing extremist, nor am I a racist. I do not have much patience for left or right extremism, and I find racism of any type moronic and evil.

I have no axe to grind with moderate Democrats. I find some of their ideas sound, and worth looking into. I am a Republican not because I think Republicans have a monopoly on the truth, but because I identify more strongly, more often, with the Republican viewpoint.

I have no interest whatsoever in slamming Obama because he is a Democrat, or black, or liberal. I do believe he is a serious threat to the United States, however—a threat of historic proportions, and potentially catastrophic consequences.

While the media pundits have been parsing statements made in the Presidential Debates and discussing "issues," Obama has been steadily positioning himself to destroy the United States as we know it. Hiding in plain sight; this trojan horse for Marxist Socialism, Islamic Extremism, and Black Racism is now poised to enter the White House. How many votes do you think Obama would get running on the "Marxist/Islamic/Black Panther" ticket? He is not stupid, you know.

Behind Obama's facade of "liberal Democrat" is a sly, intelligent, charismatic, dishonest, and implacable enemy of a free, democratic, capitalistic, and powerful United States of America.

The above paragraph is not ideologically driven hyperbole. Let us look at some of the facts. Because of the large number of areas of concern surrounding Obama, I will list only some of the more troubling areas. Every one of these areas is deeply disquieting, and should disqualify Obama from becoming POTUS.

Honesty: Obama lies like it is an Olympic event. Yes, I realize that all politicians lie at times, but Obama has raised the bar so high that even Bill Clinton is probably in awe. Obama has never met a fact he could not obfuscate; an attack he could not sidestep, or a truth he could not twist. The guy is more slippery than an eel in a vat of K-YJelly.

He lies, and lies to cover his lies, with such speed, style, and *savoir faire* that I freely admit I'm impressed. I'm concerned, angry, and distrustful—but impressed. Obama's undeniably a world-class fibber, but do we really want a President with an almost supernatural flair for mendacity?

ACORN: The "Association of Community Organizations for Reform Now" is a government funded, ballot-box stuffing, front for the Far Left. Their *modus operandi* revolves around radical activism which includes, but is not limited to, threat and intimidation.

Obama has worked for, helped organize, and legally defended ACORN. He is in ACORN up to his neck, and ACORN is committed to destroying capitalism from within. Again, that is not hyperbole, but simply the truth.

A strong case has been made that ACORN is one of the key instigators of the current financial chaos. ACORN cajoled and threatened banks into issuing loans to unqualified people – i.e. subprime loans. Banks were intimidated into making loans that no sane financial institution should ever issue. Destruction from within.

Look at what a mockery ACORN is currently making of the election process. If Obama wins, this may well be the last free election the U.S. ever holds. He is not even President and look at what ACORN is doing. Imagine what they will do with Obama *as* President. Please do not dismiss this as overblown rhetoric – investigate ACORN with an unbiased eye and see what conclusions you come to.

Racism: Black Liberation Theology (BLT) got off the ground with the publication of Reverend James Cone's book "Black Theology and Black Power" in 1969. BLT is a complex issue, but one may be forgiven for feeling that the following quote by Cone is a tad racist: "If God is not for us and against white people, then he is a murderer, and we had better kill him. The task of black theology is to kill gods who do not belong to the black community."

If you check out Black Liberation Theology on the Internet you will find a wealth of apologia. I have not seen such "bobbing and weaving" since the last Sugar Ray Leonard fight.

My favorite "bob and weave" comes from Dwight Hopkins, a professor at the University of Chicago Divinity School. Hopkins defends BLT Jeremiah "God Damn America" Wright, by saying that the word "damn" in the original Hebrew "means a sacred condemnation by God to a wayward nation who has strayed from issues of justice, strayed from issues of peace, strayed from issues of reconciliation."

OK, then—"God damn" all the egomaniacal demagogues from Bin Laden to Wright who twist, pervert, and debase spirituality so that they can further their own sick, intolerant, hate-filled agendas. I mean that, of course, in the ancient Hebrew sense.

The point here is that Obama was married by a Black Liberation reverend (Jeremiah Wright), and had his children baptized by Wright, and attended services led by Wright for twenty years. To hear Obama tell it, every service of Wright's he attended consisted of holding hands and singing "Kumbaya." I don't think so. I think that hearing twenty years of sermons espousing black racism and anti-American sentiment would leave an indelible mark on anyone.

Rabid racist and "Nation of Islam" leader Louis Farrakhan has called Obama "The Messiah." Here is a quote of Farrakhan's worth pondering: "Barack has captured the youth...That's a sign. When the Messiah speaks, the youth will hear, and the Messiah is absolutely speaking."

On multiple levels, this is really dangerous stuff— "The One," "The Chosen One," "The Messiah." Do we really want a demi-god Messiah in the White House?

Terrorism: The United States of America is currently involved in a global war with Islamic terrorists. Ring a bell with anyone?

Obama has, I believe, carried on a clandestine relationship with un-repentant terrorist Bill "just a guy in the neighborhood" Ayers. Obama's wife Michelle worked at the same law firm as Ayer's wife Bernadine ("just a gal in the neighborhood") Dohrn. Dohrn herself is no slouch when it comes to radicalism. Do you think it is a coincidence that there is a connection between these four?

Raila Odinga, Kenya's Prime Minister, is a radical Marxist, and mili-tant Muslim; he also belongs to the same tribe (Luo) as Obama's late father. Obama has conferred with Odinga in person, by phone, and by e-mail. Odinga claims to be Obama's cousin.

Obama's stepfather was a Muslim, as is Obama's half-brother Obongo (Roy) Obama. Obama's family tree is chock full of members of the Islamic faith. There is, of course, nothing wrong with that, but we are at war with rabid fringe elements of Islam that hide their all too worldly hatreds behind a cloak of religion.

I just do not think that it is real smart to have a Commander in Chief with such myriad close ties to Islam and unrepentant terrorists, when we're in the middle of a war with Islamic terrorists. Call me peculiar.

The biased liberal media will *not* investigate Obama. A hard-hitting, in-depth liberal media "investigation" would sound something like this:

Liberal Media: "Excuse us sir, but uh, well there are rumors that you have lied. "Are these accusations true?"

Obama: "Of course not."

Liberal Media: "That's what *we* thought—sorry to bother you."

Obama: "Not a problem."

No problem, indeed. The liberal press will give Obama a "free pass" on these issues until it is too late. In the meantime "Truth squads" will intimidate; liberal comedians will ridicule, pundits will dismiss, and Obama will charm.

It is up to readers such as you to get the truth circulating among the general public. A wide and rapid dispersal of the truth about Obama is urgently needed. Time is running out.

This is not some sideline distraction from the main issue. This *is* the main issue, and don't let anyone tell you otherwise. Maybe I am wrong; maybe Obama is simply some hapless bad judge of character with an unfortunate proclivity for stumbling into radical extremists. But I would not bet my country on it.

4

The Death of Journalism

October 29, 2008

Written in my callow "still friendly to Fox News" period. Ah, the halcyon days of youth — such trust, such innocence, such stupidity.

"During times of universal deceit, telling the truth becomes a revolutionary act."

George Orwell

Welcome, fellow revolutionaries—let us share some truth. Sean Hannity has said that "Journalism is dead," by which Hannity means that *objective* journalism is dead—journalism that attempts to be fair and balanced. In its place we have *partisan* journalism—journalism that acts as a mouthpiece for a particular party, candidate, or social agenda.

Okay, we have partisan journalism. The question is why is almost all journalism, *liberal* journalism? Why is the main-stream media (MSM) almost universally in the tank for Obama?

Look at some figures: Pew Research – considered the "golden standard" of polls — recently confirmed that 70% of Obama's press coverage is *positive*. The same poll showed that 60% of MSM's coverage of McCain has been *negative*. The MSM doesn't just give us biased or slanted news – they feed us "news" with quote marks around it. It is partisan propaganda, pure and simple.

Fortunately, the American people are becoming more and more aware that the MSM is feeding them a dishonest leftist version of the political scene. The same Pew poll found that 70% of voters felt that the MSM favors Obama, whereas only 9% felt that the MSM favors McCain. The MSM is solidly behind Obama, and anti-McCain. The facts and figures prove it and common wisdom acknowledges it.

To get back to my original question – why? Why does the MSM lean so heavily to the left? Is it because reporters tend to be liberal by temperament, or because the professors who taught them are so liberal, or is it peer pressure?

I believe it is all the above. I have researched polls going back to the early 1960s and they show that the vast majority of reporters have historically been liberal. It appears that reporters tend to be liberal by temperament – the profession *draws* liberals to it. That being the case, it is axiomatic that most journalism professors will be liberal and will teach journalism with a liberal slant.

That peer pressure is a factor almost goes without saying. The majority of "news" organizations are liberal from top to bottom – from the editor down to the copy boy.

Don't you think there is pressure to conform; to be "one of the gang;" to be intelligent, hip, and "enlightened?" Of course there is pressure – intense pressure.

We know that the MSM is an Obama mouthpiece and we know why. The question now becomes why does the MSM continue to claim that they are *impartial* purveyors of the news when it is obvious that they are no such thing?

The MSM is not impartial; not objective, and not balanced

The only major network with any legitimate claim to having "fair and balanced" coverage is the Fox network, and they are in a league of one. They have no serious competition —every other network is, to a greater or lesser extent, a propaganda outlet for Obama. The MSM's lack of investigative enquiry into Obama's background has put the USA at grave risk and the MSM is mostly oblivious to it.

There is reason for hope though. Barbara West of WFTV in Orlando stumped Senator Biden recently, by asking him a real question. The Obama camp is still sulking about it.

So fess-up MSM. Stop pretending you are *real* news reporters and admit that you are merely leftist sycophants who have given Obama a free pass throughout the Presidential campaign.

5

Country First

January 20, 2009

This article is a personal embarrassment — best swept under a rug and forgotten —but I include it because I want to show that the articles about Obama that came afterward were not done out of any malicious spite — I sincerely hoped that he would turn out to be no worse than Bill Clinton.

A pretty low bar I grant you, but I was perfectly prepared to put up with four years of liberal nonsense. Except that what we got, of course, was not liberal nonsense but straight, undiluted, Marxist/Fascist destruction and a historically corrupt, inept, and tyrannical regime. (The less said about my support for McCain at the time the better — live and learn).

I fully intended to hang up my writer's hat after this, and not write any more articles for the foreseeable future. If you would like to see an example of "attitude adjustment" read the rest of this book.

The United States of America has a new Commander and Chief. A new President that I did my best to see defeated in his bid for the Presidency. So, how am I dealing with it? How do I feel about it? I am cautiously hopeful.

President Obama does not appear to be the extreme left-wing radical that I had feared he was. Actually he seems to be pretty pragmatic and grounded. True, he's a leftist Democrat, and that's regrettable, but it is certainly not a cause for anger or despair.

We have dealt with Democrats in the past, and we will deal with them in the future. Democrats are sometimes unbelievably dense and misguided, but they are nonetheless a vital part of the fabric of our free and Democratic Republic.

I have seen ten Presidential Administrations come and go—six of them Republican, and four of them Democratic. Now we have the beginning of the fifth Democratic Administration of my lifetime. So the administrations are now about evened out. Which is as it should be.

Over and over I've watched the pendulum swing back and forth from one extreme to the other. The long-term end result is a nation that is balanced and on even keel. Sinking—but balanced and on even keel. It is time for us, as a unified nation, to start bailing with a will and raise our Ship of State once more.

Yes, I would have been happier if John McCain had been elected, and yes the Democrats have an inordinate amount of benighted scatterbrains in their ranks—but Obama has been elected President, and elected by a large undeniable margin.

He is now POTUS, President of the United States. I respect the fact that he was freely elected and that the majority of Americans voted him in.

The pendulum will swing back; the Republicans will regroup, rethink, reinvent themselves, and return. Sooner rather than later one hopes.

But for now President Obama is the freely elected leader of my country, and my Commander in Chief during time of war. I wish him good luck and Godspeed.

During the election I wrote an article for CFP in which I said that I would apologize to Obama if he turned out to not be the extreme radical that I feared he was. Consider this article to be that apology.

Now, lest some of you radical-left, tree-hugging nitwits think I'm going soft in my dotage, let me assure you that I fully intend on continuing to oppose your lame-brained left-wing lunacies with gusto and vigor.

I have become cautiously hopeful, not an idiot.

6

Rules for Radicals: a Blurred Vision

June 13, 2009

This was the first piece that I wrote after my kumbaya farewell article following Obama's Inauguration in January. I had resigned myself to the Obama Administration and was planning on not writing any more political commentary for some time — but like many Americans I sat up and took notice as one puzzling, confusing, and/or outrageous bill after another wound its way through Congress during the first half of 2009.

I said to myself "whoa — all stop — what in the world is going on here?" Knowing of the popularity that Saul Alinsky's book "Rules for Radicals" enjoyed among the intelligentsia and liberal elites I decided that perhaps I had better start there if I was to uncover what was happening to America.

I bought a copy of "Rules for Radicals" and read it carefully and thoroughly, page by page, line by line, making annotations and comments as I went along. It took me about a week of painstaking reading to untangle its obfuscating web of lies and deceit. I was amazed that seemingly intelligent people would give such garbage more than a passing glance. What I found was essentially a manifesto for narcissistic sociopaths.

Alinsky, because of his formal education, was able to put a thin (very thin) veneer of sophistication on what is otherwise a crude Machiavellian mish-mash of Marxism and Chicago Mob-style extortion tactics designed to create havoc and destroy civilized institutions in order to grab power.

Two of the signature ideas that he was so very proud of were the world's first "Fart In," and its first "S—t In." Liberals have all but canonized this thug.

My article was reposted when I found out that the NEA, (the teacher's union — the nation's largest), was promoting "Rules for Radicals" as suggested reading for America's teachers.

"Everyone thinks of changing the world, but no one thinks of changing himself."

Leo Tolstoy (1828-1910)

Saul Alinsky's book "Rules for Radicals," first published in 1971, has been read and assimilated by a number of those who espouse a Far Left agenda. Our current Secretary of State, Hillary Clinton, wrote her senior thesis on Alinsky while at Wellesley College. The following excerpt is from that paper.

"Much of what Alinsky professes does not sound 'radical.' His are the words used in our schools and churches, by our parents and their friends, by our peers."

Perhaps in *your* world, Madam Secretary — certainly not in mine.

My point here is that "Rules for Radicals" has had a far-reaching impact, especially on "community organizers" from Chicago — Alinsky's home turf. America's current POTUS, for example, is no doubt familiar with Alinsky's "blurred vision." This is a term I have taken from the book, where Alinsky describes the organizer's mental map as a "blurred vision of a better world." Blurred indeed.

Running throughout "Rules for Radicals" is a whiny refusal to take personal responsibility for anything. It is always "their" fault. Who "they" are, and what "their" faults are, changes from scenario to scenario, but one thing is constant — the "haves" are to blame for the state of the "have-not's."

It is a perpetrator/victim dualistic mythology straight out of Marx and Lenin. This "professional victim" mind-set caters to the infantile narcissistic ego, at the expense of spiritual and emotional growth, integrity, and character. But I'm getting ahead of myself, let me start at the book's beginning.

Alinsky begins "Rules for Radicals" with a dedication to Lucifer: "...the first radical known to man who rebelled against the establishment and did it so effectively that he at least won his own kingdom."

Right at the start of the book we get a foretaste of the vapid illogic that permeates "Rules for Radicals." Alinsky, an avowed atheist, inadvertently implies God's existence. After all, in the Luciferian mythos who does Lucifer rebel against? God, of course — a God that does not exist according to Alinsky. So *God* does not exist, but *Lucifer* who opposes God does? You figure it out, I can't.

This is as good a time as any to point out that Alinsky's book promotes what is sometimes called the Luciferic inversion — where good is bad, morality immoral, and ethics unethical — and one might add, where thinking is thoughtless. More about that in a bit.

In order to get to the essence of the subtle venom that infests "Rules for Radicals," I would like to bring attention to one of the more poisonous heroes in the Alinsky pantheon — Niccolo Machiavelli (1469-1527).

Machiavelli's book "The Prince" has the distinction of being perhaps the most evil book ever written. Stalin, who was responsible for the deaths of many millions of his country's men and women kept a copy of "The Prince" on his nightstand — just the thing for bedtime reading.

Alinsky knew his Machiavelli so well (so he thought), that he felt qualified to point out Machiavelli's "weak spots" — where Machiavelli dropped the ball, so to speak. "Machiavelli's blindness to the necessity for moral clothing to all acts and motives,,,was his major weakness," Alinsky says.

Au contraire Saul; Machiavelli had it covered. In "The Prince" Machiavelli writes that actually *having* morals and ethics was to be avoided like the plague, but the *appearance* of having such values (moral clothing) should be assiduously cultivated.

"[It is] *not* necessary for a prince to have [mercy, faith, compassion, honesty, and spirituality], but it *is* necessary to *appear* to have them. ...Having them...is harmful...*appearing* to have them is *useful.*" (Italics added)

Compare that to Alinsky's tenth rule of Ethics of Means and Ends, "You do what you can with what you have and clothe it with moral garments."

In other words, *appearance* is everything. The truth must be cloaked in glamour, verbal legerdemain; smoke and mirrors. Sound like any politicians you know?

Alinsky quotes Machiavelli in support of his (Alinsky's) position regarding selfishness, (*after* quoting that renowned advocate of egotism, Jesus Christ).

"Machiavelli with whom the idea of *self-interest* seems to have gained its greatest notoriety, at least among those who are unaware of the *tradition*, said, 'This is to be asserted in general of men, that they are ungrateful, fickle, fake, cowardly, [and] covetous...'" (Italics added).

Charming. Alinsky's point here is that Machiavelli is notorious *only* among us clueless sheep who don't comprehend the great value of the "tradition" of self-centered megalomania. Tradition? How about an infantile narcissistic pathology.

(An aside here: Freud called this sort of self-centered grandiosity the King Baby. A human infant, unable to fend for itself, comes to *expect* that all its needs will be taken care of – food, milk, diaper change, etc. This is all well and good so far as it goes, but when the infant grows into a child, and then an adult, and *still* expects the world to cater to his or her every need then we have a problem – the King or Queen Baby. Such people invariably have a God complex — more about that in a moment).

Regarding egotism Alinsky says, "Ego, as we understand and use it here, cannot be even *vaguely* confused with, nor is it *remotely* related to egotism." (Methinks he doth protest to much). (Italics added)

In the very next paragraph he writes, " The organizer is in a true sense reaching for the highest level for which man can reach — to be a great creator, to play God." So sayeth Saul "Not Vaguely or Remotely Egotistical" Alinsky.

I am speechless before such transparent duplicity. I am not sure whether to drop my jaw in awe before Alinsky's outrageous chutzpah, or shake my head in pity at his delusional blindness.

Machiavelli promotes another vile dictum — the end justifies the means. Combine an ego "playing God," with an "end justifies the means" mentality, and you have the recipe for disaster. Karl Marx combined these two attitudes; as did Lenin, Stalin, Hitler, Mao, and Pol Pot — to name a few.

Combined, these individuals have been responsible for the deaths of over 100 million people. This unholy pathological mentality is known as "malignant messianic narcissism." Sounds like something you definitely do not want to step in. Alinsky not only steps in it, he wallows in it, and urges his "organizers" to follow suit.

Does the end justify the means to Alinsky? You bet. This is from his book, where he quotes Bertrand Russell, "...obviously nothing has any value as a means unless that to which it is a means has value on its own account. It follows that intrinsic value is logically prior to value as means." Actually, Bertrand, it does not follow at all.

When you cut through Russell's pretentious jargon, what he's saying is that the end is of more importance than the means — that the goal is more important than the means you use to get there. This is akin to saying that it doesn't matter how you get from New York to San Francisco — flying or crawling — getting to the destination is what is of paramount importance. After about a week of crawling you might change your mind about that.

Contrary to what many might believe, in circumstances involving moral values the means used to get to an end are of vital importance to one's emotional, mental, and spiritual health.

Alinsky's stance regarding the ends being more important than the means is rather odd, because earlier in his book Alinsky states that the organizer's *raison d'être* — a secular utopia — is a *non-attainable* end. "If we think of the struggle as a climb up a mountain, then we must visualize a mountain with *no top*. [Like Sisyphus we are] pushing a boulder up an *endless* mountain." (Italics added)

So the "end" in Alinsky's blurred vision is *nonexistent* — but the end justifies the means? You figure it out, I can't.

All glibness aside, the whole "end justifies the means" attitude can, and has, lead to horrendous consequences. Lenin and Stalin justified their brutal regimes by claiming that all the horror they inflicted upon their "comrades" was done in order to bring into existence a worker's utopia. If you were suspected of being a hindrance to the realization of this utopian pipe-dream then you were shot or sent off to the gulags. No joke.

Alinsky would excuse such behavior, because "...in action, one does not always enjoy the luxury of a decision that is consistent with both one's individual conscience and the good of mankind. The choice must always be for the latter. He who sacrifices the mass good for his personal conscience...doesn't care enough for people to be corrupted for them."

So according to Alinsky, people like Hitler and Pol Pot must have been extremely caring people indeed. Gives me the warm-fuzzies just thinking about how caring they were.

What else can we add to this poisonous Machiavellian mix? Let's throw in some relativism — why not? Alinsky writes, "All definitions of words, like everything else, are *relative*." (Italics added)

"Like *everything else*" — got it?

This does not stop Alinsky from quoting dictionaries when he wants to define words in "Rules for Radicals." You figure it out, I...never mind.

Alinsky quotes Lewis Carroll in his book, and I'll swap quotes with him.. Here's my quote by Carroll, "When I use a word,' Humpty Dumpty said in rather a scornful tone, 'it means just what I *choose* it to mean - neither more nor less." Carroll was ridiculing such nonsense; Alinsky takes such nonsense as gospel.

When Alinsky says "like everything else," he *means* everything. He writes, "[The organizer] knows that *all values* are *relative*, in a world of political relativity." (Italics added)

It is such an attitude that enables Alinsky to write, "[Knowing] the *universal principal* that the right things are *always* done for the *wrong* reasons...the organizer...should *search* for and use the *wrong* reasons to achieve the *right* goals. He should be able to use *irrationality*...to progress toward a *rational* world." (Italics added)

That doesn't even look good on paper — let alone as a reality. Let me see if I have this right: A community organizer uses the *wrong* reasons and *irrational* thinking in order to achieve a rational *but* nonexistent goal? Oy vey.

Remember when I mentioned "thinking is thoughtless?" Well, although Alinsky was intelligent and widely read, he was no friend to logic and reason. In fact, as might be obvious by now, they were barely on speaking terms. You won't find *me* ever accusing the Far Left of being rational. Clever, duplicitous, and often intelligent? Yes. Rational? No.

Alinsky writes in "Rules for Radicals," "...a revolutionary or a man of action does not have the sedentary frame of mind that is part of the personality of the research scholar. He finds it very difficult to sit quietly and think.... He will do anything to avoid it."

Alinsky is speaking of himself. Lest we miss the point, he underlines it by writing "...the fact is that I did not want to come to grips with thinking. I welcomed...excuses to escape the *ordeal* of thinking" (Italics added). Ordeal indeed, if "Rules for Radicals" is anything to go by.

The logical fallacies that keep cropping up in "Rules for Radicals" are so numerous that one comes to expect them at every turn, and begins to feel something is amiss if a page or two goes by without *some* sort of bogus premise.

Alinsky's view of the "man of action" or *Übermensch* (Alinsky admiringly quotes Nietzsche), as being superior to the person who thinks things through before acting, is infantile at best. Contrary to Alinsky's opinion, being reasonable and logical does not automatically condemn one to a lifetime of wearing milk-bottle glasses, tweed jackets, and parsing ancient Greek.

Alinsky — no friend to thinking — advises his protégées to get arrested periodically, so as to *force* themselves to gather their thoughts. Good avuncular advice. He writes that being thrown in jail is good because, (1) it gives you that extra *caché* that every "revolutionary about town" needs, and (2) you have no option but *to* think, so you may as well write a book.

We are not talking about any *serious* jail time mind you— just enough to give you a certain *je ne sais quoi*, and maybe write a bestseller. Why not? It worked for Hitler.

Speaking of Hitler — Adolf wrote "*Mein Kampf*," while serving jail time (as per Alinsky's instructions), after a failed *putsch* or revolution. Given Alinsky's description of what makes a good revolutionary — sorry, "organizer" — you would think he would be praising Herr Hitler from the roof tops as the *ideal* community organizer template.

Hitler inflamed, agitated, organized, and was a rabble rouser *par excellence* — and to top it off, he overthrew the establishment! He is a pitch perfect example of Alinsky's man of action — the *Übermensch!* — but nary a word about Adolf in "Rules for Radicals." No doubt Alinsky was only following the Far Left's dogma that the Nazis must *always* be incorrectly associated with the *right*-wing, and that their roots in Mussolini's *left*-wing totalitarianism forever be denied and hushed up.

Moving on...but, before I move on, I should forewarn you that the next few paragraphs may seem crude to some readers. If so, please accept my apologies in advance and feel free to skip ahead a bit.

Now moving on, let us discuss some of the s—t Alinsky tries to pile up. I mean literally, as in his aborted (thank you Lord for small favors) plan to tie up the restrooms at Chicago's O'Hare airport in order to extort some concessions from the city. (Alinsky associated with Chicago's criminal element and it shows in his extortion-racket tactics). He envisioned the proposed O'Hare technique as "...the nation's first 's—t in'." Ha, ha.

He also writes about another plan that never materialized, which revolved around a bunch of folks eating huge quantities of beans and then attending a black-tie affair where they would commence a "fart in." Ha, ha.

Alinsky says that the planned "fart in" didn't happen because, "The threat of this tactic was leaked (there may be a Freudian slip here...so what?)." Ha, ha. Alinsky's rapier-like wit never fails to send a trickle down my leg. Ha, ha.

We are not out of the excrement yet. In "Rules for Radicals" we read that "The one thing that all oppressed people want to do to their oppressors is s—t on them." So sayeth Saul "Poo Poo" Alinsky, mentor to the liberal *intelligentsia*. Thanks for the visual Saul.

One cannot help but wonder what type of unfortunate potty training young Alinsky suffered through in order to have such a scatological view of life. I think that he had some unresolved issues to deal with. Rather, I *know* he had some unresolved issues.

Be that as it may, we now come to the actual "rules" in "Rules for Radicals." Here they are, all 13 of them from the chapter "Tactics:"

1. Power is not only what you have but what the enemy thinks you have.
2. Never go outside the experience of your people.
3. Whenever possible go outside the experience of your enemy.
4. Make the enemy live up to their own book of rules.
5. Ridicule is man's most potent weapon.
6. A good tactic is one that your people enjoy.
7. A tactic that drags on too long becomes a drag.
8. Keep the pressure on.
9. The threat is usually more terrifying than the thing itself.
10. The major premise for tactics is the development of operations that will maintain a constant pressure upon the opposition.
11. If you push a negative hard and deep enough it will break through into its counter-side.
12. The price of a successful attack is a constructive alternative.
13. Pick the target, freeze it, personalize it, and polarize it.

I am not going to go into each of these rules one by one. There is ample information on the Internet for those who wish to delve into them. I do, however, wish to discuss a couple of the rules.

First, a few words concerning Rule #5 — ridicule. The radical Left has taken this one to heart and polished it to a glowing luster. Alinsky calls ridicule humorous, although it usually is not. It is most often a mean-spirited venom that *masquerades* as humor, and its pernicious effects permeate our culture.

Ridicule in its most common guise is expressed in vitriolic *ad hominem* attacks. Ex-President Bush and Governor Palin are two of the best known recent recipients of such "humor."

(A short aside: One of the few bright spots to emerge from the vociferous attacks against Governor Palin has been the "outing" of the women's movement. Their blanket silence in the face of the attacks against Palin is extremely telling — you can hear crickets chirp and grass growing).

That is enough about Rule #5 and ridicule. The *key* rule in "Rules for Radicals" is Rule #13: Pick the target, freeze it, personalize it, and polarize it.

I say it is *key* because Alinsky spends a minimum amount of time explaining all of the other rules — sometimes giving no explanation at all, and at most a paragraph or two. But with Rule #13 he spends several pages describing it. Clearly *he* felt it was important, so I'll take some time discussing it.

"Pick a target" is basically self-explanatory. By "freeze it" Alinsky means to isolate it on its own. By "personalize it" Alinsky means to give a "face" to your enemy, and hopefully a derogatory nickname as well. That is, he wouldn't attack the Republican Party as such, he would attack George W. Bush, or Sarah Palin, and he would call them snide names and ridicule them. Say, that sounds familiar.

By "polarize it" Alinsky means to ignore any "common ground" you might have with the enemy, and paint him or her all black, and yourself all white. As he writes, "[The organizer must be] a well-integrated political schizoid. [He] must be able to split himself into two parts —

one part...polarizes the issue to 100 to nothing, and helps to lead his forces into conflict, and the other part knows that when the time comes for negotiations that it really is only a 10 percent difference..."

"Polarizing" in Alinsky's view is brain washing your followers into believing that they are 100 percent on the side of the angels, and the enemy is 100 percent aligned with evil. But, and here is the truly diabolical part, the organizer himself does not buy into *any* of it. *He* is not concerned with political ideology – he is *above* such things.

Alinsky continues, "[The organizer] has a strong ego, one we might call *monumental*...[though] clearly differentiated from egotism. ...Having his *own i*dentity, he has *no* need for *the security blanket of an ideology*...." (Italics added)

So if we connect the dots in Alinsky's portrait of the *Übermensch*, the ideal revolutionary/organizer, what do we see? What does Alinsky's blurred vision of the ideal community organizer look like?

A nihilistic schizophrenic with a monumental ego who uses the wrong reasons, irrationality, and any means necessary to reach a nonexistent goal.

People buy into this garbage? You bet — and they passionately promote this dangerous insanity.

Some readers may have noticed that I have been using Alinsky's techniques of ridicule and polarization throughout this article — just following the rules, you know. Truth be told, Alinsky *does* have some good ideas and intelligent observations sprinkled throughout his book.

It is this mixture of the sensible with the evil and illogical that makes his book so insidiously dangerous. There is a name for such a mixture of truth and falsehood — propaganda. Hitler's henchman Goebbels was a master at it, and so was Alinsky.

"Rules for Radicals" is a clever trap for the naïve, the idealistic, the gullible, and the unwary. And it is a clarion call for the nihilistic, the arrogant, the greedy, the self-centered, the amoral, the chronically malcontented, and those with an anti-social mind-set.

Mankind's long climb from the caves of pre-history to civilized governments has been a slow painful process (and very much an *ongoing* process). Alinsky's cavalier dismissal of "the establishment" as evil; is puerile, duplicitous, and socially irresponsible — to put it mildly. One need only look at the Machiavellian antics of ACORN to witness where the teachings espoused in "Rules for Radicals" lead.

In closing, I mentioned earlier that Alinsky quotes Jesus, and indeed he does — more than once, but there is one quote in particular that I wish to address. I'll include the sentence immediately before, and a few words that follow, in order to put it in context.

"The importance of self-interest has never been challenged; it has been accepted as an inevitable fact of life. In the words of Christ, 'Greater love has no man than this, that a man lay down his life for his friends.' Aristotle said in "Politics...," and on Alinsky goes.

I mention this in order to show how spiritually clueless Alinsky was. He quotes a verse about love and self-sacrifice in order to support his "me first," egocentric views? How ignorant is *that*?

Atheists are generally quite spiritually naïve, and Alinsky is no exception. In another part of his book he writes, "No organization, including organized religion, can live up to their own book of morality and regulations. This is what that great revolutionary, Paul of Tarsus, knew when he wrote...'Who also hath made us able ministers of the New Testament; not of the letter, but of the spirit; for the letter killeth'." [Cor. 3:6]

Great, an atheist explaining scripture to me — Jesus wept.

Alinsky would have done well to have contemplated the verse immediately preceding the one he quotes: "Not that we are competent in ourselves to claim anything for ourselves, but our competence comes from God (II Cor. 3:5).

At any rate, Paul's words are about the importance of experiencing an *inner* spiritual transformation; as opposed to merely following *outward* formulas and customs by rote while leaving the inner-self unchanged.

It is the same issue Jesus raised with the Pharisees: "Blind guides; who strain out a gnat, and swallow a camel! ...For you cleanse the *outside* of the cup...but *inside*...they are full of robbery and self-indulgence" (Matt. 23:24,25).

I believe that Paul would agree that the most important thing that we can change and improve is *ourselves*, our *inner* selves, and that is the absolute truth.

Laus Deo.

7

The Storm Upon Us

Aug 27, 2009

This is, I believe, my earliest call to action — and I did not know the half of it yet. The country's conservative patriots were of course the first ones to wake up and start sounding the alarm, but eventually even moderate Democrats felt that the downward direction that the Obama Administration had America directed toward was not what they had signed on for. The awakening continues, but will enough people awaken in time to save America?

One of three possible scenarios is currently being played out in the United States: The first option is that the Obama Administration is the most corrupt, dishonest, and inept administration that America has ever been burdened with. That is the "best case" scenario. Unfortunately, this is the option that I think least likely.

I suppose it is possible that Obama has simply had a phenomenal run of bad luck; that the various bills and laws passed by his Administration have by some fluke been accidentally anti-small business, anti-free enterprise, economically suicidal, and have worsened the economic crisis. I might also mention that there has been a, how shall I put this — lackadaisical — attitude toward an American debt of biblical proportions.

The second option is that the Obama Administration despises individual freedom, capitalism, free-enterprise, and is hell-bent on transforming the United States into a fascist/communist collective — a regime that will be run by a venal, ruthless, power-hungry elite. That actually sounds more plausible to me.

The third option is that the Obama Administration is part of a global restructuring process (New World Order) in which the world will be turned into a fascist/communist collective — run by a venal, ruthless, power-hungry elite.

My guess is — take your pick between options two and three. If you are surprised by my analysis then you have not been paying attention to what has happened, and is happening, to the United States. Let me roll out some facts and figures for you.

The SEIU (Service Employees International Union) is run by Andy Stern, a militant Far-Left thug, and Anna Burger another Far-Left radical. The SEIU has increased its size and power through arm-twisting intimidation tactics and other nefarious means. Two years ago Obama said before an SEIU rally "I've spent my entire adult life working with SEIU."

That is not good news. Once you have looked into the corruption, ruthlessness, and Far-Left agenda of the SEIU leadership you will know that it is not good news at all.

Let's discuss ACORN. Wade Rathke, who "cut his teeth" in the left-wing radical group SDS (Students for a Democratic Society) in the 1960s, founded ACORN and also SEIU Local 100. These and numerous other Far Left groups under the Rathke "umbrella" are funded by our taxpayer dollars.

And let us not forget the hundreds of "advocacy groups" connected with ACORN: groups such as the WFP (Working Families Party), — which, according to an Associated Press report was created in 1998 to help push the Democratic Party toward the left."

Many of our taxpayer dollars are funneled to various Far-Left organizations which, after the "bosses" get their cut, distribute the money among hundreds, possibly thousands, of groups which advocate the destruction of the United States as a free republic and the installation of a welfare collective. It is a con game that is going on, and has been going on, for years — with the assistance of radical leftist foundations like Arca and Tides.

What a deal, huh? Collect the money earned by some bourgeois chump, and then spend your time destroying the system that enabled the chump to make the money in the first place. Sweet!

Although I have been talking exclusively about the Far Left influence I don't want to be remiss and forget to mention that greed, corruption, and duplicity are non-partisan vices. The right-wing has its share of snakes in the grass as well.

I watched a town hall meeting yesterday where Senator McCain was asked a question about Obama disrespecting the US Constitution. Senator McCain replied, "I'm sure that he respects the Constitution." Senator McCain's comment was booed and I turned off the TV.

How can a person with as many years on Capitol Hill as Senator McCain say with a straight face that Obama respects the Constitution? I guess that it takes all those years in Congress to be able to state such a bald-faced lie with a straight face.

With all due respect to his heroic service record, Senator McCain is either an inattentive dolt or he thinks that the American public are morons. I am not especially fond of either conclusion.

Obama and his ilk have been trying to tear down the Constitution for decades. It is an axiom that the Far Left hates the Constitution, and the liberal-left is no friend to it. They see it, and always have, as an obstacle to implementing their collectivist social engineering agendas.

The Far Left has an undeniable panache for naming things as they are not. Calling the government takeover of health care, the "public option," is one example. Another gem is calling the "death by a thousand cuts," of the US Constitution the "Living Constitution." As Bubba Clinton might have said, "Just how do you define the word — *living*?"

By the term "living Constitution" the Left means a pliable, moldable, elastic Constitution — a Constitution that can be stretched and formed to mean anything that they want it to mean. They mean the death of the US Constitution as it was written by the Founding Fathers.

Instead of a bulwark protecting the American public from government interference, the Constitution will become a means for enacting Draconian laws to oppress the people. The "living Constitution" means a perverted travesty of the US Constitution.

It is rapidly coming down to this: either there will be a number of anti-American individuals who will be tried for treason against the United States during a time of war — and I believe that the penalty for that is death — or the United States as a free republic and world power will perish.

As Abraham Lincoln eloquently put it "We shall nobly save, or meanly lose, the last best hope of earth." The time is upon us and we cannot vacillate any longer.

I live in Florida, and we are used to getting ready for hurricanes. We buy portable radios, flashlights, and batteries. We stock up on nonperishable foods and bottled water. There is most definitely a "hurricane" coming, and for this storm you might want to add arms and ammo to your shopping list.

Godspeed — and may God bless America.

8

George Soros: Republic Enemy #1

Sept. 15, 2009

The popularity of an article was part of the criteria weighed in selecting it for inclusion in this book. Judging from the emails I have received, this is the most popular, or at least the most widely read, of my articles. Over the years since it was first posted folks have sent me this article as a "must read" — attributed to someone else — usually Steve Kroft of "Sixty Minutes" (Mr. Kroft, I am sure, knows nothing about any of this).

When this article first appeared there was not a great deal on the Internet regarding Soros. That is not to say that he was not well known, indeed Soros was famous, or infamous if you prefer — but he was not exactly a household word. He has gained much more notoriety since then. He and Maurice Strong (Agenda 21 and the Aspen Institute) are perhaps the two most visible faces of the Nazi/Marxist NWO elite (Strong scurried away to Red China a few years back and has not been seen much in the limelight since).

"The main obstacle to a stable and just world order is the United States."

George Soros

"George Soros is an evil man. He's anti-God, anti-family, anti-American, and anti-good."

Rev. Jesse Lee Peterson

Is it possible to lay the global financial meltdown, the radicalizing of the Democratic Party, and America's moral decline, at the feet of one man? It is indeed possible.

If George Soros is not the world's preeminent "malignant messianic narcissist," he'll do until the real thing comes along. Move over, Hitler, Stalin, Mao, and Pol Pot. There's a new kid on the block.

What we have in Soros is a multi-billionaire atheist with skewed moral values and a sociopath's lack of conscience. He considers himself to be a world class philosopher, despises capitalism, and just loves social engineering. Uh oh — can you say "trouble" boys and girls?

Soros is a real life version of Dr. Evil — with Obama in the role of Mini-Me. This is not as humorous as it might at first sound. In fact it is bone-deep chilling.

György Schwartz, better known to the world as George Soros, was born August 12, 1930 in Hungary. Soros' father, Tivadar, was a fervent practitioner of Esperanto — a language invented in 1887, and designed to be the first global language — free of any national identity.

The Schwartz's, who were non-practicing Jews, changed the family name to Soros in order to facilitate assimilation into the gentile population as the Nazis spread into Hungary during the 1930s. Soros is an Esperanto word meaning "to soar."

In 1944 Hitler's henchman Adolf Eichmann arrived in Hungary to oversee the murder of that country's Jews. The Soros children were all given fake identity papers and were shipped out to various Christian families. George Soros ended up with a man whose job was confiscating property from the Jewish population. Soros went with him on his rounds. Soros has repeatedly called 1944 "the best year of his life."

In an article in the Wall Street Journal, Joshua Muravchik notes that, "70% of Mr. Soros's fellow Jews in Hungary, nearly a half-million human beings, were annihilated in that year. They were dying and disappearing all around him, and their numbers no doubt included many whom he knew personally. Yet he gives no sign that this put any damper on his elation, either at the time or indeed in retrospect."

During an interview with "Sixty Minute's" Steve Kroft, Soros was asked about his "best year:"

KROFT: My understanding is that you went out with this protector of yours who swore that you were his adopted godson.

SOROS: Yes. Yes.

KROFT: Went out, in fact, and helped in the confiscation of property from the Jews.

SOROS: Yes. That's right. Yes.

KROFT: I mean, that sounds like an experience that would send lots of people to the psychiatric couch for many, many years. Was it difficult?

SOROS: Not, not at all. Not at all.

KROFT: No feeling of guilt?

SOROS: No.

Of course he didn't feel guilty. Soros has the moral depth of a clam. Nonetheless, he has said, "my goal is to become the conscience of the world."

In his article, Muravchik describes how Soros has admitted to having "carried some rather potent messianic fantasies with me from childhood, which I felt I had to control, otherwise they might get me in trouble." Can you imagine the results of this messianic sociopath being "the conscience of the world?" Yikes.

Be that as it may, after WWII Soros attended the London School of Economics (LSE), where he fell under the thrall of fellow atheist and Hungarian, Karl Popper, one of his professors. Popper was a mentor to Soros until Popper's death in 1994. Two of Popper's most influential teachings concerned "the open society," and Fallibilism. Fallibilism is the philosophical doctrine that all claims of knowledge could, in principle, be mistaken. Then again I could be wrong about that.

The "open society" basically refers to a "test and evaluate" approach to social engineering. Regarding "open society" Roy Childs writes, "Since the Second World War, most of the Western democracies have followed Popper's advice about piecemeal social engineering and democratic social reform, and it has gotten them into a grand mess."

In 1956 Soros moved to New York City, where he worked on Wall Street, and started amassing his fortune. He specialized in hedge funds and currency speculation. Soros is absolutely ruthless, amoral, and clever in his business dealings, and quickly made his fortune. By the 1980s he was well on his way to becoming the global powerhouse that he is today.

Kyle-Anne Shiver writes, "Soros made his first billion in 1992 by shorting the British pound with leveraged billions in financial bets, and became known as the man who broke the Bank of England. He broke it on the backs of hard-working British citizens who immediately saw their homes severely devalued and their life savings cut drastically...almost overnight."

In 1994 Soros crowed that "the former Soviet Empire is now called the Soros Empire." The Russia-gate scandal in 1999, which almost collapsed the Russian economy, was labeled by Rep. Jim Leach, then head of the House Banking Committee, "one of the greatest social robberies in human history." The "Soros Empire" indeed.

In 1997 Soros almost destroyed the economies of Thailand and Malaysia. At the time Malaysia's Prime Minister, Mahathir Mohamad, called Soros "a villain, and a moron." Thai activist Weng Tojirakarn said, "We regard George Soros as a kind of Dracula. He sucks the blood from the people."

The website Greek national Pride reports, "[Soros] was part of the full court press that dismantled Yugoslavia and caused trouble in Georgia, Ukraine and Myanmar [Burma]. Calling himself a philanthropist, Soros' role is to tighten the ideological stranglehold of globalization and the New World Order while promoting his own financial gain.

He is without conscience; a capitalist who functions with absolute amorality." France has upheld an earlier conviction against Soros for felony insider trading. Soros was fined just under 3 million dollars.

Recently, his native Hungary fined Soros 2.2 million dollars for "illegal market manipulation." Elizabeth Crum writes that "The Hungarian economy has been in a state of transition as the country seeks to become more financially stable and westernized. [Soros'] deliberately driving down the share price of its largest bank put Hungary's economy into a wicked tailspin, one from which it is still trying to recover."

My point here is that Soros is a planetary parasite. His grasp, greed, and gluttony have a global reach.

But what about America? Soros told Australia's national newspaper "The Australian" that "America, as the centre of the globalised financial markets, was sucking up the savings of the world. This is now over. The game is out," he said, adding that the time has come for "a very serious adjustment" in America's consumption habits. Ready to tighten your belts America?

Soros also told "The Australian" that the world financial crisis was "stimulating" and "in a way, the culmination of my life's work." Stimulating? Have you found the job losses, house foreclosures, and incredible national debt — stimulating? Me neither.

Obama promised 2 billion of our tax dollars to Brazil (yes, billion with a "b"), in order to give them a leg-up in expanding their offshore oil fields (while shutting down our own in the Gulf of Mexico). Obama's largesse towards Brazil came shortly after Soros invested heavily in Brazilian oil (Petrobras).

Tait Trussel writes, "The Petrobras loan may be a windfall for Soros and Brazil, but it is a bad deal for the U.S. The American Petroleum Institute estimates that oil exploration in the U.S. could create 160,000 new, well-paying jobs, as well as $1.7 trillion in revenues to federal, state, and local governments, all while fostering greater energy security." Do you get the feeling that American taxpayers are being treated like gullible suckers?

A blog you might want to keep an eye on is SorosWatch.com. This is their mission: "This blog is dedicated to all...who have suffered due to the ruthless financial pursuits of...George Soros. Your stories are many and varied, but the theme is the same: the destructive power of greed without conscience. We pledge to tirelessly watch Soros wherever he goes and to print the truth in the hope that he will one day stop preying upon the world's poor...that justice will be served." (Note: Since this article was first published SorosWatch has gone offline. Try SorosMonitor.com instead).

Back to America: Soros has been actively working to destroy America from the inside out for some years now. People have been warning us. Two years ago Bill O'Reilly said on "The O'Reilly Factor" that "Soros [is] an extremist who wants open borders, a one-world foreign policy, legalized drugs, euthanasia, and on and on. This is off-the-chart dangerous..."

In 1997 Rachel Ehrenfeld wrote, "Soros uses his philanthropy to change — or more accurately deconstruct — the moral values and attitudes of the Western world, and particularly of the American people. *His 'open society' is not about freedom; it is about license* [italics added]. His vision rejects the notion of ordered liberty, in favor of an ideology of rights and entitlements."

Perhaps the most important of these "whistle blowers" are David Horowitz and Richard Poe. Their book "The Shadow Party" outlines in detail how Soros hijacked the Democratic Party and now owns it lock, stock, and barrel.

Soros has been packing the Democratic Party with radicals and ousting moderate Democrats for years. I don't have time to do the subject justice in this article, but FrontPage's Jamie Glazov has an excellent interview with Richard Poe, which will fill you in on many of the facts. The Shadow Party became the Shadow Government, which became the Obama Administration.

DiscoverTheNetworks.org writes, "By his [Soros'] own admission, he helped engineer coups in Slovakia, Croatia, Georgia, and Yugoslavia. When Soros targets a country for 'regime change,' he begins by creating a shadow government — a fully formed government-in-exile, ready to assume power when the opportunity arises. The Shadow Party he has built in America greatly resembles those he has created in other countries prior to instigating a coup."

The above quote was written before the Presidential Election. So was the following quote from the November 2008 edition of the German magazine "Der Spiegel" in which Soros gives his opinion on what the next POTUS should do after taking office. "I think we need a large stimulus package...." Soros thought that around 600 billion would be about right. Soros also said that "I think this is a great opportunity to finally deal with global warming and energy dependence. The U.S. needs a cap and trade system with auctioning of licenses for emissions rights." Any of this sound familiar?

Although Soros doesn't (yet) own the Republican Party like he does the Democrats, make no mistake his tentacles are spread throughout the Republican Party as well.

Soros is a partner in the Carlyle Group where he has invested more than 100 million dollars. According to an article by "The Baltimore Chronicle's" Alice Cherbonnier the Carlye Group is run by "a veritable who's who of former Republican leaders," from CIA man Frank Carlucci, to CIA head [and ex-President] George Bush, Sr. In late 2006 Soros bought about 2 million shares of Halliburton — Dick Cheney's old stomping grounds.

When the Democrats and Republicans held their conventions in 2000, Soros held Shadow Party conventions in the same cities, at the same time. Republican Senator John McCain was the keynote speaker at the "Soros Convention" (so labeled by the late Robert Novak) in Philadelphia. Soros has dirtied both sides of the aisle, trust me. And if that were not bad enough, he has long-held connections with the CIA — and I mustn't forget to mention Soros' involvement with the LSM (Lame Stream Media), the entertainment industry (e.g. he owns 2.6 million shares of Time Warner), and the various political advertising organizations he funnels millions to.

As Matthew Vadum writes, "The liberal billionaire-turned-philanthropist has been buying up media properties for years in order to drive home his message to the American public that they are too materialistic, too wasteful, too selfish, and too stupid to decide for themselves how to run their own lives."

Richard Poe writes, "Soros' private philanthropy, totaling nearly $5 billion, continues undermining America's traditional Western values. His giving has provided funding of abortion rights, atheism, drug legalization, sex education, euthanasia, feminism, gun control, globalization, mass immigration, gay marriage and other radical experiments in social engineering."

Some of the many NGOs (None Government Organizations) that Soros funds with his billions are: MoveOn.org, the Apollo Alliance, Media Matters for America, the Tides Foundation, the ACLU, ACORN, PDIA (Project on Death In America), La Raza, and many more. For a more complete list, with brief descriptions of the NGOs go to DiscoverTheNetworks.org.

Poe continues, "Through his global web of Open Society Institutes and Open Society Foundations, Soros has spent 25 years recruiting, training, indoctrinating and installing a network of loyal operatives in 50 countries, placing them in positions of influence and power in media, government, finance and academia."

As I have said before, America currently faces the greatest challenge to its existence as a free republic since the Civil War. And as we go, so goes the world.

So is Soros to blame for *all* of America's woes?

Without Soros, would the Saul Alinsky Chicago machine still be rolling? Would SEIU, ACORN, and La Raza still be pursuing their nefarious activities? Would Big Money and lobbyists still be corrupting government? Would our college campuses still be retirement homes for 1960s radicals? Yes, yes, yes, and yes — but to much less of a degree.

The purpose of this article is to point out that without the financial skullduggery and Machiavellian manipulations of Soros, America would be a considerably safer, saner, more stable place to live.

America stands at the brink of an abyss and that fact is directly attributable to Soros. Soros has vigorously, cleverly, and insidiously planned the ruination of America.

His conduct has been immoral, duplicitous, and traitorous. Stripping Soros of his US citizenship should be one of the first steps taken during the upcoming courtroom trials.

And trials there must be. No matter the cost the nest of vipers on Capitol Hill and all of the traitors in the government at large must be brought to task for their behavior, or a free America is doomed.

The words of Patrick Henry (1736-1799) are apropos: "Is life so dear, or peace so sweet, as to be purchased at the price of chains and slavery? Forbid it, Almighty God! I know not what course others may take, but as for me, give me liberty, or give me death!"

These days Patrick Henry's sentiments are more than quaint hyperbole from long ago — they articulate a slow-burning intense glow that fires our courage and hearts.

Laus Deo.

9

Taking Back America II

September 28, 2009

When I visited St. Louis, Missouri in the fall of 2009 for the convention described here, I had the honor of meeting Phyllis Schlafly (a brief photo-op really), and heard some wonderful speakers. I was perhaps most impressed by Michelle Bachmann, who seemed to possess more energy than ten "normal" people.

This article wraps up my report on the HTBA (How to Take Back America) conference that I attended. On Saturday, the final day of the conference, speeches were given by Mike Huckabee, Phyllis Schlafly, Janet Porter, and House Representatives Michelle Bachman, Trent Franks, and Tom McClintock.

In any other venue, each of the talks that these individuals gave would have been considered the keynote speech and the highlight of the event. At the HTBA conference however, there was a plethora of oratorical excellence. To put it in the vernacular, there was a lot of darn good talking going on.

The general mood of the audience was summed up by one attendees comment, "I've never heard so much bad news, and felt so good at the same time" — a worried but hopeful feeling. The "bad news" imparted by the speakers and in the workshops, was more than offset by the ambiance of enthusiasm, faith, and patriotism that pervaded the conference.

Permit me to say a few words regarding faith and patriotism. You cannot support changing the Constitution, and call yourself a patriot. You cannot extol globalization at the expense of American sovereignty, and call yourself a patriot. You cannot demean entrepreneurial freedom, and call yourself a patriot. You cannot support the removal of God from our government and culture, and call yourself a patriot.

The liberals endorse all of those things and many other concepts, doctrines, and actions that belittle and diminish the United States. They are *ipso facto* unpatriotic, if not traitorous — any blather about their "patriotic" use of the First Amendment notwithstanding.

At best, liberals are occasionally nationalistic. Nationalism is a pugnacious mental stance — a thing of the mind. Nationalism according to Wikipedia "is a type of collectivism emphasizing the collective of a specific nation." And as we know, collectivism — Marxism, Fascism, Socialism, et al. — is a doctrine of the Left.

True patriotism is a love for America — it is a thing of the heart and soul. A true patriot loves and supports America and American values. Although the right-wing has its share of unpatriotic individuals, it is primarily the left-wing that attacks and devalues America.

The liberals are in close proximity to the Far Left. And the Far Left, being atheists who believe that "the end justifies the means," are manipulative liars of the first order. Liberals are guilty by association if nothing else. If you are a liberal and consider yourself patriotic, then you need to either give up your political stance, or give up your claim to truth and patriotism. You cannot belong to a group that trumpets love for the planet over love for America and call yourself patriotic.

This is not to say that the two feelings are mutually exclusive. One can love America and still — indeed should — love the planet. It is a question of priorities — which comes first in your heart?

One of the perks of attending the conference was simply being in the company of so many dedicated, enthusiastic, God-loving patriots. I didn't attend the conference in order to "network," but nonetheless I kept running into "movers and shakers."

As I was checking out of the hotel early yesterday, Joe "The Plumber" Wurzelbacher was checking out as well, and we chatted a bit about "his" NFL team (the Bengals), and "my" team (the Tampa Bay Bucs). Not an earth-shaking conversation to be sure, but rubbing shoulders with committed patriotic Americans like Joe, coupled with the electrifying speeches that I heard, left me with a renewed sense of purpose, enthusiasm, and direction.

Perhaps the most important message of the HTBA conference was the plea for each of the attendees to spread the "word" upon returning home. By the "word" was meant both the danger America is in (which is extreme), and the need for Americans to embrace "God, flag, and country," and get *active*.

America is in mortal danger, make no mistake — and if there ever was a time for conservatives to rise up, band together, and take action, this is it. The place is here, the time is now, and we are chosen to be the ones who will defend "the world's last best hope." Let's get to it.

Laus Deo.

10

Agenda 21: The Death Knell of Freedom (The Plan)

Oct 17, 2009

A co-worker at my younger brother's place of employment suggested that I look into Agenda 21 early in 2009. Eventually I did and this article was the result. The more I researched the subject the more alarmed I became.

Although several individuals had been sounding warning bells for some time, there was not a great deal on the Internet dealing with Agenda 21 at the time I was doing my research. Two valuable resources were the website "The Green Agenda," and the articles and videos by Michael Shaw (who should receive a medal for his efforts).

I am glad to report that there has been a rapid expansion in interest about Agenda 21 — among both conservatives and liberals alike. Several counties have opted out of ICLEI, and it looks like many more will follow suit. TPTB want our land and water and they have been successfully taking it, unop- posed for the most part. "We the people" need to put a stop to all that ASAP.

This article was revised and reposted in February of 2011.

"The common enemy of humanity is man. In searching for a new enemy to unite us, we came up with the idea that pollution, the threat of global warming, water shortages, famine and the like would fit the bill. ...The real enemy then is humanity itself."

From the Club of Rome's "The First Global Revolution" p. 71,75 1993

"Therefore, send not to know for whom the bell tolls, It tolls for thee."

John Donne (1572-1631)

The death knell for freedom has been tolling for some time, and only now are people starting to hear it. It started tolling faintly, decades back, and has slowly progressed in volume until today its tolling is impossible to ignore.

The United States of America — that "shining city on a hill" — had a good run of it and made a gallant effort at establishing liberty for all. But as the old saw would have it, all good things must come to an end.

Liberty, after all, is an aberration in mankind's history — a light that has flared here and there over the centuries only to dissolve back into the darkness.

America is barreling toward becoming a bit player on the world's stage, and its vaunted middle class — once the envy of the world — is on the verge of being eliminated. For the good of the planet, for the good of Gaia. for the good of the collective — freedom is being replaced by servitude, capitalism by socialism, and property rights by "sustainable development."

I am not talking about something we need to be on guard against. It is all already in place. It has been going on for quite some time, and it will continue to go on at a greatly accelerated pace. We are at the endgame point.

The Globalists know it. Why do you think the Democratic (and many Republican) political hacks on Capitol Hill are so dismissive of "we the people?" They are essentially putting on a dog-and-pony show for public consumption while the final pieces for America's defeat are slid into place.

To a great extent the Globalists own the mass media, the entertainment industry, and the Judicial, Executive, and Legislative branches of government. Why should they worry?

Already, several generations have been indoctrinated via our school systems to value globalization and "social justice" over personal responsibility and free enterprise. They have been repeatedly sold the idea that they should "Think globally, act locally."

God has been demeaned, marginalized, and eradicated, at every turn. Our religions are in many cases a watered down and diluted mimicry of true spirituality.

The Globalists have come out from the closets, the woodwork, and from under rocks. They know that their time of hiding is at long last over. They are brazen about, and proud of, their anti-American/pro-globalist stance. Their arrogance and hubris is palpable.

Call them Communists, Marxists, Fascists, or Globalists — call them what you will, they are collectivists who despise America's middle class, capitalism, and free enterprise.

They have been duplicitous, Machiavellian, clever, and patient — and it has paid off. The trap has been sprung. America got hit high, and America got hit low. We suffered sudden catastrophic sneak attacks from without and insidious long-term betrayal from within.

We were hit low by Alinskyesque "community organizers" in our streets and propagandists in our schools. We were hit high by "think tanks" like the Trilateral Commission, the CoR (Club of Rome), and the CFR (Council for Foreign Relations).

They have divided us with special interest groups, vociferous "talking point" attacks, and identity politics. They have infiltrated our schools and indoctrinated our children.

They have opened floodgates using the Cloward-Piven Strategy — overwhelming our judicial system, banking establishment, border security, and more. They have encouraged corruption and greed from the lowest to the highest levels of government. They have twisted and perverted the US Constitution. They have promoted and encouraged anything and everything that would help bring America down.

They intend on taking over the planet, but first they need to destabilize, and then destroy, the United States of America. Because we are a powerful bulwark of freedom, we have to go first. And to a large extent, go we have.

The Club of Rome (CoR) was founded in 1968 in Italy by Aurelio Peccei, an Italian scholar and industrialist, and Alexander King a Scottish scientist.

Over the years the list of its members has included ex-presidents, prime ministers, kings, queens, diplomats, and billionaires. Its membership roster reads like a "who's who" of the world's movers and shakers. It includes UN bureaucrats, scientists, economists, and business leaders from around the globe.

After its inception it split into two additional branches: The CoB (Club of Budapest), and the CoM (Club of Madrid). The CoB focuses mainly on social and philosophical/religious issues, while the CoM concentrates more on political issues. In addition, there are over thirty affiliated organizations in other countries—such as the USACoR in the United States.

The CoR first garnered public attention with its 1972 report "The Limits to Growth," which went on to become the best selling environmentalist book of all time. Simply stated, its main thesis is that economic growth cannot continue indefinitely because of the limited availability of natural resources, particularly oil. It is a sort of industrialized version of the Malthusian nightmare.

Twenty years later the CoR published "The First Global Revolution" — a quote from that book appears at the start of this article. This book made a big splash as well, and helped to re-energize and expand the whole environmentalist movement.

Another quote from the book worth keeping in mind is, "It would seem that humans need a common motivation, namely a common adversary...such a motivation must be found to bring the divided nations together to face an outside enemy, either a real one, or else one invented for the purpose..."

"One invented for the purpose." Enter global warming and greenhouse gases. But something even more important happened the year before "The First Global Revolution " came out. At the instigation of the CoR and their ilk, in 1992 the United Nations held the Conference on Environment and Development — informally known as the Earth Summit — in Rio de Janeiro, Brazil.

At the Earth Summit, 178 nations signed an agreement called Agenda 21 — so named because it dealt with the United Nation's agenda for the 21st century.

Agenda 21 consists of numerous chapters detailing the role that different parts of society should play in implementing "sustainable development." There are chapters for central governments, local governments, businesses, and community organizations.

George Bush senior, then President of the United States, flew down and committed the United States to the UN's FCCC (Framework Convention on Climate Change) agenda.

Ever since then the Executive Branch — Republican or Democrat — has been bypassing Congress and passing "soft laws" foisting Agenda 21 on the American public. No matter where you go environmentalism permeates the US Government bureaucracy. Sometimes it is blatant and out front; other times you may need to dig a little, but it is always there.

The Agenda 21 Globalists wine and dine each other, and hold conventions and conferences around the world. They give each other praise, pats on the back, and prestigious awards. The Norwegian Globalists gave Obama the Nobel Peace Prize for the same reason that they gave one to Al Gore — promoting globalization and Agenda 21.

Gore's movie "An Inconvenient Truth" also received an Oscar from the liberal Hollywood elite. These honors have been bestowed on Gore, not for exposing the truth — for "An Inconvenient Truth" is merely a slickly packaged lie — but because the film spreads the falsehoods of Agenda 21 so well.

It can only be shown to school children in the U.K. if accompanied by a disclaimer. The U.K.'s "The Daily Mail" reports that "...teachers will have to warn pupils that there are other opinions on global warming, and they should not necessarily accept the views of the film."

"The Daily Mail" also noted that the lawyer who successfully sued to have the disclaimer attached, said it did not go far enough. "He said 'no amount of turgid guidance' could change the fact that the film is unfit for consumption in the classroom." Yet American students are forced to view this blatant propaganda — with no disclaimer.

In June of 2009, NASA said that global warming is caused by solar cycles — i.e. the sun. Left unmentioned was the fact that the greenhouse gas theory is full of holes. Actually it is a fairy tale, a convenient lie used to force the world to bend to the will of the Globalists.

Under pressure from the Obama Administration NASA now teaches that global warming is caused by the greenhouse effect, and "bad" gases like CO_2 — which we humans unfortunately emit each time we breathe. Bad humans!

Al Gore, the CoR, the UN, and all of the environmental organizations and their adherents, don't care what the truth is. They could care less about what causes global warming, or if there even *is* such a thing as global warming. They have their "outside enemy...invented for the purpose," and they are not about to let go of it.

The Globalists actually tried Global Cooling first, but for various reasons it didn't fly. Look at page 22 in the 1974 Annual Rockefeller Report, and you will find the mention of a conference called to investigate "...the future implications of the global cooling trend now underway..." Things sure warmed up in a hurry.

So what is the purpose behind all this? What is really behind all the global warming hoopla? Power. It is the same old Marxist/Communist/Fascist collectivist shtick, dressed up in new clothes.

Global warming is all about a power grab by a wealthy elite and their collectivist sycophants — using the UN as a cover and tool.

As always, there are numerous "useful idiots" who swallow the party line whole. Some of them are simply misguided idealists, and some of them are nuts — dangerously so.

Behind it all, is a relatively small group of people who are manipulating the world for their own twisted narcissistic ends. It is a perfect cover. Think about it — who does not feel that fresh air, clean water, and a healthy environment are admirable ends to work toward? Any sane person supports such ideals. But hidden behind the admirable goals are some diabolical designs.

Don't take my word for it, and don't dismiss what I write without doing your own homework. We all need to know what is headed our way shortly. If you are not aware of these facts already, then please educate yourself.

What have we seen since the Obama Administration took over? The brainiacs in charge of America's finances have been ignoring our debts and eagerly proposing ways to sink us deeper into a financial quagmire — a lot deeper. At first I thought that they were simply corrupt, venal, self-serving idiots — all of which is undoubtedly true — but they're also destroying America's financial foundation, cleverly and intentionally.

They want the American dollar replaced by a new global currency. They want America's middle class to hang in the wind and then die on the vine. They are Globalists, and they want America to fail. It is so easy to see once you realize what is going on.

Why else would they add trillions to an already staggering debt? Why else did they try to rush through a Cap and Trade bill that will, in Obama's words, make electricity prices "skyrocket." Why else would they jam ObamaCare down America's throat? Why else would Obama say he would bankrupt anybody who built a new coal plant?

Once you grasp Agenda 21 and the sly machinations of the United Nations and globalizing NGOs like the CoR it all makes sense. It is all part of the "The Plan:" Ruin America's economy, destroy her middle class, and put a stranglehold on her energy grid.

At the UN Summit at Rio in 1992, the Conference Secretary-General, Canadian billionaire Maurice Strong, said "Isn't the only hope for this planet that the industrialized civilization collapse? Isn't it our responsibility to bring that about?"

He also said, "Current lifestyles and consumption patterns of the affluent middle class — involving high meat intake, the use of fossil fuels, electrical appliances, home and workplace air-conditioning, and suburban housing — are not sustainable."

Club of Rome member, multi-billionaire George Soros echoed Strong's statement last fall when he told an Australian newspaper, "America, as the center of the globalized financial markets, was sucking up the savings of the world. This is now over. The game is out,' he said, adding that the time has come for 'a very serious adjustment' in American's consumption habits."

We will be forced to cut back on fossil fuel consumption. Forced to cut back on water usage. Forced to give up our property. Forced to eat less. Forced to warm or cool our homes less. Forced to give up driving.

We *will* be forced to give up these and many other things that we currently take for granted. It is "The Plan" — you had better believe it.

Look at what is happening to California's Central Valley—once "the world's breadbasket" and now a dust bowl. All due to Agenda 21. I assure you that the Globalists will not help the farmers. As the saying goes, "You can't make an omelet without breaking a few eggs." The Globalists *want* the land unplowed. They *want* it to go "back to nature." They *want* to increase the price of food. They *want* to ruin the middle class farming community. It is all part of "The Plan."

It is not just America this is happening to of course. Australia, Great Britain, Japan, Canada, Germany... Every country is on the verge of being converted into a vassal state — part of a global hegemony run by the UN and a Power Elite.

All this will be more easily accomplished with a greatly reduced population. Did I mention population reduction and control? Behind all of the warm and fuzzy terminology about "smart growth," "sustainable development," and "think green," lies a very chilling fact: the Agenda 21 folks want to reduce the earth's population — a lot.

In 1996, Club of Rome member and CNN founder, Ted Turner, told Audubon magazine, "A total population of 250-300 million people, a 95% decline from present levels, would be ideal." A 95% reduction!

More recently he has said that getting rid of a mere two thirds of the world's population would suffice. Getting mellow in his old age no doubt.

The hard-core environmentalists are all bio-centrists. That is, they believe that humanity is no more important than any other species on this planet. In fact, to hear them tell it, the world would be much better off without any people at all.

Anthropologist and anarchist David Graber put it like this in an L.A. Times book review, "Human happiness, and certainly human fecundity, are not as important as a wild and healthy planet. ... We have become a plague upon ourselves and upon the Earth. ...Until such time as Homo sapiens should decide to rejoin nature, some of us can only hope for the right virus to come along."

Because most of these Globalists are atheists they do not respect the divine spark in man, or unalienable rights, or divine retribution. In short, they do not have many qualms about killing people — which they have proven time and again whenever, and wherever, their ilk have come to power. Something to keep in mind.

You know the sardonic comment "Well excuse me for breathing?" These people take that statement literally — and probably will *not* excuse you. After all, you are adding to the earth's carbon dioxide level every time you exhale.

ICLEI (International Council for Local Environmental Initiatives) even has a personal CO_2 calculator you can use. ICLEI (pronounced "ick-lee") believes you should know (and of course *want* to know) the amount of "your yearly direct personal carbon dioxide emissions." To which I say, personally and directly, "f—k off."

My favorite eco-friendly slogan is "Save the Planet—Kill Yourself." There is something deeply disturbed and disturbing about too many of these folks. For example, Yale professor and eco-nut, Lamont Cole is of the opinion that "To feed a starving child is to exacerbate the world population problem."

Many of these "useful idiots" may be crazy and harmless, but they can also be crazy and dangerous. Behind them, pulling the strings, and waiting to take over are the Global Elite and their one world government.

Whether or not America will last as a free republic until the 2012 presidential elections is debatable. Iran's leadership is aching to nuke Israel and Israel's only going to wait so long before taking preemptive measures — and there goes a large chunk of America's oil supply. And what happens if Egypt comes under the control of the Muslim Brotherhood and they decide to close the Suez Canal? (Remember that Obama's drilling ban (declared unconstitutional) is still in effect).

Long lines for gas — if you can get any at all. America's power grid flickers and intermittently fails. Time for the Globalists to make their final moves. So America, freedom, and Western civilization go down the drain on our watch. It is nothing to be proud of, that is for sure.

Is there no hope then? Well, if there are still enough patriotic Americans who value personal integrity, responsibility, and freedom, then there is a slim chance we can turn this thing around, but it will not be easy — far from it.

Make no mistake though, if we lose to the globalists then America and the world will sink into an abyss of amoral tyranny for a very, very long time.

Laus Deo.

11

Hey, Let's Talk About Islam!

January 22, 2010

When I sent this article into CFP at the beginning of 2010 I had the title all in caps, but they "turned down the volume" a bit by replacing the caps with lower case letters. I had used the caps as a way of saying "Wake up! We need to talk about this!"

At the time there was, to my mind, waay too little discussion going on (even on the Internet) about the dangers posed by Islamists (and Islam in general). While writers such as Daniel Pipes, Robert Spencer, Pamela Geller, and Brigitte Gabriel had been sounding the alarm for years, they were at the time that I wrote this article still largely "voices in the wilderness." The surge in commentary since then has been nothing short of explosive (excluding the MSM, of course) — seems that I "caught the wave" just as it was forming.

I suppose that technically speaking this piece should be considered a compilation of quotes, as opposed to being a bona fide article. I included quotes by Leftists such as Bertrand Russell and Hitler in order to briefly showcase the history of liberal fawning over Islam and their disgust with Christianity.

It is wise to bear in mind that Islam is not a right-wing phenomena – it is left-wing all the way (anti-freedom, anti-democracy, and pro-totalitarian theocracy – hello?). Anyone who tells you that Islam is right-wing is either ignorant of the facts or purposefully trying to mislead you.

If one goes by the Pentagon's recent report on the Ft. Hood terrorist attack, the Pentagon's PC putzes wouldn't recognize a Muslim terrorist if one jumped up and bit them on the butt. So in the interest of national security I have collected some statements made by folks over the years which might point the Pentagon in the right direction. One lives in hope — the poor dears can be awfully slow on the uptake though.

"Ever since the religion of Islam appeared in the world, the espousers of it...have been as wolves and tigers to all other nations, rending and tearing all that fell into their merciless paws, and grinding them with their iron teeth; that numberless cities are raised from the foundation, and only their name remaining; that many countries, which were once as the garden of God, are now a desolate wilderness; and that so many once numerous and powerful nations are vanished from the earth! Such was, and is at this day, the rage, the fury, the revenge, of these destroyers of human kind."

John Wesley (1703-1791)
Methodist leader

"Bolshevism combines the characteristics of the French Revolution with those of the rise of Islam... Marx has taught that Communism is fatally predestined to come about; this produces a state of mind not unlike that of the early successors of Mahommet... Among religions, Bolshevism is to be reckoned with Mohammedanism, rather than with Christianity and Buddhism. Christianity and Buddhism are primarily personal religions, with mystical doctrines and a love of contemplation. Mohammedanism and Bolshevism are practical, social, unspiritual, concerned to win the empire of this world."

Bertrand Russell (1872-1970)

"Adopting from the new Revelation of Jesus, the faith and hope of immortal life, and of future retribution, he [Mohammed] humbled it to the dust by adapting all the rewards and sanctions of his religion to the gratification of the sexual passion. He poisoned the sources of human felicity at the fountain, by degrading the condition of the female sex, and the allowance of polygamy; and he declared undistinguishing and exterminating war, as a part of his religion, against all the rest of mankind. THE ESSENCE OF HIS DOCTRINE WAS VIOLENCE AND LUST.— TO EXALT THE BRUTAL OVER THE SPIRITUAL PART OF HUMAN NATURE....

Between these two religions, thus contrasted in their characters, a war of twelve hundred years has already raged. The war is yet flagrant ... While the merciless and dissolute dogmas of the false prophet shall furnish motives to human action, there can never be peace upon earth, and good will towards men." [The words in caps are as originally printed].

John Quincy Adams (1767-1848)
Sixth President of the United States

"How dreadful are the curses which Mohammedanism lays on its votaries! Besides the fanatical frenzy, which is as dangerous in a man as hydrophobia [rabies] in a dog, there is this fearful fatalistic apathy. ...The fact that in Mohammedan law [sharia] every woman must belong to some man as his absolute property, either as a child, a wife, or a concubine, must delay the final extinction of slavery until the faith of Islam has ceased to be a great power among men. Individual Moslems may show splendid qualities — but the influence of the religion paralyzes the social development of those who follow it. No stronger retrograde force exists in the world."

Sir Winston Churchill (1874-1965)
British Prime Minister

"Only in the Roman Empire and in Spain under Arab domination has culture been a potent factor. Under the Arab, the standard attained was wholly admirable; to [Islamic] Spain flocked the greatest scientists, thinkers, astronomers, and mathematicians of the world, and side by side there flourished a spirit of sweet human tolerance and a sense of purist chivalry. Then with the advent of Christianity, came the barbarians. Had Charles Martel not been victorious at Poitiers—already you see the world had already fallen into the hands of the Jews, so gutless a thing Christianity!"

Adolph Hitler (1889-1945)

"Today [1950], the hatred of the Moslem countries against the West is becoming hatred against Christianity itself. Although the statesmen have not yet taken it into account, there is still grave danger that the temporal power of Islam may return and, with it, the menace that it may shake off a West which has ceased to be Christian, and affirm itself as a great anti-Christian world power."

Archbishop Fulton J. Sheen (1895-1979)

"Islam makes it incumbent on all adult males, provided they are not disabled and incapacitated, to prepare themselves for the conquest of [other] countries so that the writ of Islam is obeyed in every country in the world. But those who study Islamic Holy War will understand why Islam wants to conquer the whole world... Those who know nothing of Islam pretend that Islam counsels against war. Those [who say this] are witless. Islam says, kill all the unbelievers just as they would kill you all! ...Whatever good there is, exists thanks to the sword, and in the shadow of the sword! People cannot be made obedient, except with the sword! The sword is the key to Paradise, which can be opened only for Holy Warriors! ...Does all that mean that Islam is a religion that prevents men from waging war? I spit upon those foolish souls who make such a claim."

Ayatollah Khomeini (1902-1989)

"[Islam] is essentially an obstructive, intolerant system... It has consecrated despotism; it has consecrated polygamy; it has consecrated slavery. It has declared war against every other creed; it has claimed to be at least dominant in every land... When it ceases to have an enemy to contend against, it sinks into sluggish stupidity and into a barbarism far viler... It must have an enemy; if cut off...from conflict with the infidel, it finds its substitute in sectarian hatred of brother Moslems..."

Edward Augustus Freeman (1823-1892)
British historian

"Qur'an... an accursed book... So long as there is this book there will be no peace in the world."

William Gladstone (1809-1898)
Prime Minister of Great Britain 1868 – 1894

"In the mid 1970s, the KGB ordered my service, the DIE — along with other East European sister services — to scour the country for trusted party activists belonging to various Islamic ethnic groups, train them in disinformation and terrorist operations, and infiltrate them into the countries of our "sphere of influence." Their task was to export a rabid...hatred for American Zionism by manipulating the ancestral abhorrence for Jews felt by the people in that part of the world. Before I left Romania for good, in 1978, my DIE had dispatched around 500 such undercover agents to Islamic countries. According to a rough estimate received from Moscow, by 1978 the whole Soviet-bloc intelligence community had sent some 4,000 such agents of influence into the Islamic world."

Gen. Ion Pacepa
Former head of the DIE —
the Romanian equivalent of Communist Russia's KGB

"Am I calling for a war between Christianity and Islam? Certainly not. What I am calling for is a general recognition that we are already in a war. ...What we are fighting today is not precisely a "war on terror." Terror is a tactic, not an opponent. To wage a "war on terror" is like waging a "war on bombs": it focuses on a tool of the enemy rather than the enemy itself. A refusal to identify the enemy is extremely dangerous..."

Robert Spencer

"Arise. O sons of Arabia, fight for your sacred rights. Kill the Jews wherever you find them. Their spilled blood pleases Allah, our history, and religion."

From a radio broadcast by **Amin el-husseini**,
the Grand Mufti of Jerusalem.

After instigating a pro-Nazi putsch in Baghdad in 1941, he left for Germany, where he spent the remainder of WWII broadcasting Nazi propaganda to the Middle East.

"Will not perhaps the temporal power of Islam return and with it the menace of an armed Mohammedan world, which will shake off the domination of Europeans — still nominally Christian — and reappear as the prime enemy of our civilization? The future always comes as a surprise, but political wisdom consists in attempting at least some partial judgment of what that surprise may be. And for my part I cannot but believe that a main unexpected thing of the future is the return of Islam."

Hilaire Belloc (1870-1953)

"We should fully understand our religion. Fighting is a part of our religion and our Sharia [Islamic legal code]. Those who love God and his Prophet and this religion cannot deny that. Whoever denies even a minor tenet of our religion commits the gravest sin in Islam."

Osama bin Laden

""I view Islam not as a religion, but as a dangerous, totalitarian ideology — equal to communism and fascism. Aren't I allowed to say so?"

Geert Wilders

"Christianity was saved in Europe solely because the peoples of Europe fought. If the peoples of Europe in the seventh and eighth centuries, and on up to, and including, the seventeenth century, had not possessed a military equality with, and gradually a growing superiority over, the Mohammedans who invaded Europe, Europe would at this moment be Mohammedan and the Christian religion would be exterminated.

Wherever the Mohammedans have had complete sway, wherever the Christians have been unable to resist them by the sword, Christianity has ultimately disappeared. From the hammer of Charles Martel, to the sword of Sobieski, Christianity owed its safety in Europe to the fact that it was able to show that it could, and would, fight as well as the Mohammedan aggressor.

The civilization of Europe, America, and Australia, exists today at all, only because of the victories of civilized man over the enemies of civilization — because of victories through the centuries from Charles Martel, in the eighth century, and those of John Sobieski, in the seventeenth century. ...There are such "social values" today in Europe, America and Australia only because during those thousand years, the Christians of Europe possessed the warlike power to do what the Christians of Asia and Africa had failed to do — that is, to beat back the Moslem invader."

Teddy Roosevelt (1858 -1919)
Twenty-sixth President of the United States

"Islam isn't in America to be equal to any other faith, but to become dominant. The Qu'ran should be the highest authority in America, and Islam the only accepted religion on earth."

Omar Ahmed
CAIR (Council for American Islamic Relations) Founding Chairman

"Ladies and gentlemen, we have to recognize that Islam is not a religion. It is a worldwide political movement bent on domination of the world. And it is meant to subjugate all people under Islamic law. In the Quran, it says it very clearly. There are two spheres. One is the Dar al-Harb, which is the realm of war. The other is Dar al-Islam, which is that part that's under submission to Islam. There is no middle ground. You're either at war, or you're under submission."

Pat Robertson

I hope these quotes help to clear things up for the Pentagon. If I did not know better I would think that they were more concerned with political correctness than with honor, oaths, or country. The United States already has semi-dhimmi status — note the lack of free speech when it comes to Islam. I strongly urge the Pentagon to get on the ball and stop playing with themselves ASAP.

Laus Deo.

12

The Constitution, Nazis, and the Corpse Man

February 6, 2010

In this article I once again hammer on the fact that fascism, and the Nazis in particular, are a left-wing phenomenon. I believe that redundancy is needed in order to sweep away the decades of liberal lies surrounding the issue. All but forgotten today is the fact that for years liberals lauded fascism and compared it favorably with communism.

The "nutshell version" of how and why the liberals distanced themselves from the fascists begins when Stalin decided that the fascists were no longer part of the communist "fold" and put out word to the party faithful that fascism was to be shunned. What better way to underline the "untouchable" status of fascism then to label them as right-wing, even though they were nothing of the sort? Lies and obfuscation are, after all, the stock in trade of the Far Left, so they went about the process of slandering the fascists with a will.

The atrocities of the Nazi death camps, work camps, and eugenics program made it all the more important for the Far Left to separate themselves from fascism and blame the Nazis on the "reactionary right." The resulting liberal propaganda resulted in unavoidable confusion (e.g. why was such a committed leftist like Ezra Pound such a staunch advocate of a "right-wing" fascist like Mussolini?), but the odd glitch and inconsistency was cleverly swept under the rug and ignored.

The "Great Lie" went largely unopposed and was "accepted wisdom" until the publication of Jonah Goldberg's watershed book "Liberal Fascism" a few years ago, which finally brought light to bear on decades of lies and disinformation.

Recently I have noticed several things that the Progressives are having trouble with. Well, actually a *lot* of things, but this article will focus on just a few of them. First of all Obama, like most Progressives, seems to have a problem identifying the US Constitution.

In his State of the Union address Obama stated that "We find unity in our incredible diversity, drawing on the promise enshrined in our Constitution: the notion that we are all created equal..."

Darn near made me want to stand up and salute (something our POTUS could use some lessons in by the way). There is a problem here however. It turns out that "the notion that we are all created equal" is not "enshrined in our Constitution" — it is from the Declaration of Independence.

This mistaken attribution is an understandable *faux pas* for your average "Joe six-pack," but Obama is supposed to be a Harvard-trained Constitutional lawyer. It does not say much for Harvard Law School, or Obama's grasp of the Constitution, when he confuses the US Constitution with the Declaration of Independence.

(Note to the White House (and Harvard Law School): they are two totally different documents, with different wording, and different purposes. They are not interchangeable. I know — bummer). One can imagine Obama's final exam on Constitutional Law:

Harvard Law professor: "Mister Obama, what are the opening words of the US Constitution?"

Obama: "Uh, 'When in the course of human events...'"

Harvard Law professor: "Close enough! You pass!"

No wonder these folks have so much trouble following the Constitution. Next, I would like to discuss the Nazis — again.

The Progressives, and their Islamic buddies, are still showing a fondness for equating conservatives with Nazis. It has been repeatedly pointed out to liberals that conservatives are *not* Nazis — that if anyone is a Nazi, it is *them*. All to no avail.

Disparaging a conservative, by calling them a Nazi, is no doubt insulting, but it is also misleading, misguided, and nonsensical. Nazis are a Far Left phenomenon all the way, but this obvious point is simply not registering with the left-wing. So once more unto the breach, dear friends. I will write this slowly so our Progressive friends can follow along, and hopefully, finally see the light. (It is worth a try, right?)

To understand the roots of Nazism is simplicity itself. NAZI is an acronym (in German) for Adolph Hitler's political party, the "National Socialist German Workers Party." Take out the words "National," and "German," and you are left with the "Socialist Workers Party."

The "Socialist Workers Party." Hello? That is unequivocally *not* a conservative outfit folks — that is as Far Left as you can get (well, I suppose you *could* nudge it a little farther left by calling it the "*Communist* Workers Party," but that is really quibbling over semantics). I can easily picture a "Socialist Workers Party" being a voting bloc at a *Democratic* convention — but at a *Republican* convention? Puh-leeze.

Adding the terms "National" and "German," is the main reason why Nazism a fascist, as opposed to a communist, variation of Marxism. The German Nazis (like Mussolini's Italian fascists) practiced a *national* brand of Marxism, as opposed to the Russian communists, who practiced a *global* brand of Marxism.

There are other differences as well, but the key point is that both communism and fascism are big-government *totalitarian* (Mussolini coined the term) doctrines. (Totalitarian: *adj.* of or relating to a system of government that is centralized and dictatorial and requires complete subservience to the state).

Fascism and Communism are closely related, and Progressivism has links to them both. So you Progressives can take back your swastikas, Hitler moustaches, and "Sieg heils." They are yours, and always have been. Here — don't forget your arm-bands.

The inextricable link between the Nazis and Progressives helps to explain the Progressive's fondness for abortion, euthanasia, and population control. It is nothing more than the "same old, same old" — the same old Nazi song and dance hidden behind new labels, new "clothes," and the passage of time.

It is no coincidence that George Soros, the most visible of the puppet masters behind the modern Progressive movement, and founder of "Project on Death in America," was once a Nazi collaborator. The Progressive's link with the Nazis also helps to explain their ever-increasing anti-Semitic/anti-Zionist stance.

If you doubt that anti-Semitism/anti-Zionism is rampant, and growing in Progressive Europe, then you have not been paying attention to what is going on in "Eurabia" these days. I strongly suggest that any Jews who consider Progressives to be the best thing since sliced matzah reconsider their position — excepting those with a taste for masochism and suicide, of course.

Study some history — preferably from a history book not written by a Western civilization hating, Judeo/Christian-culture despising, capitalism deploring, left-wing Progressive academic. You may have to search far and wide for such a book, but it is well worth the effort.

In closing, there is one last thing I would like to touch on. The other day Obama repeatedly referred to a US military corpsman, as a "corpse-man." The use of such a misnomer needs to be nipped in the bud before it catches on.

Yelling out "Hey I need a corpse-man over here!" in the thick of battle, would not only prove unnecessarily alarming to any wounded, but would no doubt be detrimental to troop morale as a whole. Someone needs to inform the POTUS that corpsman is pronounced "core-man" — with the "p" and "s" silent.

In all seriousness, Navy corpsmen (and Army/Air Force medics) have historically been among some of the bravest people in the U.S. military; often putting their lives on the line in order to help others, and at times paying the ultimate price for doing so. Many vets and active duty personnel are alive today only because of some corpsman's heroic and timely efforts.

The POTUS would do well to read up on some of the many corpsmen who have received the Medal of Honor over the years. At the very least, the CINC (Commander in Chief) should learn how to pronounce the honorable name of "corpsman" properly.

Laus Deo

13

The Real American Narrative

February 14, 2010

Written some months before the 2010 elections, if anything this article is truer today than when it was first written — just substitute the year 2012 for 2010.

"I fear all we have done is to awaken a sleeping giant and fill him with a terrible resolve"

> *Japanese Admiral Yamamoto after the attack*
> *on Pearl Harbor (from the film "Tora! Tora! Tora!")*

"You've awakened a sleeping giant."

> *Katy Abram to Sen. Arlen Specter*
> *at a Town Hall meeting, early August, 2009*

In a recent article in "The Weekly Standard," Jeff Bergner wrote about the American Narrative — how it has been written by the Left; adopted by our culture, and accepted by Democrats and Republicans alike.

Bergner says that the Narrative goes something like this: From its founding, America has been working towards the ideal of equality for all. This goal is an inevitable certainty, although it must be aided now and again by the use of will, and power. The best means of ensuring equality for all is through the auspices of strong government entitlement programs.

Those who oppose the Narrative are evil, backward, selfish rubes, who place their own self-interest before the welfare of others. The Narrative also says that the idea of American exceptionalism is nothing but a misguided, parochial elitism which thwarts world peace and encourages a divisive American arrogance.

The Left wrote the Narrative in order to supplant America's *real* Narrative, and it has been disseminated via Progressive journalists, academics, and politicians for over a century. It has been repeated so pervasively and insistently that it is now taken as a matter of course by most people. It is, however, a lie.

In his article, Bergner quotes Progressive scribe and pundit, Walter Lippmann, opining in 1932. "In the name of progress, men who call themselves communists, socialists, fascists...progressives, and even liberals, are unanimous in holding that government with its instruments of coercion, must by commanding the people how they shall live, direct the course of civilization..."

Got it? That is progressivism in a nutshell. "We the people" are to be "commanded" and "coerced" by a tyrannical government into doing what a Progressive elite feels is best for the collective. Social engineering at its reprehensible and vile best.

I should be noted that Lippmann shows no hesitation in lumping fascists in with communists, progressives, socialists, and liberals. Before the advent of WW II it was accepted wisdom among the left-wing *intelligentsia* that fascism was one of "their" doctrines. Hitler and Mussolini were lionized by the Left.

So when you are adding up the bloody body-count of failed leftist regimes of the last century, don't forget to add Hitler and Mussolini to the list of Lenin, Stalin, Mao, and Pol Pot. Left-wing totalitarian governments always work out so well (that's sarcasm).

The Left never learns. It is as if they have some sort of selective amnesia when it comes to their innumerable murderous screw-ups — so we need to remember for them. "We the people" need to constantly remind ourselves that these morally stunted, ethically challenged, fiscal morons are dangerous to themselves and humanity as a whole.

These regressive Progressives are forever "running with scissors," and if they don't hurt themselves, they will certainly hurt *you*. They are about as future-oriented as a twig hut. Their "Progressive" agenda consists of an updated, snazzy, "new and improved" return to serfdom for "we the people."

NWO (New World Order) Progressives come in both left and right-wing varieties, of course — although the left-wing takes "pride of place" for blind adherence to the idiotic notions of progressivism.

The hothouse conceptual inbreeding of the left-wing *intelligentsia* has resulted in more economic fiascoes than any other political entity — nobody else even comes close. I get the feeling that they take some sort of perverse pride in this fact. "We are too smart to be distracted by facts, history, or common sense."

America's current crop of Progressives looks to Eurabia (formerly Europe) as the ideal that America should strive toward. Yes indeed, a veritable cornucopia of largess, wealth, and equality. Not.

Greece is on the brink of civil war, Spain's "green jobs" initiative is a disaster, France is a simmering multicultural pressure-cooker, free speech is ever more muzzled, and the European Union's economy is falling apart. This is the Progressive's vaunted political template? Well, they can keep it — "we the people" want nothing to do with that mess.

So what *do* we want? What is America's *true* Narrative? There are several variations, but the basic story-line goes something like this:

America was started as a great experiment — one believed by its founders to be divinely ordained. The world had never seen such a country before, and to this day it is in many ways still unique.

America was founded upon the bedrock foundation that God had endowed its citizens with certain unalienable (therefore untouchable) rights. Among these untouchable rights were liberty (personal free-dom), life, and the pursuit of happiness.

The Founding Fathers wrote a legal document (the Constitution), designed to protect the rights of the citizens and restrict the role of government. The Constitution and Bill of Rights were specifically written to protect American citizens from the stifling interference of an overreaching and tyrannical government.

All of America's citizens were considered to be equal — not in any physical sense, of course, but because each of them had a similar divine spark from their Creator. On the mundane physical level, America strove for equality by attempting to build a level playing field of equal opportunities for all. Opportunities — not entitlements.

Personal-responsibility, honesty, charity, hard work, courage, and faith were watchwords for individual conduct. An entrepreneurial spirit, a capitalist market economy, and a merit system based on performance were important elements of a hugely successful national character.

Most importantly, America was founded with a profound appreciation of God, based on Judeo/Christian principles. This, of course, meant a deep respect for truth, for "...the truth shall set you free." George Washington's admonition to "seek truth and pursue it steadily," applied to the country as well as individuals.

With God, personal liberty, and truth as a personal and national North Star, Americans haltingly, but steadily, prospered as individuals and as a nation. Then along came the Progressives.

The Progressives started rewriting the American Narrative at the turn of the last century and they've been at it ever since. They have downplayed, minimized, and ignored America's greatness, while they isolated, magnified, and exaggerated any of her faults.

Because the main tomes of the Left are all atheistic, their stock in trade is half-truths, perversions of the truth, and outright lies. Their ultimate fallback position is nihilism, chaos, and a bleak void. Make no mistake; they are in direct opposition to honor, integrity, and spiritual truth — truth in any form, for that matter.

One need only look at the Progressive lie of "man made global warming" in order to see their duplicitous *modus operandi*. The whole "green agenda" — Agenda 21, sustainable development, climate change, et al. is nothing but an elaborate ruse designed to steal our freedom, break the back of the middle-class, and destroy America's sovereignty.

Progressives would have us narcissistically immerse ourselves in "Sex and Soma," and worship at the feet of Gaia (Mother Earth), while they strip away our last remnants of freedom, honor, and dignity. How thoroughly Progressive: to praise glitter, exalt the crass, worship the creation, and ignore the Creator.

It is past time "we the people" took back the American Narrative and replaced the perverted lie fed to us by Progressive journalists, entertainers, academics, lawyers, and politicians over the decades.

It is time to return to America's roots, to our original Narrative. It is an old Narrative, but because it is based on truth it is an ever green and fresh Narrative. It is the only Narrative that will return America to sanity and allow us to face the future with vigor, inspiration, and hope. It is America's *real* Narrative.

It is time to again extol the virtues of personal-responsibility, honesty, charity, hard work, courage, and faith. It is time to eradicate the insidious spread of sustainable development, social justice, political correctness, entitlements, and all of the other Progressive horses—t."We the people" — a sleeping giant — have indeed awakened from a long slumber. And we did not awaken in a good mood.

We do not much like the fact that the Rockefellers, Rothschild's, Bilderberg's, Soros', etc. and international banking cartels have been gutting our economy, robbing us, and stealing our children's future. We do not like the fact that America is in hock to foreign interests — whether through financial ineptitude or design is beside the point.

We do not like the fact that our borders are open to all comers; that we are *still* dependent on foreign oil, and that the current Administration treats enemy combatants with more respect than our own troops. Nor do we like the government's fiscal insanity, which is either (1) a sign of greed and economic idiocy, and/or (2) an intentional ploy to destroy America as a world power.

We do not like the politically correct "hands off" policy toward Muslims who are seeking America's destruction in order to create a world-wide Islamic caliphate. We do not like the anti-American indoctrination that has replaced education in our schools. We do not like the fact that we have a POTUS whose past history is largely a cipher to "we the people" — except for two self-serving "autobiographies" of course.

Well, the list does goes on — we have been lulled to sleep for a long time. But we are awake now, and you had better believe it. "We the people" are up; getting our bearings, and preparing for the long haul.

The press, political pundits and TV "talking heads" are talking about how the elections this November might be as dramatic as the elections of 1994. Trust me, 1994 was nothing. You wait until November 2010 and you will see something to write home about. And November will just be the opening salvo.

Republicans take note; you are no safer than the Democrats. Although the stink gets worse the farther left you go, there is nobody in Congress that is above scrutiny, and Republicans will be replaced as needed — and there is a need.

Republican bigwigs say that we need to appeal to moderates — that the Republicans need a "big tent." Well, "we the people" don't want a frigging tent — we want our country back.

"We the people" have a message for the Progressives, or whatever label the anti-American NWO scumbags are hiding behind — whether they are smooth talking politicos, or violent radicals. "We reject your perverse left-wing agendas, and if you have a problem with that, bring it on."

On second thought, there is no need to bring it on — we will bring it to you. Just wait.

Laus Deo.

14

The Intelligentsia, Intellectuals, and Other Idiots

March 3, 2010

Almost all of the articles that ended up in this book were very close to being as good as they were going to get, and only needed a modicum of revising. This one, however, probably would have ended up on the cutting room floor had I realized at the onset just how much rewriting it would require. But the "rightness" at its core kept bringing me back to it.

This article is fundamentally unchanged from the version posted online, but it is certainly a much more polished effort and consequently a better read IMHO.

"Whoever takes it upon himself to write an honest intellectual history of twentieth-century Europe [and America] will need a strong stomach."

Mark Lilla "The Reckless Mind"

"Calling [conservatives] defenders of the status quo is a triumph of verbal virtuosity over plain and demonstrable facts. That such a lazy way of evading critics should have prevailed unchallenged from the eighteenth century to the present, among those who consider themselves "thinking people," is a sobering sign of the power of a vision and rhetoric to shut down thought."

Thomas Sowell "Intellectuals and Society"

I am reading Thomas Sowell's "Intellectuals and Society," and he uses the term "verbal virtuosity" to describe the *intelligentsia's* use of misdirection, obfuscation, and outright lies. Because his book deals with left-wing intellectuals he is called upon to use the term a lot.

Personally, I prefer the term "bulls—t," but out of regard for my readers sensibilities I will follow Mr. Sowell's lead and use *his* term throughout this article. Before we wade too deep into the "verbal virtuosity" allow me to define some other terms as used by Mr. Sowell.

"Intellect" is simply the capacity to think — there is high intellect, low intellect, and everything in between. "Intelligence" is the combination of intellect with good judgment. And finally, "wisdom" is the combination of intellect, judgment, knowledge, and *experience.*

Left-wing intellectuals have intellect in abundance — intelligence not so much, and are notoriously lacking when it comes to wisdom. So what do left-wing intellectuals possessing fine intellects, but only rudimentary intelligence and scant wisdom actually do? Well, they think — a lot.

They come up with ideas and "notions." The folks who "ooo" and "ahhh" at the notions that intellectuals arrive at are called the "*intelligentsia.*" The *intelligentsia* not only "ooo" and "ahh," but they also try to introduce the intellectual's ideas into society at large.

The right-wing has its own intellectuals — some notable examples being Adam Smith, Edmund Burke, F.A. Hayek, Milton Friedman, and Thomas Sowell himself. Because right-wing intellectuals generally inject intelligence and wisdom into their ideas, they are fewer in number than the "dime a dozen" left-wing intellectuals. Also, we must take into account the long-standing animosity toward conservatives in academia and the press. All this has resulted in a plethora of *left*-wing intellectuals and a relative dearth of right-wing intellectuals.

Given their greater numbers, when I refer to intellectuals and the *intelligentsia* from now on I am referring exclusively to the *left*-wing variety. The *intelligentsia* consists of those teachers, journalists, politicians, lawyers, judges, and "others who base their beliefs or actions on the ideas of intellectuals."

The *intelligentsia* does not *chiefly* consist of greedy, ruthless, power addicted idiots, nor radical, violent, asocial idiots, but mainly bleeding-heart "useful idiot" idiots.

Please do not make the mistake of confusing the intellectual's often impenetrable and Byzantine pseudo-logic for intelligent discourse. It is designed to cover up the fact that their puerile narcissistic doctrines are ultimately based on nothing at all, as are all atheistic philosophies — how could it be otherwise?

There can be no real meaning in a purposeless universe, and there can be no purpose in a Godless universe. In the atheist's universe there is only pointless egocentrism to delude yourself with while awaiting the end of your meaningless existence (which is an illusion anyway). As the ego-game is the-only-game-in-town to the atheist, they treat it with the utmost seriousness.

This is the main reason why the Left is so intent on fixing the *outside*. Their *inside* remains largely untouched by introspection or honest self-appraisal — it is an *old* game. Jesus observed of the *intelligentsia* of his day: "You clean the *outside* of the cup...but *inside* you are full of greed and self-indulgence."

Because intellectuals deal with abstract ideas concerning abstract people in an abstract world, their notions are lacking in any "real world" experience, constraints, or common sense. Consequently, intellectuals and the *intelligentsia* are infamous for their "unintended consequences."

"Sorry about wasting trillions of your tax dollars — oopsie." Actually the *intelligentsia* would never make such a remark as they are world-class hypocrites and *never* admit to doing anything as plebeian as making a mistake. A "mistake" to their way of thinking is getting caught — bad form.

Intellectuals are professionals at covering up, minimizing, and denying their innumerable screw-ups through the use of their finely honed talent for verbal virtuosity. The *intelligentsia* never hold intellectuals accountable for their f—kups.

As Eric Hoffer puts it, "One of the surprising privileges of intellectuals is that they are free to be scandalously asinine without harming their reputations." It is less than good news that the Obama Administration has more intellectuals and fewer folks with real world experience than any other administration in US history.

Perhaps the most dangerous element of the intellectual-*intelligentsia* circle is that no *external* criteria are brought into play. That is, the intellectuals get feedback about their notions, not from any "real world" consequences (like losing their job, status, or money), but from the "thumbs up" or "thumbs down" of the like-minded *intelligentsia*. They march in lock-step groupthink — generally toward oblivion. This would be all fine and good except for the fact that they have this penchant for taking everyone else with them.

They are convinced that they know what is best for us all, and if "we the people" need to be bent, spindled, and mutilated in order to get us to conform properly to the collective template — well, that is only because we are too dim to appreciate their superior good sense, *savoir faire*, and social standing.

The fact that "we the people" are actually pretty darn sure about what is good for us, and it does *not* include the *intelligentsia's* lame-brained notions, does not compute with them. To their arrogant, utopia-addled minds we simply just don't get it. But we *do* get it — they are morons, we *get* that.

As Sowell points out, "it is doubtful whether the most knowledgeable person on earth has even one percent of the total knowledge on earth, or even one percent of the consequential knowledge in a given society. There are many serious implications of this which may, among other things, help explain why so many leading intellectuals have so often backed notions that proved to be disastrous."

Because the intellectuals and *intelligentsia* have such a deluded and exalted view of their intelligence (minimal), and wisdom (imaginary), "they have often overlooked the crucial fact that the population at large ["we the people"] may have vastly more total knowledge...than the elites, even if that knowledge is scattered in individually unimpressive fragments among vast numbers of people," says Sowell.

In other words, "we the people" possess a type of real world "collective consciousness" that is vastly superior at arriving at pragmatic solutions then the abstract groupthink of the insulated, inexperienced, inbred intellectuals and their sycophants.

Sowell continues, "If no one has even one percent of the knowledge currently available [not to mention the infinite amount of knowledge yet to be discovered], the imposition from the top down of the notions in favor among the elites, convinced of their own superior knowledge and virtue, is a formula for disaster." Can I hear an Amen?

What we are talking about here is the collective wisdom culled from the *experiences* of the many ("we the people"), versus the abstract *notions* of an arrogant few.

It really comes down to one of the key elements of wisdom — *experience*. "We the people" have it, and the intellectuals and *intelligentsia* do not. And without experience you cannot have good judgment (intelligence), let alone wisdom.

In short; intellectuals and the *intelligentsia* are generally dumber than dirt when it comes to any number of subjects outside of their area of expertise — most infamously the specialty of economics, about which they *all* consider themselves to be experts. (Though I suppose if you consider an economic expert to be someone who takes money from other people and squanders it while enriching themselves in the process, then they have a legitimate claim to the title).

The *intelligentsia* often refers to government by the euphemism "society" — as in President Johnson's "Great Society" (i.e. "Big Government"). Sowell notes that "what is called 'social' planning are in fact government orders over-riding the plans and mutual accommodations of millions of other people."

The *intelligentsia* dictates economic policy that is in line with their groupthink. They are generally idiots when it comes to economics but this does not deter them in the slightest. They are oblivious to the economic wrack and ruin they often inflict on those they "help." They set themselves up to profit in any event.

They are quick to implement any policies that make them appear to be "on the side of the angels," no matter the unintended consequences. Look at the current state of Detroit's economy if you wish to see the results of such willful blindness and smug hubris. Easier yet, check your wallet.

"We the people" are being financially squeezed in order to bail out Wall Street, the banks, large corporations, and other fat cats. At the same time, we are being squeezed to pay for entitlements to the poor.

The *intelligentsia* may call it "social justice" — I call it legalized robbery. Basically it is a government-run extortion racket — pay up or else.

Sowell calls this reckless behavior the "vision of the anointed" — *self*-anointed to be sure. The anointed vision is largely based on Rousseau's idea of the noble savage who "was born free, and...is everywhere in chains." This ties in with the *intelligentsia's* idea of an egalitarian society where everyone is equal.

The fact that a primitive society of Rousseauian savages has never been found, or that a successful egalitarian society has never existed, does little to dampen their ardor for considering such societies to be our *natural* state.

They are convinced that it is only capitalism, Christianity, and the other social institutions of Western civilization which keep us from experiencing a utopian bliss — naturally.

Sowell sagely observes that the *intelligentsia's* empirical case for an egalitarian society runs the gamut from "feeble to non-existent." Nonetheless, the anointed feel justified in their fantasies because they are very smart you know — just ask them.

Opposing the vision of the anointed is what Sowell calls the "tragic" vision — tragic because it sees life as a constant struggle against the baser elements of human nature. He writes "the tragic vision regards itself as something that requires constant great and constant efforts merely to be preserved — with these efforts to be based on actual experience, not on 'exciting' new theories."

The tragic vision, which considers barbarism to be always waiting in the wings, and civilization to be a hard-won fragile prize to be protected, is the *conservative* vision.

It is a "constrained" vision, in that the acquired knowledge of the ages and the collective experience of billions of people, past and present, shows that certain societal constraints are needed in order to promote the most freedom for the most people.

I can picture a smooth PR pundit taking Mr. Sowell aside and saying something like: "Tommy, baby, now don't take this the wrong way, but calling conservatives "The Party of Tragedy and Constraint," stinks on ice. It's not working for me; sounds like a mortician's convention for crying out loud. Gotta lighten things up and think *big* — think Super Bowl half-time!"

Rather than the "anointed" vision versus the "tragic" vision, a perhaps more felicitously named match-up would contrast the "mature" vision versus the "immature" vision. The intellectual's vision is certainly an immature one — complete with hissy fits when thwarted, and temper tantrums when wants are denied.

Their "vision" is one of lies, manipulation, self-indulgence and duplicity. They remind me of nothing so much as Freud's spoiled King Baby — whose adult narcissistic demands make life miserable for all around them.

The conservative stance is the mature vision; it is the adult's vision. It champions self-responsible behavior, integrity, and choices based on a mature weighing of empirical evidence. Russell Kirk writes, "A people's historic continuity of experience, says the conservative, offers a guide to policy far better than the abstract designs of coffee-house philosophers."

We do not need any more abstract solutions for abstract people with abstract problems in an abstract world. "We the people" are *real* people with *real* problems in a *real* world clamoring for *real* solutions.

The *intelligentsia* say that they are "on the side of the angels," but you know they lie. Intellectuals are responsible for some of the most ruthless and horrific episodes in human history — from the French Revolution's Reign of Terror, to Cambodia's Killing Fields. On the side of the angels? I think not.

Contrary to what the *intelligentsia* would have us believe, empirical studies have shown that it is conservatives, in fact, who are the most generous giving people.

Outside of the *intelligentsia*, I do not see anyone rushing to support their claim to the moral high-ground. I have news for them: destroying the economic foundation of the middle-class is ethically reprehensible; turning the poor into an entitled class of welfare drones is insidious poison, and creating an elite to rule over "we the people" is morally vile.

It's a jungle out there kiddies, and you had best believe that there are individuals, corporations, and governments that would love nothing more than to take America down. Destroying us economically would suit them just fine.

Contrary to the view expressed by the *intelligentsia*, the United States of America faces far graver concerns than whether or not we win the world's "Miss Congeniality" contest.

The intelligentsia would have us believe that conservatives are a reactionary force that protects the status quo and puts the brakes on any forward progress. Nothing could be farther from the truth. As Sowell notes in his quote at the beginning of this article, it is a lie that has been operative for at least the last two centuries. It is nothing but a big pile of intellectual...verbal virtuosity.

The idea that conservatives have done nothing more than resist the inevitable rising tide of Progressivism is manure dished out by the *intelligentsia*. The truth is that subversive forces in favor of a massive centralized government — a global regime — have been slowly eroding the freedoms, virtues, and principles that conservatives defend.

It is these very freedoms, virtues, and principles that stand in the way of the New World Order's one-world government. The New World

Order is not some enlightened stride toward a future utopia — it's a huge step backwards, away from freedom, liberty, and hope.

Far from merely protecting the status quo, conservatives have been the driving force behind America's growth, strength, hope, and *constructive* change. It has been the intellectuals and *intelligentsia* that have been trying to reverse history and drag us back down to tyranny and lives as chattel.

If you are not familiar with world history then I suggest that you read up on how well all of the previous attempts at "people's utopias" have worked (not). The larger these "utopias" were, the fouler the consequences. One shudders to think what would result from attempting the same failed stratagems on a *global* scale. (And do not forget to add the German Nazis and Italian Fascists to the list — both came out of big government (*left*-wing) social engineering designs).

Conservatives are the agents of *positive* change, and always have been — change that does not end in economic ruin, chaos, and bloodshed; change that is based on fiscal responsibility, experience, integrity, and common sense — not deceit and "notions."

The duplicitous *intelligentsia* can keep their bloated totalitarian governments, their corrupt political elites, their trickery, and their fool's utopias. "We the people" demand that our power be returned to where the Founding Fathers placed it — in the hands of the people.

Power to the people!

Laus Deo.

15

It's the Illegality Stupid

April 29, 2010

I try to "wear the world like a loose robe," and most of the time I do, but occasionally the world gets the best of me and I bite back. This article is an example of that. The reason for my anger was not illegal immigration, or the federal government's tyrannical opposition to Arizona's SB1070 (which basically stated that Arizona was going to do what the federal government was supposed to do but was not).

The reason why I was so upset when I wrote this is because in the process of researching the article it hit me that the same sort of vile backstabbing crooks who had made such a bloody mess of the 20th century, were setting the world up for another bloody conflagration. The realization that the bastards were doing it AGAIN infuriated me. If profanity offends you please feel free to skip this "chapter."

My anger has since largely burned itself out — and in its place is an implacable resolve to oppose their arrogance, greed, and cupidity wherever, whenever, and however I can.

I bang on the "the Nazis are left-wing" drum once again, as I will continue to until it has become common knowledge — I believe it to be that important.

Illegal immigration, illegal aliens, illegal immigrants — *illegal*. Illegal: meaning not authorized by law; unlawful, criminal.

Good grief, what part of *"illegal"* do these morons protesting Arizona's SB1070 not understand? And the protesters are comparing Arizona's courageous (and commonsense) stance to fascism; Nazism; racism; to the holocaust, and to the Jim Crow laws of the Old South.

The charges of "racism" are blatantly absurd and the rest of their rubbish is just as puerile, mendacious, and ignorant. In each case, when the Lame Stream Media, protestors, or demagogues use these appellations all they are doing is pointing fingers right at themselves.

Fascism, both the Italian and German varieties, was a left-wing big government doctrine all the way. Fascist leader Mussolini put it like this: "Everything for the state [government], nothing outside the state, nothing above the state." (*"Tutto nello Stato, niente al di fuori dello Stato, nulla contro lo Stato"*).

The fascists (ergo German Nazis) were strictly a *left*-wing phenomenon; always have been, and always will be. So you duplicitous liberal putzes can stop pointing fingers, and simply go to the nearest mirror if you want to see a *real* Nazi. *Keep* your swastikas, and all your other Nazi gear. They are *yours*, and we refuse to take them off your bloody hands.

Hey morons! The racist "Jim Crow" laws were instituted by — guess who? The *left*-wing! That's right, the Democrats who controlled the Old South for decades. So take your Jim Crow racist bull-s—t, and shove it up where you keep your Nazi armbands, "Little Red Books," hammers and sickles, Muslim burkhas, and La Raza pins.

All of the millions of deaths caused by communism can be laid directly at the feet of the *left*-wing; all of the millions of people killed in the Nazi holocaust can be laid directly at the feet of the *left*-wing, all of the millions of deaths caused by abortion can be laid directly at the feet of the *left*-wing. Eugenics — *left*-wing. Jim Crow — *left*-wing. Killing Fields — *left*-wing, etc., etc., etc.

And now the spiritually warped, morally stunted, lying sacks of s—t that comprise the Far Left are prepared to once more immerse millions in bloodshed just so that they can satiate their ego-driven lusts and fulfill their perverted delusions. All of you left-wing dolts protesting Arizona's illegal immigration laws are obviously nothing but strident anti-American freedom hating a—holes. F—k each and every one of you traitorous dips—ts, from Boston to San Francisco, from sea to shining sea!

All that Arizona has done with SB1070 is to stand up and protect its LEGAL American citizens — *legally* — because the federal government has failed to do so. GOOD FOR ARIZONA! And f—k you if you don't like it!

If you oppose SB1070 then know that I despise you and all you stand for, and I am prepared to fight for myself, my family, and my country.

Laus Deo

16

Racism and the Never-ending Storm

July 25, 2010

It was around the time this article came out that the "race card" started to lose its effectiveness. No longer would it be the guaranteed show-stopper that it once was. Liberals had cried "Wolf!" one too many times and "we the people" were increasingly hip to the scam.

"Long as I remember, the rain been coming down.
Clouds of mystery pouring, confusion on the ground.
Five-Year plans, and New Deals, wrapped in golden chains.
And I wonder, still I wonder, who'll stop the rain?"

John Fogerty "Who'll Stop the Rain"

"Five-Year plans, and New Deals" — yeah buddy — where do I sign up, not. The Far Left always has a plan — a plethora of plans. The fact that their plans ultimately never work, does not dissuade them in the least. They are always prepared to go "back to the drawing board," and begin tweaking some new variation of the same old stuff.

If it's true, as the saying goes, that the definition of insanity is "doing the same thing over and over again, expecting different results," then the Far Left is certifiably insane. No surprise there.

In fact the insanity of the Left is so pervasive, so blatant, and so historically evident, that it is amazing that more people have not commented on it. Long-term proximity to nihilism will do that to you — ask

Nietzsche. Having the abyss stare back at you for any extended period of time, is just bound to put a kink or two in a person's psyche.

Actually, it's not so surprising that more folks aren't aware of the depraved nature of the Far Left. They are extremely clever, in a reptilian way, and have been very successful at hiding their screw-ups, or (and this is one of their favorite ploys) blaming them on conservatives. I think of the Far Left as being like an ever-present, never-ending storm. Wherever they go, they bring *strum und drang*; wrack and ruin — a "hard rain" indeed.

There are so many areas of life, culture, and society, which the Marxist/Fascists have damaged or ruined, that it's hard to know where to begin. Because the issue of race has been in the news lately, why don't we start there?

Would it surprise you to learn that the Ku Klux Klan was revived, and given its virulent racism by the left-wing? Are you aware that Progressive icon Margaret Sanger was a closet racist, and that the Planned Parenthood organization that she started was conceived of as a vehicle for racial genocide against blacks?

Seeing as how the Left is so fond of calling conservatives racists, let's take a look at those two topics, and a few others. We will see who has been chiefly responsible for keeping blacks "on the plantation." You may be surprised at what we find.

Long-time US Senator, and "liberal lion," Robert Byrd recently passed away. His days spent as a proactive heavyweight in the Klan, were largely swept under the rug by the media. One can be forgiven for wondering how he transitioned so smoothly from the Klan, to the Democratic Party — purportedly the party of, and for, the blacks. Well, wonder no more.

First a few facts: An article on revisionist history by Scotty Starnes lays some of the more pertinent facts out nicely: "What party was founded on a pro-slavery platform? Who was the party that supported and enforced [Jim Crow] laws from 1876 to 1965? What party voted against the passing of the 13th, 14th and 15th amendments, not to mention voting against every single piece of civil rights legislation up until 1965? The Democratic Party!"

The Democratic Party has a long history of racial bigotry of the vilest sort. No wonder there's such a thing as "liberal white guilt." I'd feel guilty too, if the political party I associated myself with, had a history like theirs. Sen. Byrd merely was following a path blazed long before he came along.

Revered Progressive icon, Woodrow Wilson, 28th President of the United States, was an especially rabid racist, and white supremacist. His enthusiastic endorsement of the cockeyed racist film, 'Birth of a Nation" (ostensibly about the Civil War) was largely responsible for the films popularity, and an especially brutal revival of the Klu Klux Klan.

The movie, which was silent, used several quotes from Wilson, that it flashed onscreen. Here's an example of one: "The white men were roused by a mere instinct of self-preservation... until at last there had sprung into existence a great Ku Klux Klan, a veritable empire of the South, to protect the Southern country." The Progressives were emphatically anti-black for several decades, and heavily promoted eugenics — especially the extermination of "inferior races."

Jonah Goldberg points out in his book "Liberal Fascism" that "In 1934, when the [Nazis] had sterilized over fifty thousand "unfit" Germans, a frustrated American eugenicist exclaimed, 'The Germans are beating us at our own game." Indeed, Hitler "took notes" from the eugenics' teachings of American Progressives.

Left-wing "saint," Margaret Sanger, the founder of Planned Parenthood, was another Progressive racist — and eugenicist. Another Progressive icon, FDR, appointed Klansman Hugo Black (D-AL) to the Supreme Court. You should check out the short video about Hugo Black made by Kevin Jackson as part of his "Great Moments in Democrat Racist History" series.

Michael Zak notes that, "In the 1950s, the Klansmen against whom the civil rights movement struggled were Democrats. The notorious police commissioner Bull Connor, who attacked African-Americans with dogs and clubs and fire hoses, was both a Klansman and the Democratic Party's National Committeeman for Alabama."

The list of Progressive/Democratic racist behavior is long, lurid, and loathsome, but in the 1960s they underwent a sea-change. What happened? A lot of things happened, but mainly Lyndon Baines Johnson (D-TX), the 36th President of the United States, happened.

Sensing the way the wind was blowing (due primarily to civil rights efforts made by conservative Republicans), LBJ (himself a racist) decided to co-opt the black vote. In a typical left-wing ploy, the Democrats positioned themselves to "solve" a problem largely created by them. The welfare programs initiated under FDR, were massively expanded under LBJ, and the modern "welfare state" as we know it was born.

The result of several generations living under the government's thumb has been devastating to black communities. Check out the number of one-parent families with no decent male role models and the dropout rates in the inner-city schools.

Their thinking has been so twisted and warped by Far Left propaganda that instead of valuing freedom and their right to succeed, they clamor for handouts and their "right" to be enslaved by a "nanny state." "Wrapped with golden chains" they suck from the teat of big government and consider themselves "entitled."

"We the people," work to support them, as the Far Left continues to exploit them (and us). Like concentration camp kapos, black "overseers" make sure that their charges stay on the plantation (in ghettos, on welfare), for "massa" (the Democratic Party). (Religious trappings seem to be favored by these "overseers").

Increasingly, the Left is playing "the race card," and increasingly, patriotic Americans are not buying it. "We the people" refuse to be labeled racist simply because we are voicing our non-racially motivated opinions. You want some racial bigotry? Try this quote on for size. It's from James Hal Cone, the founder of the Marxist, racist doctrine of Black Theology. Cone was a mentor of Jeremiah Wright (Obama's ex-pastor).

"If God is not for us [the blacks] and against the white people, then he is a murderer, and we had better kill him. The task of black theology is to kill Gods who do not belong to the black community..."

Hmm — you don't say? This is the same Jeremiah "God D—n America" Wright, in whose congregation the Obamas sat for over twenty years, without noticing anything untoward? Hmm. The Obamas must be more than a little dense is all I can say — or if they are *not* dense, then that would mean that they are (oh my gosh) racist. Perhaps they simply went through a phase (a 20-year-phase) of enjoying sermons given by a bigoted Marxist.

As American patriots awaken from being in thrall to the insidious effects of political correctness, they are noticing that the Democrats are still racists, but now the shoe is on the other foot. Now whites (and Asians) are discriminated against, and black bigotry is fostered and encouraged, via such channels as Black Theology, "social action," and most recently, the DOJ.

I suppose now would be a good time to underline the fact that I am not prejudiced. I believe that we are all God's kids, and skin color is certainly no reason for negative feelings, or positive ones for that matter ("content of character," and all that). I abhor racism; whether it comes from whites or blacks.

How I deal with left-wing folks who call me a racist, has changed from what it used to be. Back in the day, I might have said something crass like "F—k off," and then gone on to explain the racist nature of the Progressives to them. I have mended my ways though, and these days, I just say "F—k off," and leave.

I have've learned that it never pays to get into a debate with one of these dolts, as they are generally not interested in the truth — only in pushing their agenda. One does, occasionally, run into a liberal that is open-minded, and therefore salvageable, but they are a *rara avis* indeed.

The Far Left are masters of misdirection, lies, and subterfuge — they have to be, because once their agenda is exposed, people overwhelmingly reject it; as a matter of course. As I mentioned earlier, one of their favorite ploys is to lay the blame for their more flagrant failures at the feet of conservatives. They have successfully obfuscated the truth about a thousand-and-one things — primarily through the venues of a compliant academia, media, and entertainment industry. They sow lies, disinformation and confusion wherever they go like some deranged Johnny Appleseed.

This helps to explain such paradoxes as Sen. Byrd's racist Klan past, being so readily "forgiven" by the Democratic Party — or Hitler being both a "right-wing reactionary," and a Far Left founder of Germany's socialist worker's party (NAZI). The Far Left lies, cheats, steals, extorts, obfuscates, misdirects — and then has the gall to claim the moral *high* ground. Their two-faced hypocrisy knows no bounds — *none.*

Aside from the fact that they live in a delusional hothouse atmosphere where they are constantly telling each other how wonderful they are, (and giving each other prestigious awards to "prove" as much), liberals suffer from a host of other factors that contribute to their irritating, and dangerous, hubris. We need to know more — we need to know our enemy and make no mistake the Far Left, and to a lesser extent liberals, are every liberty-loving patriot's enemy.

The hundred million deaths attributed to the Far Left in the "Black Book of Communism" only tell the half of it. Add the deaths caused by Far Left fascist dictator, Hitler, to the list; add the deaths Mussolini was responsible for to the list; add the lynchings and burnings of the Ku Klux Klan to the list. Add all of the wrecked, poisoned, shattered and stunted lives that the Far Left has been responsible for — from the French Revolution up to the present day.

The Far Left "storm" has been going on for some time — waxing and waning over the years. Many scholars trace its beginnings to Jean-Jacques Rousseau (1712-1778), and the French Revolution. Others trace it back farther. For example, in his book "Moral Darwinism," Benjamin Wicker makes a convincing case that the "storm" is actually an ages-long war, waged between spirituality and materialism, with its roots in the teachings of Epicurus (341 BC-270 BC). Be that as it may, the storm has been with us for a long, long time.

In closing, we should remember that it's not just the left-wing that has problems; the right-wing has its own concerns, such as our own in-house Progressives, RINOs, and other issues — but that's a topic for another article.

For now, I'm keeping a weather-eye on the Far Left and liberals, and carrying my umbrella with me.

Laus Deo.

17

What Exactly Is It We Are Doing In Afghanistan?

July 29, 2010

Perhaps the way that our involvement in Afghanistan has been handled by Congress is not treasonous — perhaps it only appears treasonous as the result of monumental stupidity and incompetence. Your call.

"Hey, I have a great idea — let's colonize an opium-rich cultural backwater half the world away surrounded by countries that the enemy can hide in and get resupplied by! And while we are getting shot at, maimed, and killed, we can make sure that they practice recycling and becomes eco-conscious comrades of Gaia! Whadda ya think?"

I think it is insane by anyone's measure — and some of America's best and bravest have paid dearly to implement this asinine "strategy."

I opened this article with Rep. Gabrielle Gifford's quote in order to give some idea of the skewed priorities at play in the Afghanistan war. I, of course, had no idea that she would be gunned down in the Tucson tragedy early the next year. I wish her only the best and pray that she is blessed with a miraculously full recovery.

"[General Petraeus] we know that a major part of the Kandahar offensive will include some serious repairs, and upgrades to the energy system, which will include small-scale solar and hydro-power systems, and also

some solar-powered street lights. I'm just curious if [there are] plans to utilize any of those same technologies at our bases around Afghanistan, and wouldn't that greatly reduce our need for fuel?"

Gabrielle Giffords (D-AZ) (questioning Gen. Petraeus during a Congressional briefing June, 2010)

Allow me to suggest that America bring our troops home from Afghanistan, and get our own house in order before we even think about exporting "what we have" to other countries. What exactly is it that we *have* anyway, that the world is in such dire need of?

Our floundering economy? Our social-activist trial lawyers and judges? Our racially bigoted justice department? Our corrupt and venal Congress? Our pathetic educational/indoctrination system? Our multibillion dollar porno industry? Hollyweird? Our shredded US Constitution? Our.... What is it exactly that is so precious, so important, so vital that we absolutely *must* gift Afghanistan with it? I'm listening.

(Crickets chirping. Sagebrush rolling across a ghost-town's dusty street. A soft breeze blowing over the Greenland icecap).

I didn't think so. So if America does not really have much to offer — *until we get our own house in order* — wouldn't you say *that* should be our first order of business? Otherwise, I suspect that all we are doing is exporting the mess and not the message.

And what is our message, or rather, what *should* our message be? The message is the US Constitution. The message is free enterprise and capitalism. The message is the rule of law in a free republic. The message is one man, one vote. The message is lost. America's identity is lost and we need to get it back — now, before it is lost for good.

Coach Dave Daubenmire recently said about Americans, that "we have a sense of emergency, but not of urgency." If Americans had any idea — *any* idea — how bad things are in this country, especially *vis a vis* the Islamist stealth jihad being waged against us, they would sit up and pay attention. They would acquire a "sense of urgency" in a heartbeat. America needs to wake up *now*, yesterday would have been better.

We need to deal with the threat the Islamists pose right here in America. Right *here*, right *now*. And we need to deal with an invasion taking place across our southern border — right *here*, right *now*. We need to deal with a corrupt and traitorous Congress — right *here*, right *now*. We need to deal with an economy in a nose-dive — right *here*, right *now*.

We need to deal with a POTUS and an administration that are destroying America as a free republic, as a world power, as a "beacon of light" to the world. We have quite enough on our plate *right at home* — right here, right now.

I am not saying that we should withdraw *all* of our troops from overseas. We are, after all, involved in a global war with Islamists (GWWI). (Calling it a "war on terror" is not only an anathema to the current administration, it is — not to put too fine a point on it - stupid).

As Robert Spencer points out, we have never actually fought "a war on terror." He writes "Terror is a tactic, not an opponent. To wage a 'war on terror' is like waging a 'war on bombs': it focuses on a *tool* of the enemy rather than the enemy itself."

The enemy is Islamists, not terror. Terror is just one weapon in their arsenal. And America d—n well better wake up to this fact — quickly. The stealth jihad in the United States is well underway.

Understanding Islamist tactics and goals will go a long way towards explaining why I do not believe that Afghanistan can ever successfully be "colonized" by the US — either directly, or by proxy.

(Sidebar: There are a number of good books concerning the threat posed by the Islamists. I especially recommend Robert Spencer's books. Ralph Peters' "Endless War" is a personal favorite. "The Grand Jihad" by Andrew McCarthy is excellent, and covers a lot of bases. Also, there are several good websites out there — "Jihad Watch" "Creeping Sharia," and "Act for America" are three of the better ones).

We should take each member of Congress, lock them in a room; sit them down and require them to read "Radical Islam for Dumb F—ks," or any other suitable book, such as "The Politically Incorrect Guide to Islam: and the Crusades." And not let the morons out — not even for a latte break, or pedicure — until they have finished reading the entire book. (A handful of Congress-critters can be excused from having to attend such a class — Sue Myrick (R-NC) springs to mind).

Getting back to US involvement in Afghanistan: Do you think we are going to "win the hearts and minds" of the Afghan people? Oh really? What makes you think that such a thing is either plausible or possible? Have you given any thought to what is involved in such a lame-brained undertaking? The cost to our men and women in uniform?

I do not wish to give anyone the wrong idea here — it is not like I am an anti-war activist or something. I mean, of course I deplore war, any sane person does, but I feel that war is sometimes an unavoidable necessity. Sometimes evil must be *physically* beaten.

However, I am also a firm believer in — get in, do your business, and get out. I'm from the Vietnam era — call me "gun shy" regarding long-term "hearts and minds" overseas military entanglements.

Am I for a long term commitment to defeating the Islamists? Absolutely, you bet. Am I for a long term commitment to "colonizing" the Islamic world? No frigging way.

Here is an idea: Bring our troops home from Afghanistan and deploy them along the US southern border and start kicking some drug cartel butt! Now there's a war that makes sense to me. Bring our troops home and give them some sane ROE (Rules of Engagement), and leaders who take their oaths to defend the Constitution earnestly. We need to deep-six the current crop of court eunuchs running the show at the Pentagon these days. We need patriotic warriors by God, not arrogant quisling career dweebs.

There are some questions that bother conservatives about leaving Afghanistan. Perhaps some of the following questions have crossed your mind:

Are you reluctant to appear to be agreeing with the Left?

Are you afraid of looking like you don't support our men and women in uniform?

Are you afraid that the Taliban will take over Afghanistan if we leave?

Are you afraid of America "losing" — losing face, if nothing else?

No doubt the most difficult question is: What about the US military men and women who have already sacrificed limbs, mental health, or lives. Are we supposed to just write off their loss — like it never happened, like it doesn't matter?

Let me attempt to answer each of these in turn.

Not wanting to support a US withdrawal from Afghanistan because it might appear that you are agreeing with the Left is the lamest of these positions. Withdrawing from Afghanistan is a question of sound reasoning, priorities and national interest; it is not simply a defeatist leftist ploy.

Although the Left may at times do the right things for the wrong reasons (usually they do the wrong things for the wrong reasons), that does not negate the fact that the things that they promote are sometimes right. Even a broken clock is right twice a day. We just want to make sure that we, as conservatives, are doing the right things for the *right* reasons.

As far as support for our troops goes — do you think that supporting a cock-eyed effort to colonize a barbarous, corrupt, stuck-in-the-middle-ages country is supporting our troops? Do you think that sending them into harm's way with one arm tied behind their back by idiotic ROE is supporting our troops? Do you think that pairing them up with a Taliban-infiltrated "ally" such as Pakistan is supporting our troops? Think again.

Will the Islamists take over Afghanistan when we leave? No doubt — they seem to be thriving everywhere else. We have to rethink this whole scenario from the get-go, and we need to get out of Afghanistan in order to best do that. If the Islamists come waltzing back in after we leave, then so be it.

We have more important fish to fry. America is going down the tubes — I could not care less about Afghanistan. Screw Afghanistan — and please feel free to tell them I said so. We need to save America first and foremost.

The whole "losing," or "losing face" deal is a red herring, and a sophomoric trap. If we have gained knowledge, wisdom, and experience from our time in Afghanistan, how is that "losing?" If we leave on our own terms, on our own time-table, after having kicked the Taliban and Bin Laden out of the country, how is that "losing face."

The Taliban may consider it a "loss" for the US, and the Taliban might consider it "losing face," but if you give a tinker's damn what the Taliban's opinion of us is then you have some serious self-image issues to deal with. F—k what the Taliban think of us.

I said that the last question was the hardest to answer, and indeed it is. I'll do my best. Let me say first of all that I honor all of our service men and women. I especially honor those who have sacrificed physically, or mentally/emotionally (or spiritually) on behalf of our country. And most of all, I honor those who "gave the last full measure" and died in the service of the United States; I am proud of them and grateful for them. May God bless them all and their families.

As I mentioned before, I am from the Vietnam era, so I long ago had to make peace with the idea that brave and patriotic men and women can be misused, mislead, and misdirected for less than noble reasons. Such treatment does not diminish in the slightest, the valor, integrity, and sacrifice of those who fought in Vietnam. *They* did not fail — their country failed them.

Those who fought in Vietnam were not *allowed* to win that war — for political reasons — but that in no way takes away from their honor. I feel the same way about those who have fought in Afghanistan. Their honor is intact — win or "lose," that is a given.

Saying "win or lose" is actually a misleading way of phrasing things — because we *already* won in Afghanistan some years ago. The US went in there to kick the Taliban's butt, and kill or capture Bin Laden. We did kick the Taliban's butt — from Kabul to Herat — and we chased Bin Laden out of the country with his tail between his legs. But then — then when we should have pulled our troops out, we screwed up and stayed.

I grant you, the situation in Afghanistan is a mess, with no easy clear-cut solutions. Yet surely getting bogged down "winning hearts and minds" in a brutal "tar-baby" backwater is near the bottom of anybody's list of smart moves.

If by some miracle we start to pull things together in Afghanistan what then? What is next — Yemen? Let us go to Yemen then, and colonize Yemen. But you know those darn Islamists will just scoot on over to Somalia. Somalia then? Let us go and colonize Somalia. Where to next? Decisions, decisions.

I do not know about you, but I have less than zero (we are talking negative numbers here) interest in colonizing the entire Muslim world. As much as I like Muslims that would just be too much of a good thing. It is insane to even contemplate it.

America is collapsing. America is being invaded — both from Mexico, and through stealth jihad. America is teetering on the brink of hyper-inflation and financial ruin. America is being transformed into an also-ran. America will soon be unrecognizable.

To let the United States of America become a shadow of its former self, *that* would be disrespecting our troops in Afghanistan. To allow the US to be invaded by drug cartels from Mexico, (while our DOJ attempts to aid and abet them), *that* would be betraying our troops in Afghanistan.

Pretending that the wholesale destruction of America's economy is not happening under our noses — *that* is letting down our troops in Afghanistan. Permitting America to go down the tubes on our watch, while our brave men and women fight for us overseas is the ultimate cowardly copout. *That* is disrespecting the sacrifices made by our military personnel in Afghanistan and around the world.

It disrespects not only the troops who are serving or have served in Afghanistan, it dishonors the memories of everyone who has ever fought for the United States of America — from the Revolutionary War on up until the present day. If America falls, all of their sacrifices throughout time — *all* of them — will have been for naught. Which do you think is more important — Afghanistan or America?

We should use the remaining time spent in Afghanistan to make necessary arrangements to facilitate any post-occupational surgical strikes and sallies that may be warranted in the future. I sympathize with the plight of the Afghan people, but their untrustworthy, corrupt, opium-spoils bloated government can go to h—l. I am much more concerned with the problems besieging the USA than with the fate of Afghanistan.

Let me reiterate, my problem with our involvement in Afghanistan is not with our men and women in uniform — they represent the best that America has to offer. Whether the US stays or goes they will always have my unwavering support.

"We the people" need to get our *own house* in order before we even *think* about exporting "what we have." Forget "*Pax Americana*," we need to save "*E Pluribus Unum*."

It's time to, in the time-honored tradition of America, take the United States and transform it into something better than we received — something that we can pass on to future generations with pride. And those future generations will say of us, "*They* were the ones who saved America in her darkest hour." No joke.

We must, and we will, restore the Framer's vision of a vital, ever-evolving, pluralistic society of laws and freedom under God's providence.

Laus Deo.

18

Semper Fidelis:
Jerry McConnell at Guadalcanal

August 8, 2010

This article came about when I discovered that fellow CFP columnist Jerry McConnell would be celebrating (if that's the word) the anniversary of his landing on the beaches of Guadalcanal during WW II. This article was polished up a bit and reposted in 2011 as "Still Fighting for His Country." Semper fi Jerry — always faithful.

"The circle of life begins at home midst family, then sometimes it ends away from home, but still in midst of family, now called friends. They were as much my brothers as if we shared the same last name. I couldn't have loved them more."

Jerry McConnell — First Marine Division,
First Marine Regiment, 3rd Battalion, K Company

It is important that as many Americans as possible wake up to the dire straits we are in, and it is especially important that the young adults of America wake up to how they are being led down a path to servitude, poverty, and mediocrity by the political/banking/corporate elites.

It is equally important that they understand that freedom is not free, and that they will have to fight for their liberty — one way or another. Patriotic Americans who have gone before them have left a long and proud tradition to draw inspiration from.

Readers of Canada Free Press are familiar with the articles of CFP columnist Jerry McConnell. He has been effectively using his pen to fight for America and exposing traitors, thieves, and scoundrels for years.

Many readers may not be aware that Mr. McConnell's fight to defend America began many years ago — with a gun, not a pen. August 7, 2010 commemorates the 68th anniversary of Jerry McConnell's arrival on Guadalcanal, and the start of that epic WW II battle. After his initial landing on the beach, it would be over four months before Jerry got to take a deep breath and step back from the constant strain of battle.

When he departed the 'Canal he weighed 35 pounds less than when he left the United States. He was weak from dysentery; wracked with malaria, and had seen and done things that he never imagined before Guadalcanal. He was 18 years old.

Before getting any deeper into Mr. McConnell's experiences on Guadalcanal I would like to thank Kent Cooper and the folks at Seacoast Marines. Without their efforts I would not have been able to piece together this article. It was Mr. Cooper who, a few years ago, persuaded Jerry that it was important for future generations that he write down "...a period of my life that had been put behind me to be forgotten. Too ugly to be remembered. Too unimportant to anyone but myself, and the others who went through it."

Guadalcanal is part of the Solomon Islands group, and is approximately ninety miles long by thirty-five miles wide. It is located to the northeast of Australia, around 600 miles east of Papua New Guinea.

The island was picked as the primary launching point for the beginning of the US "island-hopping" push toward Japan. The invasion of Guadalcanal was arguably the first major land offensive by the US in WW II — preceding the invasion of North Africa by three months. Such discussions are beyond the scope of this article, as are the great sea battles that took place around Guadalcanal.

Nor will I be going into detail about the day-to-day travails of the Marines and soldiers on Guadalcanal. That subject has been well covered in the past — most famously in war correspondent Richard Tragaskis' book "Guadalcanal Diary."

This article's focus is Mr. McConnell — a foot grunt in the thick of things. No grand scenarios here — just blood, sweat, fear, misery, bone-deep weariness — and a unit *espirit de corps* and *camaraderie* to die for.

Following several hours of US bombing and shelling of the invasion area, Jerry hit the beach with the 1st Marines on the morning of August 7, 1942. His unit, "...the Third Battalion of the First Marines, was among those given the objective of capturing a large 'grassy knoll' [Mt. Austen] just to the south of the airstrip that butted up against the mountains." The "grassy knoll" overlooked a captured Japanese airstrip (soon named Henderson Field), and its capture was of great importance.

Jerry recalls "Those first three days spelled out a lot of the entire story of the Guadalcanal campaign. We experienced large doses of fear, anxiety, near-death thoughts and encounters, punishing damage to our bodies, extreme thirst and hunger, and almost no sleep for the entire time."

That first night on the island, after an exhausting, adrenaline-pumping day, "...word was passed down the columns that every other man would sleep for two hours, while the others would remain awake and alert - hah!"

After a second day of fighting "the second night was a sleepless night for all — Japs and Americans. Some of our units continued to move forward up the hill, trying to gain an advantage. The resistance was severe, and the sharp crack of rifle-fire echoed all night long."

Following the third day of fighting, that night Jerry recalls "after we had secured the knoll, we were able to rest, and as a result, only those whose turn it was to stay awake, saw the naval flashes out on the bay. The rest didn't even hear the roar of the big naval guns." (The Battle of Savo Island).

"Of course, we had no idea who was who, and we naturally thought that our guys were winning. Wrong!"

Sleep became a matter of catch-as-catch-can. Jerry even mastered the trick of sleeping while awake. "I became quite adept at sleeping while I was awake. As strange as it sounds, it's true. I could doze off in seconds and wake just as quickly. Night sleep often proved deadly, so we avoided dropping off, keeping alert as much as we could."

McConnell throws some light on a little noted, or discussed, aspect of combat on Guadalcanal — or anywhere — personal hygiene. "We were unable to relieve our bowel demands for the entire [first] three days. It was something that was done only when the body would not allow any alternative."

"There just were no opportunities, or convenient places, for such necessities. You didn't dare wander off from the main body of troops, for fear of being killed or captured — or worse, mistakenly shot by one of your own men!"

Mr. McConnell explains that "I only mention it here, because over the years, in many stories, I have never seen it addressed. And yet, it was a very serious problem, that had many side effects, and repercussions, that contributed to deteriorated performance. Little did I know at the time, that it would set a pattern of behavior and living, that would become all too familiar to us in the coming months."

Getting, and keeping, Henderson Field operational became crucial after the US Navy left — a couple of days into the invasion — taking around half of the Marines' much-needed supplies with them. The ships would not return for another two months.

The Navy had been badly beaten-up in the waters off of Guadalcanal ("... the worst naval defeat ever suffered by the US Navy") in the early morning hours of August 9th. That, coupled with the fear of Japanese submarine attacks, aerial attacks, and other considerations, prompted the Navy to withdraw their support ships from Guadalcanal.

The waters offshore became known as "Iron Bottom Sound" due to the large number of ships and planes laying on the sea floor. All that the Marines on Guadalcanal knew was that they were stranded and screwed

The Marines on Guadalcanal were totally cut off from support and "we controlled about one-half of one percent of the total island, and the Japanese controlled the other ninety-nine and one-half percent."

It would be two weeks before Henderson Field would be operational and air support could fly in to Guadalcanal. "We filled the holes, and graded the strip, mostly with our bare hands, mostly during moments when we weren't engaged in some form of combat, which added to the delay."

"Getting that strip ready to receive our planes was a priority exceeded only by engaging in direct combat with enemy ground forces." Still, because of the atrocious conditions, and the lack of proper equipment, it was a couple of weeks before planes would, or could, fly into Henderson. In the meantime the Marines stranded on the island were on their own.

McConnell takes the time to explain some of the minutia of his life on the 'Canal. Things you might not think of:

The nights were often "quite chilly."

Because they had few machetes, they had to use their bayonets to cut through the tall (6'+), razor-sharp kunai grass.

Boot-laces rotted away, and "in a lot of cases were replaced with jungle vines."

When they ran into colonies of the large (1") red fire-ants, "we quickly learned to tuck the pant legs down inside our socks and knock them off as they climbed upwards."

"The sand-flies were about as bad as [those 'damned mosquitoes'], if not worse. They delighted in getting...in your ears, nose, mouth and eyes."

Speaking of sand, one night Jerry was dug-in with his battalion on the beach, being held in reserve about 100 yards behind the front lines. Soon rifle shots, machine-gun fire, grenade explosions, screams and yells from the front lines told them that a serious battle was going on nearby.

You might think that being behind the front lines is a piece of cake, "but it's not knowing what's going on, when you hear all of the shooting that gets real 'tough' — or to be blunt — scary!"

"When the fierce shooting would momentarily cease, the quiet lulls would make you even more tense. You begin to wonder if the Japs had killed all of our men and were sneaking up behind, or all around us ready to pounce at any moment. Even the click of the sand crabs made us jump. You pray awfully hard for daylight."

During the night, many of dead Japanese soldiers were washed out to sea via the creek they had been crossing, and their bodies carried by an incoming tide, lay half-buried along the beach. "Imagine our surprise in the morning to see all the dead bodies in front of us."

The battle that Jerry is referring to is shown in the HBO series, "The Pacific." It is known by several names, including: Battle of the Tenaru, Battle of the Ilu River, and Battle of Alligator Creek.

Jerry and his mates "were elated that our fellow regimental battalion Marines had stood the test, and held out on their own, and, of course, the situation was reversed at times, when we were the ones under siege, while our reserve battalion was heaving a sigh of relief, and giving thanks to our stalwartness."

One of the times that Jerry's unit was in the front lines involved an engagement at the Matanikau River. "The 3rd Battalion and my Company (K), was on the eastern side of a sand bar when ten tanks tried to come across in October. The noise of the tanks was bad enough, but the insane screaming of the charging Jap soldiers who came alongside, and behind the tanks, was mind-bending and nerve wracking. I often wondered how we survived that night. There were times that...I wished the earth would swallow me up whole and protect me."

"[One] memorable-forever occasion, occurred when two Japs were charging at me at the same time. From somewhere behind I heard a loud scream, 'Drop, Mac!' which I did without delay. In less than a second, I heard the rapid 'burp-burp-burp' of a BAR [Browning Automatic Rifle] cutting down the two Japs, one of whom landed almost on top of me. But such actions were common that night."

When Jerry left Guadalcanal in December, there was still a battle going on for control of the island, but with an influx of fresh troops (both Marines and US Army), the island was under Allied control by early February.

Wikipedia notes that "after Guadalcanal the Japanese were clearly on the defensive in the Pacific. The constant pressure to reinforce Guadalcanal had weakened Japanese efforts in other theaters... The Allies had gained a strategic initiative which they never relinquished."

It seems fitting to me, that Jerry conclude this article in his own words:

All of those men were like my brothers. We all cared for, looked out for, and protected each other, like family members do. Being in a depressed state didn't always mean that you were worried about yourself. Often I would think to myself, 'God, I hope John, or Elmer, or Gary, doesn't get hurt.' I was unable to use the word 'killed,' it was just unthinkable.

Whenever there was a serious wound or injury, it hurt nearly as much as if it had been ourselves. The death of a very close buddy was like a knife in the heart. You just didn't want to believe it, even if you actually saw, and knew that it was true.

I mean those guys were like a part of you. You had been with them twenty-four hours a day, seven days a week, for many, many months. And now they were gone. And it felt like a big hole was right in the middle of your heart.

But, oh my God, what a wonderful feeling when you looked around and saw everyone that mattered still there, still grinning at you with a wink and a nod, that showed their happiness at making the same discovery. Man, family doesn't get any closer than that.

It was feelings like those that drove us to excel under the vilest of conditions.

The circle of life begins at home midst family, then sometimes it ends away from home, but still in midst of family, now called friends. They were as much my brothers as if we shared the same last name. I couldn't have loved them more.

Semper fi Jerry.

19

Timothy of Baghdad's Lost Christian Empire

September 25, 2010

We are so used to the propaganda spewed forth by leftist "news" sources, radical academics, Hollyweird, and liberal books that many of us are surprised to learn that the Middle East, large swaths of Africa, and even parts of Asia were at one time under Christian control. In fact, Muslims stole much of their territory from Christians.

"In terms of the number and splendor of its churches and monasteries, its vast scholarship and dazzling spirituality, Iraq was through the late Middle Ages at least as much a cultural and spiritual heartland of Christianity as was France or Germany, or indeed Ireland."

Philip Jenkins from "The Lost History of Christianity: The Thousand-Year Golden Age of the Church in the Middle East, Africa, and Asia — and How It Died"

Centuries before Islam was a gleam in Muhammad's eye much of the Middle East was part of a vast Christian empire. In fact, this Christian empire continued for centuries after the Muslims took over the region.

Christianity carried on as a powerful cultural force under Muslim control for centuries. As Philip Jenkins points out in "The Lost History of Christianity, like Christian Egypt, the conquered Middle Eastern lands were "still effectively a Christian society under a Muslim military elite." It wasn't until the 1300s that the axe finally fell — more about that in a bit.

First, let's take a look at the lost empire. In 780 AD (a little over a hundred years after the Muslims conquered Baghdad), Timothy became patriarch of the Nestorian Church of the East — a Christian branch that held sway over a vast area that ran from the Mediterranean Sea in the west to China and the Pacific Ocean in the east.

Timothy ruled over churches near the Caspian Sea in the North, down to Yemen in the south. The Nestorian rabban, or priests (closely aligned to the Hebrew word "rabbi," obviously), looked to Baghdad in present day Iraq as the seat of the Church, although Jerusalem was considered to be their spiritual home.

The Nestorian empire was immense and quite diverse. They included a group in India who claimed direct lineage from a mission started by the apostle St. Thomas. Around 1275, (shortly before the axe fell), two rabban from China traveled west to visit the seat of the empire in Iraq.

After arriving in Iraq one of them, Markos, was elected patriarch of the church in 1281 (Yaballaha III). The other Chinese rabban, Bar Sauma, traveled on to Europe, where he was given Communion by the Pope in Rome (Nicholas IV), held his own mass in that city, and "the king of England himself (Edward I) took Communion from his hands."

So what became of the Nestorian Christians? Until a year ago, when I ran across some information written by Robert Spencer, I had never heard of them — and I am fairly well informed as regards world history. They seem to have been erased from the earth and largely scrubbed from the history books. What happened?

What happened — is Islam. What happened is the control of the media and academia by anti-Christian forces that downplay, ridicule, twist, and erase the role of Christianity in current affairs and world history.

Up until the 14th century, violent suppression by Muslims of *dhimmi*, or non-Muslims, under their rule had been limited to what Jenkins refers to as "surges" or "booms." One especially savage "boom" was directed toward the Armenian Christians, whose males were ordered to convert to Islam or suffer "branding, blinding in one eye, and castration."

These "surges and booms" were awful enough, but after 1300 widespread intolerance was the order of the day. This intolerance "lingers to the present day, as the vigorous Muslim legalism that emerged in just these years has largely shaped modern fundamentalist movements," according to Jenkins.

One of the Muslim scholars of this period has been especially influential — Ibn Taymiyyah. He is "regarded as the spiritual godfather of the Wahhabi movement, and of most modern extremist and jihadi groups." Wahhabism, of course, is the state religion of the USA's "good buddy" Saudi Arabia. You know — the country whose ruler Obama bows to?

(Sidebar: In case you are not aware, Jihadi Muslims or Islamists, have been playing a "good cop/bad cop" game with the US for decades. The game goes like this: There are two "types" of jihadists — terrorists and "moderates." Although their *tactics* are different the *goal* is the same — a global Caliphate. The "moderate" jihadists play off of the terrorists by saying in effect "You had better listen to our "moderate" demands, or we cannot be held accountable for what those crazy terrorists will do." Different tactics — same goal).

After the 14th century Muslim violence went into "remission" for the next few centuries (barring the odd "boom" or "surge"), until about a century ago when it returned with a vengeance that continues to this day.

During the Hamadian massacres of 1894-95 an especially brutal genocide of Turkish Armenian Christians resulted in a number of horrific events — including 3,000 Christians being burned alive in the cathedral where they had sought sanctuary (a scene reminiscent of the recent burning alive of about fifty Christians [mostly women and children] locked in a church in Kenya. They were killed by Muslim followers of Obama's "cousin" Raila Odinga).

The Nestorian Christian empire is now nothing but a memory, and a dim one at that. As recently as 1970, 5 to 6 percent of Iraq's population was still Christian. Today it is around 1 percent, and "shrinking fast." As Jenkins recounts, "Just between 2003 and 2007, two-thirds of Iraq's remaining Christians left the country, and the population will certainly sink farther in coming years."

The Muslim jihad against Christians is hardly limited to the Middle East. It is global, and ongoing: Nigeria, Indonesia, Sudan... Sudan!

I just had an epiphany. You know how upset Obama's old pastor Jeremiah "God Damn America" Wright is over the injustices of slavery? Well, Muslims have been enslaving black Christians for centuries – in fact, they are doing it *right now in Sudan!*

What a golden opportunity to take a real-time stand against the slave trade! I'll bet once he finds out, Wright will be on the next plane to Africa to stamp out this evil. Go get 'em tiger! Take the Reverends Jackson and Sharpton with you, as I know that they would not want to miss out on any of the action. But I digress.

The only non-Muslim geographic areas to go head-to head with Islam over the centuries and remain non-Muslim, are Europe and India in the west and east, and Russia and Ethiopia in the north and south (and the beat goes on).

Europe first turned back the Muslims at the battle of Tours in 732, and nine centuries later beat them back in eastern Europe, at the gates of Vienna.

US President Teddy Roosevelt knew what he was talking about when he wrote, "There are such 'social values' today in Europe, America and Australia only because during those thousand years, the Christians of Europe possessed the warlike power to do what the Christians of Asia and Africa had failed to do — that is, to beat back the Moslem [sic] invader."

Given Islam's history, why are the liberals, government, and academia not more alarmed? Are they stupid? No, for the most part they are not stupid, but they have been cleverly and deeply indoctrinated, and are enmeshed in social and/or business environments that encourage thinking of Islam in a certain politically correct way.

The established media (or more correctly, propaganda outlets) follow the party line because they are, for the most part, idiots (of the "useful" variety). They have been thoroughly indoctrinated to think and behave in a certain manner that would do Pavlov proud.

They and most of the political elites actually think that they are doing good by being cookie-cutter clones of NWO group-think. Many of them see their betrayal of America as a *good* thing, and they are *good* people (or good *dhimmis*, as the case may be). Their puppet-masters are something else again — but that is the topic for another article.

Most puzzling to me is the submission of "liberated" liberal females to the party line regarding Islam. Their deference is an impressive, if disturbing, sign of the depth of their indoctrination. Islam treats women as breed-stock chattel. Talk about a "keep 'em barefoot and pregnant" attitude! Muslims wrote the book on the subject; or rather they follow the book written on the subject.

Technically speaking each Muslim man can acquire up to four wives, but in actual fact the sky's the limit if you are very wealthy. Divorces are literally as easy as 1-2-3 (for men only). Child brides, sharia-approved wife abuse — well, the list just goes on. One can see the allure for a certain type of guy (or gal).

The women's rights organization NOW, has been curiously quiet about the misogynistic nature of Islam. Actually not so curious, as NOW is really the Far Left's Women's Auxiliary, and the Far Left has been working in collusion with Islamists to destroy Western civilization for some time. ("Hey, hey, ho, ho, Western Civ has got to go!" is not just a catchy meme aimed at changing academic curriculums).

If you doubt the truth of that last bit — about the Far Left and Islam working together to destroy Western civilization — then you are either an idiot (of the "useful" sort, if you like), or you are simply ignorant and need to educate yourself on the subject.

If some education is in order then I strongly suggest that you get cracking, because the time left for you to get up to speed is rapidly running out — if it has not run out already.

Laus Deo.

20

1776: Victory or Death

December 23, 2010

After so many years of purposefully neglecting to teach the true history of America in our schools, and perverting what little is taught, I thought it might be a good idea to revisit the beginning stages of the United States of America. I believe that we are again at a point where our options are as stark as those that Washington faced – victory or death.

"[Future generations] you will never know how much it has cost my generation to preserve your freedom. I hope you will make good use of it."
John Quincy Adams (1767-1848)
Sixth President of the United States of America

"The [Revolutionary] war was a longer, far more arduous, and more painful struggle than later generations would understand or sufficiently appreciate."
David McCullough "1776"

The frigid scene by the Delaware River was illuminated by flickering camp-fires, a few dim lanterns, and a scattering of storm-tossed torch-lights.

George Washington sat on his horse with his back turned to the wind and sleet. It was early morning on the day after Christmas, 1776. He and his ragged band of soldiers had just crossed the Delaware River into New Jersey from Pennsylvania. They were gathering for an assault on German mercenaries — the Hessians — hired by Great Britain to help stamp out the revolt in their American colonies. The Hessians were stationed about ten snow-covered miles away in Trenton, New Jersey.

The crossing of the Delaware had been more difficult than anticipated and Washington and his force were now several hours behind schedule.

They were one tine of a planned three pronged attack on Trenton, and Washington knew that his force would no longer be able to meet up with the other two groups in time. He had to decide, and decide quickly, whether or not to go ahead with the attack.

Unknown to Washington, if they pushed ahead, he and his men would be facing the Hessians alone. The other American commanders had called off their attacks due to the extremely bad weather.

The Nor'easter that blew in late Christmas Day had increased in fury until it was perilous simply to stand outside for any length of time. Freezing to death was a very real possibility, and indeed two colonial soldiers died from the cold that night. How many suffered from frostbite will never be known.

John Greenwood, a sixteen-year-old fife player from Boston later recalled "...it rained, hailed, snowed, and froze, and at the same time blew a perfect hurricane..." Greenwood stood by a fire to warm himself, but found that he had to keep changing which side faced the fire. As he described it, "...by turning myself round and round I kept myself from perishing." This was no place for a fife player, and young Greenwood was like all of the other soldiers, carrying a musket and three-days-worth of food.

Washington made his decision — they would go ahead and attack the Hessians. He really had no choice, as the fragile fire of American liberty was close to being extinguished. In his book "1776" David McCullough notes "By all reasonable signs, the war was over and the Americans had lost."

After a series of defeats in New York at the hands of the British and Hessians the Continental Army had crossed the Hudson River, and then retreated down the length of New Jersey hounded by the British every step of the way. McCullough writes, "So destitute of shoes that the blood left on the frozen ground, in many places, marked the route they had taken."

In early December Washington's diminished army had crossed over the Delaware into Pennsylvania and had stopped to catch their breath and gather such strength as they had. Washington's friend and aide, Gen. Nathaniel Greene, wrote to John Adams "But give me leave to tell you sir, that our difficulties were inconceivable to those who were not eyewitness to them."

Philadelphia artist, Charles Wilson Peale, along with a small militia unit, made the short trip north to reinforce Washington's exhausted force and give what aid and succor they could. Washington's army was in bad shape. Peale was especially struck by one pitiful wreck who "was in an old dirty blanket jacket, his beard long, and his face so full of sores that he could not clean it."

It was several moments before Peale realized that he was looking at his own brother James, who had been serving in the army's rear guard.

Fearing the advancing British forces the Continental Congress had fled Philadelphia — the city itself was largely abandoned. In less than a week's time the enlistment period for most of Washington's soldiers was due to expire.

Washington's attack on Trenton was much more than just a clever jab at the enemy, it was a last ditch — do or die — attempt to save the revolution from withering away. As Washington put it to his aide Joseph Reed, "...necessity, dire necessity...must justify an attempt." How had the young republic come to such a sorry state? The year had started out so well.

At the beginning of 1776 the American patriots had the British bottled up in Boston; Colonel Henry Knox was on his way with 58 mortars and cannon from Ft. Ticonderoga; Thomas Paine published "Common Sense," and George Washington had declared on New Year's Day a "...new army, which in every point of view is entirely continental."

Thus, the rag-tag band of colonial forces under Washington's command became known as the Continental Army.

During the previous spring fifteen-year-old John Greenwood had heard of the events at Boston, Lexington, and Concord. He repaired a broken fife he found, taught himself to play, and walked 150 miles to join the fray.

He arrived at the outskirts of Boston in May of 1775 in time to see the wounded and beaten patriots retreating from Bunker Hill. The sight shocked and terrified him. "I could positively feel my hair stand on end" he recalled years later.

Greenwood ran across a wounded black patriot bleeding profusely from a neck wound. Greenwood asked him if "it hurt him much," and the man replied that it wasn't bad, and that all he needed was a band-age to stop the bleeding and he would be ready to get back into the fight.

The man's response and demeanor had a profound effect on Greenwood. He later wrote that "I began to feel brave and like a soldier from that moment, and fear never troubled me afterward during the whole war."

Bunker Hill was a Pyrrhic victory for the British, and once they had Bunker Hill under their command they were in no rush to enter into another such bloodbath. The Americans were not too keen on another bloodbath themselves, and consequently the strategically important Dorchester Heights, which overlooked Boston, remained a sort of "no man's land" that neither side bothered to take.

It wasn't for lack of bravery on the British side. The General in command of the British forces, William Howe, had personally led his men in three charges up Bunker Hill. After one particularly wicked volley during the third assault up the hill Howe was the only man in the front line left standing. Courage was not an issue for Howe; he simply did not want to waste any more of his troops.

Nor was bravery an issue for the Americans. Their problem was that they lacked the cannon that would make the taking of Dorchester Heights a worthwhile endeavor. It did not make any sense to occupy this strategic hill if they lacked the cannons to bombard Boston — but Colonel Knox was about to fix that.

It had been Henry Knox's idea to pick up some cannons at Ft. Ticonderoga in upstate New York, and transport them back to Boston — no mean feat in the middle of winter (or in any season for that matter).

Knox arrived back in the Boston area with his cannons in late January, and plans began in earnest to occupy Dorchester Heights. The night of March 4th was decided upon as being the soonest the Americans could make their move.

Starting on March 2nd, the Americans started firing night-long salvos at the British (who returned the fire with vigor). The cannonade's noise would be used on the 4th to cover the sound of all the men and cannon being moved into position on the heights.

On the morning of March 5th the British awoke to find that the Americans had erected fortifications and installed cannon on Dorchester Heights. General Howe felt that Boston had become an untenable position and decided that it was time to leave.

On March 17, St. Patrick's Day, the British fleet pulled anchor and left Boston behind. Over a hundred ships filled with close to 9,000 troops and over a thousand Loyalists sailed toward Canada to regroup, reorganize, and await reinforcements.

The British would be back, and when they returned they would come prepared to thoroughly crush the American Revolution.

Washington and his staff thought (correctly), that the next major move the British would make would be directed toward New York City, so after leaving a small force behind to watch over Boston, Washington and the 20,000 strong Continental Army headed south to New York in high spirits.

The army made between 15-20 miles a day and arrived in New York City in mid April. They immediately started to fortify the city, which was at the time the second largest in the colonies. Of its population of around 20,000 most were Loyalists — loyal to the British crown.

Washington and his staff assumed (again correctly) that the British would probably make their main amphibious landing on Long Island. Consequently, they fortified the high-ground surrounding Brooklyn (a small village consisting of eight buildings).

The British sailed into New York harbor on June 29; took over Staten Island, and used it as their base of operations. General Howe's brother, Admiral Richard Howe, was in charge of the British fleet, which included five warships whose combined firepower alone dwarfed the American shore batteries.

Over 32,000 British troops disembarked onto Staten Island — this was greater than the population of Philadelphia, the largest city in America. Although the troops were generally well behaved, rape and pillage were not unknown.

British officer Lord Rawdon was pleased by the rapes, as they seemed to indicate a proper disdain for the Americans and an admirable "spirit" in his troops. Nonetheless, the British soldiers were often punished for these lapses in discipline.

Rawdon wrote of the American women that "they are so little accustomed to these vigorous methods that they don't bear them with proper resignation, and of consequence we have most entertaining courts-martial every day."

He also wrote "We shall soon have done with these [American] scoundrels, for one only dirties one's fingers by meddling with them." The "American scoundrels" were working furiously to complete their fortifications around NYC and the Brooklyn area of Long Island.

With prophetic foresight Henry Knox wrote to his wife, "We are fighting for our country, for posterity perhaps. On the success of this campaign the happiness or misery of millions may depend."

While the British and American troops prepared for the battle to come, the Continental Congress declared independence from the British crown. In Philadelphia, on July 4th 1776 the Declaration of Independence was read in public and the Liberty Bell rang for the first time.

The Declaration proclaimed that the people had endured a long list of "abuses and usurpations" by the British government, and that " it is their right...their duty, to throw off such government. " No longer were the patriots merely fighting to address some grievances held against Great Britain — they had declared themselves fully and irrevocably free.

On the morning of August 22 the long-anticipated British invasion of Long Island began. The landing itself went unopposed and the British used the next few days to finalize their plans and prepare their troops and artillery. At the same time, the Americans were feverishly completing their fortifications, and deciding if the British landings on Long Island were a feint or not — they were not.

On August 27 the British and Hessians attacked and by nightfall the American troops had been defeated and had retreated to Manhattan Island. Although the Americans had fought bravely and tenaciously, they had been outmaneuvered, overpowered, and out-gunned. The British and Hessian troops captured over a thousand American prisoners

American John Jewett, who had commanded a company of patriots, was bayoneted in the stomach and chest. That night, as he lay dying in a Staten Island POW camp, his friend Jabez Fitch comforted him as best he could. He later recalled that Captain Jewett "...was sensible of being near his end, often repeating that it was hard work to die."

The American defeat at Brooklyn was only the first of a series of defeats for the Americans. The British soon landed at the southern end of Manhattan and began moving northwards, hard on the heels of the retreating Continental Army. Although there were several battles of note, (Kip's Bay, Harlem Heights, White Plains), Washington's army was defeated at each turn, and by November he was forced to retreat over the Hudson river.

Many things of note happened during this period, but I would like to briefly direct attention to three in particular. First: on September 7 American patriot David Bushnell's "Turtle" launched the world's first submarine attack against Admiral Howe's flagship, HMS Eagle.

Second: on September 21, twenty-one-year-old Yale graduate and patriot Nathan Hale was hung as a spy by the British. He famously said "I only regret that I have but one life to lose for my country" — or words to that effect — before the noose tightened. One wonders what he would think of his fellow "Elis" today.

Third: on November 16 as the Battle of Ft. Washington raged, John Corbin who had come north with his Pennsylvanian artillery unit was killed while firing his cannon. His wife Margaret who had accompanied her husband north "...stepped into his place," and loaded and fired the cannon until she was severely wounded.

(Sidebar: A similar instance occurred at the Battle of Monmouth in 1778 when Mary Hays took her husband's place at his cannon after he had collapsed (either wounded or from heat exhaustion). Prior to that Mary (Molly) had been "carrying water to soldiers and artillerymen, often under heavy fire from British troops." Not only did the men require drinking water carried to them in pails and pitchers, but the cannon and ram-rods needed to be doused with water occasionally to keep them from overheating. Because of the real-life exploits of women like Mary Hay and Margaret Corbin the generic name "Molly Pitcher" was coined to describe such brave and patriotic women).

Washington and a force of around 2,000 soldiers reached Ft. Lee, New Jersey on November 13 (named after his second-in-command, British army veteran and "odd genius" Major General Charles Lee).

After the fall of nearby Ft. Washington, just across the Hudson, Washington and his soldiers, who had been strengthened by the addition of some fresh troops, began the long march south to Pennsylvania on November 21. They surrendered Ft. Lee without a fight.

It was at the start of this retreat that newly arrived eighteen-year-old James Monroe got his first glimpse of George Washington. "I saw him...at the head of a small band, or rather in its rear, for he was always near the enemy, and his countenance and manner made an impression on me which I can never efface." Judging from this and other similar descriptions of him, Washington must have radiated charisma like a lighthouse.

Monroe's impression of Washington included the illuminating comment that, "A deportment so firm, so dignified, but yet so modest and composed, I have never seen in any other person."

Washington had not sought, nor wanted, the command of the Revolutionary Army. After receiving the position he had written to his wife Martha, "...far from seeking this appointment, I have used every endeavor in my power to avoid it...it has been a kind of destiny that has thrown me upon this service."

Later he wrote to her that "I have often thought how much happier I should have been if...I had taken my musket upon my shoulders and entered the ranks, or if I could have justified the measure to posterity, and my own conscience, had retired to the back country, and lived in a wigwam." As appears to be the case with everything this extraordinary man said, he meant it.

Washington lead his cold, hungry, exhausted troops south toward temporary sanctuary across the Delaware, and in their wake followed enemy troops, rape, and pillage.

David McCullough observes of these atrocities, "The British blamed the Hessians...The Hessians blamed the British, [and] the Americans blamed both the British and the Hessians..." This finger pointing was of little, if any, comfort to those who suffered.

The ragged remnants of the Continental Army reached and crossed over the Delaware into Pennsylvania on December 7. They either took with them or burned any boats that they found. General Howe's troops pursued Washington as far as Trenton; situated along the river bank on the New Jersey side. Both armies stopped to take stock of things.

On December 13th General Howe decided to call off the chase for the time being, and hunker down until spring. Although he was now within striking distance of Philadelphia he decided to retire to New York City, and left a string of British garrisons along the route they had followed south. At the southernmost outpost, Trenton, Howe left behind 1,500 Hessians under the command of General Johann Gottlieb Rall (Rahl).

On Christmas Day Washington had his soldiers assemble and had Thomas Paine's new tract "The Crisis" read to them. Paine had accompanied the soldiers along the march south and knew firsthand of the hardships they had endured. He was all too aware of the precarious state of the young republic — a "crisis" indeed.

The first words of Paine's pamphlet echo down to us through the years. "These are the times that try men's souls. The summer soldier and the sunshine patriot will, in this crisis, shrink from the service of their country; but he that stands by it now, deserves the love and thanks of man and woman. Tyranny, like hell, is not easily conquered..."

During the course of the day Congressman Dr. Benjamin Rush had a private meeting with Washington. Rush recalled years later that Washington kept writing something down on slips of paper. One of the papers fell to the floor, and Rush saw that Washington had been writing "Victory, or Death" over and over. These were the passwords for that night. They also, of course, signified much more than that — they were the stark options available to Washington and his army.

Washington and his troops started crossing the Delaware, back into enemy-held New Jersey, a bit after nightfall Christmas day. By 3 a.m. the next morning everything, including men, horses, and artillery were finally across the river. Washington made the decision to go forward with the attack against the Hessians. They set off in the dark, moving slowly toward Trenton amid the wind, rain, sleet, snow, and hail.

The young ex-fifer, John Greenwood, would write years later that the men figured that they might as well forge ahead, "...for it was all the same, owing to the impossibility of being in a worse condition than their present one."

Washington and his soldiers arrived at the outskirts of Trenton later that morning. When informed by one of his Generals that the men's muskets were too wet to fire Washington told him to "use the bayonet." This battle would be Washington's first time as a field commander with the Continental Army. The attack began at around 8 a.m. December 26.

Henry Knox recalled that "The storm continued with great violence, but was [at] our backs, and consequently in the faces of the enemy."

Knox placed his cannon at a strategic intersection in Trenton and rapidly cleared the streets of the Hessians who had run out of the houses and barracks.

General Rall was mortally wounded while trying to rally his men, and after a fierce if relatively brief engagement, the battle was over. The Americans had killed 21 Hessians, wounded 90, and captured over 900.

No Americans were killed in the battle, and only four were wounded. The surprise attack had been overwhelmingly successful.

After searching the town and securing their prisoners the Americans retraced their route. They made the trek back to where they had first crossed over into New Jersey, and that night repeated the process in the other direction. It had been a long day, or rather a long two days.

Soon Washington would take his weary soldiers back into New Jersey to attack the British at Princeton, but that battle took place in early 1777 which is beyond our concerns here.

As for the year that was drawing to a close, I am sure that many patriots would have agreed with Robert Morris when he wrote to Washington, "The year 1776 is over. I am heartily glad of it, and hope you, nor America, will ever be plagued with such another."

As exhilarating and badly needed as the Trenton victory surely was, the struggle for independence was far from over. The next winter would see the Continental Army suffer through the brutal experience of Valley Forge, and it would be seven more long years until the Treaty of Paris was signed in 1783, ending the war.

George Washington was a profoundly religious, even spiritual, man. He was a man with a deep sense of duty, honor, and integrity. He felt honor-bound to lead "we the people" in the fight against an indifferent, arrogant, and tyrannical government. He never trusted governments, being of the opinion that "government is...a dangerous servant and a fearful master."

It would appear that God was on his side — or rather, that Washington was on God's side. As McCullough says at the end of "1776" "...for those who had been with Washington and who knew what a close call it was at the beginning...the outcome seemed little short of a miracle."

Laus Deo.

Post Script: Almost all of the quotes in this article are from David McCullough's book "1776." Indeed, this article can be considered something of a synopsis of the book — any misquotes, faulty attributions, in short any mistakes are mine alone. As "we the people" start our own contemporary revolution, perhaps one of the many targets we can set our sights on is to have "1776" taught in American schools, rather than Saul Alinsky's "Rules for Radicals" — just a thought.

21

Atheism Means Never Having To Say You're Sorry

December 29, 2010

Because the three articles on atheism in this book form something of a trilogy and are relatively short I thought about combining them into one "chapter" for this book — but seeing as how so many people these days have the attention span of rats on crack, and there is so much vying for our attention, I thought that I had better keep the "chapters" short, so I have kept the articles separate.

"The liberties of our country, the freedoms of our civil Constitution are worth defending at all hazards; it is our duty to defend them against all attacks. We have received them as a fair inheritance from our worthy ancestors. They purchased them for us with toil and danger and expense of treasure and blood. It will bring a mark of everlasting infamy on the present generation – enlightened as it is – if we should suffer them to be wrested from us by violence without a struggle, or to be cheated out of them by the artifices of designing men."

Samuel Adams (1722-1803)

Among other things, liberals believe that it is colder because it is warmer, that you save money by spending it, and that shackling people to the government via handouts frees them. In short, they believe anything and everything that their accepted vendors of propaganda dish out and that their oh-so-brilliant fellow liberals concur with. No wonder "Sauron" (aka George Soros) funnels millions to NPR, "The Huffington Post," "Media Matters," etc. One must keep the sheeple "informed" you know.

As amusing as some of the liberal fantasies may be, in their own bizarre way, for those of us living in the real world it has become increasingly obvious that their immature notions of How Things Should Be are driving America off of a cliff — both through ignorance, and intent. Well playtime is over and their "toys" must be returned to the care of responsible adults — liberal temper tantrums notwithstanding.

"We the people" must take back control of America, or we will be complicit in the ruination of the greatest and most successful social experiment in human history. Contrary to the lies spewed forth by secular humanist Progressives, America is a country founded on Judeo/Christian principles and aligned with God. It is no wonder that the atheistic Far left abhors us, and seeks our destruction.

They have slowly and cleverly targeted certain areas of our culture for infiltration and subversion. First and foremost, they have subverted our university and college campuses and thereby stocked our professions full of indoctrinated sheeple. Of special interest to them, has been the indoctrination of students of law, journalism, and education. (The relative few who have successfully resisted the Progressive indoctrination are to be applauded for their integrity).

These indoctrinated Progressives have slowly, but surely, infiltrated America's political process, court system, and media outlets to such an extent that they are now the *de facto* "establishment." Hence conservatives (which comprise the vast majority of Americans) have largely been forced "underground," and find themselves fighting for their survival against government "representatives" that no longer represent them.

"We the people" have been betrayed by our public servants and we are now under the heel of a cleverly disguised tyranny. Our concerns are given lip service while the Power Elite go about the business of implementing social engineering programs designed to shut us up, shut us out, and shut us down.

(I must not neglect to mention the Far Left's ongoing and longstanding effort to "dumb down" America, nor their efforts to subvert both religion and science. They leave "no tern unstoned," as Ogden Nash might have said).

You know what the Declaration of Independence has to say regarding what "we the people" are to do when confronted with tyranny right? Does the phrase "it is their *right*, it is their *duty*, to throw off such Government" ring any bells? Yeah well, talk is cheap is it not?

The collusion of educated professionals, big government, big business, big banking, Wall Street, and special interests has resulted in the phenomenon of the "Washington Beltway Bubble," where Progressives (left and right) speak to other Progressives in a closed loop that excludes the traditional American values of conservative "fly-over country."

The "Beltway Bubble" of Liberalese thought and speech (duplicitous, polysyllabic, arrogant) is not limited to Washington D.C. George Sauron's tentacles reach everywhere, and wherever two or more are gathered in his name, the religion of the "Beltway Bubble" exists — from sea to shining sea, and all around the world. Can I hear an amen?

At the "core" of their religion (I would say its "heart" but it does not have one) is atheistic Fascism/Communism — *both* of which are Far Left ideologies need I remind you. (Somewhere I hear a liberal cry "No way, you're the Nazi dude." To which I reply, "Sure thing, Adolph — have another toke").

To the Far Left, atheism means never having to say you're sorry. In case you have not noticed, the Far Left is never, ever, wrong — in their opinion at least — they are merely sometimes guilty of being caught.

As Dinesh D'Souza observes, "[Far Left atheist] Pol Pot killed a larger percentage of his countrymen than Stalin and Mao killed of theirs. Even so, focusing only on the big three — Stalin, Hitler, and Mao — we have to recognize that atheist regimes have in a single century murdered more than one hundred million people. Religion-inspired killing simply cannot compete with the murders perpetrated by atheist regimes."

In the race to see which conceptual framework is the bloodiest, atheism leaves religion in the dust, and Christianity itself, as an "also ran." Bravo — way to go Far Left atheists! You must be so proud.

(Sidebar: I do not have anything against atheism *per se*; it can be a legitimate, if false, step on a quest for truth. But all too often atheism is simply an excuse to pursue a hedonistic amoral lifestyle, and/or is simply the result of willful delusion augmented by ego-driven hubris).

Certain left-wing apologists for atheism claim that because Far Left luminaries such as Hitler, Stalin, Mao, etc., made a religion out of their anti-religious atrocities they were, in fact, religious — that their murderous anti-religious regimes were actually examples of an anti-religion religion. So it is all religion's fault you see — especially Christianity somehow. (Please read D'Souza's chapter "A License To Kill: Atheism And The Mass Murders Of History" in "What's So Great About Christianity" before emailing me on this point).

To the "it's colder because it's warmer" crowd this all makes perfect sense I suppose. The rest of us need to pick our jaws off the floor and be about our business — the business of protecting and advancing America and restoring true American values.

America is making a bee-line for a cliff — with corrupt, unbalanced Progressive bozos (both left and right wing) driving the bus. "We the people" must wrest back control of the steering wheel.

Laus Deo.

22

Atheism Revisited

January 3, 2011

In recent years my feelings in regard to atheism have undergone a profound change similar to my feelings about Islam. That is, I have gone from a rather blasé attitude of "live and let live," to one of deep concern and antipathy.

It has become all too evident that the secularization of America has resulted in a national tragedy. The hatred of the Far Left for Christianity is on display wherever one looks — from the constant lawfare against Jesus to the blatant promotion of Islam.

The resultant lack of morals and ethics is everywhere around us — the zeitgeist of our times. Corruption and greed have been given free rein and whether or not something is legal has largely replaced any concern over ethics. Worse yet, increasingly the main question for all too many is "will I get caught?" Worst of all are the powerful scumbags and their shills who consider themselves to be above the law altogether, and could not care less about questions of legality, let alone ethics.

Religion and morality are the essential pillars of civil society."
George Washington (1732-1799)

"To claim that [his] rhetoric makes Hitler a Christian is to confuse political opportunism with personal conviction. Hitler himself says in "Mein Kampf" that his public statements should be understood as propa-

ganda that bear no relation to the truth, but are designed to sway the masses."

Dinesh D'Souza "What's So Great About Christianity"

"The heaviest blow that ever struck humanity was the coming of Christianity."

Adolf Hitler (1887-1945) "Hitler's Table Talk"

"Everyone thinks of changing the world, but no one thinks of changing himself."

Leo Tolstoy (1828-1910)

I want to thank the atheists who attempted to straighten me out regarding some points I made in my last article. I did not realize that Adolph Hitler was a staunch compassionate Christian, or that the Founding Fathers were such a confused bunch of sanctimonious old farts, or enlightened closet-atheists. Nor did I realize that atheist Ayn Rand was such a paragon of virtue, or that atheists are such upright pillars of society. I think that is all just groovy. (If your Sarcasm Detector is not blaring shrilly then you either do not have one or it is turned off).

It is all the more commendable that atheists are such exemplars of moral rectitude when you take into account that there is no particular reason for them to be that way; seeing as how their lives have no ultimate purpose, and that they putter away their meaningless lives in a mindless, soulless, heartless, pointless universe. *Ex nihilo nihil fit —* out of nothing comes nothing (going nowhere). Bravo atheists, again I say, bravo!

By the way, is there any chance that you virtuous atheists could pass the word along to your brethren regarding just how virtuous you all *are*, as the vast majority of atheists seem to be doing a bang-up job of pretending to be self-serving a—holes? I would especially appreciate your making a point of passing along the word to Wall Street in general, and Goldman Sachs in particular — especially the former Goldman

Sachs employees currently running US finances into the ground while enriching those "in on the action." TIA.

I love the atheists who grandly stride onto a soapbox and passionately give a spirited defense of atheism — describing how wonderful, rational, and virtuous it is — all the while knowing that they have no skin in the game, so to speak. How can they, when ultimately nothing matters in a Godless universe?

My amazement continues to grow. Is there nothing the ego will *not* do, no lies it will not tell, no gambit it won't try, in order to protect its paranoid positionality. For make no mistake the ego is by its nature fear-based and paranoid. How could it be otherwise, when the ego is surrounded by everything that is not ego, i.e. the rest of the universe? One against infinity — bad odds indeed. One against a heartless, intelligence free, soulless universe — how noble, how heroic, how mindlessly pointless.

Let's see, should I choose a moral/ethical system grounded on nihilism, hubris, and ego gratification, or should I choose one leading to truth, spirituality, and freedom? If your ego is leading you around by the nose then the "right" choice is an obvious no-brainer. It takes dedication and commitment to follow the spiritual path — it is so much easier to just relax and fall back into our "default position" of egocentricity.

Science (whose practitioners are largely atheist) prides itself in its pristine search for truth and a firm reliance on intellect. (I do not include "scientists" who have allowed themselves to be co-opted by ideology and/or greed and are content to serve as shills for various Far Left ploys such as the AGW global warming scam).

Regarding the intellect, excuse me for pointing out the obvious, but when René Descartes famously wrote "I think, therefore I am," he missed the mark by a wide margin. After all, how could he even know he was thinking unless he was *aware* of it?

Consciousness (aka "state of being," aka "awareness") is *a priori* to thought, obviously, and yet science continues to largely dodge the whole intellect/awareness issue — dated but important findings in quantum mechanics notwithstanding. It is almost as if science has been blinded by Ego.

(Sidebar: I should mention that one needs be careful when using the terms "consciousness" and "mind," as they both can have vastly different meanings depending on the context in which they are used. For example, the word "mind" means something quite different in a psychiatric clinic as opposed to a Buddhist monastery).

All sarcasm aside I have no doubt that there are decent, well-meaning atheists who are valuable additions to society. However, after around six decades on this planet I also have no doubt that the vast majority of people who live Godless lives are self-serving egotists — and the worst are Machiavellian scum-bags who are only "in it for themselves," and are restrained by no ethical or moral limits whatsoever. As the saying goes, "99% of Democrats give the others a bad name," and so it is with atheists — the majority give the minority a bad rap.

Such decency and sanity as the world currently has (granted, nothing to write home about) are due almost exclusively to the influence of the world's major religions. I do not include Islam, which is more properly understood as a non-evolving religious/cultural/legal system of totalitarian control then as a religion *per se.*

(Sidebar: Islam's totalitarian nature and its desire to eradicate Judeo/Christian culture are what make it so attractive to the atheistic Far Left, which would otherwise despise Islam for its theology and treatment of homosexuals. The Far Left is also "on board" with the subservient role of women in Islam — note the deafening silence of NOW in this regard).

As I was saying, the world's religions (none more-so than Christianity) are largely responsible for whatever decency and sanity the world possesses. This, despite the fact that the world's religions, being open to everyone, have historically been infiltrated by any number of charlatans, grifters, narcissists, and a plethora of other undesirables.

Such people have either deluded themselves about their own religiosity, or were/are knowingly using religion as a cloak for their ego-driven duplicity. One can be forgiven for considering them to be atheists in sheep's clothing. After all, hiding amoral narcissism behind a cover of respectability is *de rigueur* for an atheist weasel on the prowl (not that all atheists are weasels – I am not saying that).

Nonetheless, because the spiritual truth at the heart of these religions is so powerful, the "wolves in sheep's clothing" have so far proved incapable of destroying these vehicles of truth (religions, which are in themselves *not* truth, provide a means of carrying truth).

The attack on Christianity, both from within and without, by atheists has been unremitting, clever, vicious, and ongoing for centuries — going back at least as far as the French Revolution. A good case can be made (and has been, by Ben Wiker) that the atheistic attack goes back at least as far as the Medieval Renaissance, and Lucretius's poetic translation of the atheistic doctrines of the Greek philosopher Epicurus.

Given all of that, it is indeed remarkable that Christianity (especially Catholicism; by far the oldest and largest Christian sect) has held up as well as it has, for as long as it has. Which bespeaks the power of the truth that Christianity carries at its core — all of the various "wolves," frauds, false dogmas, orthodoxical missteps, and theological dead-ends notwithstanding.

Be that as it may, because atheism is essentially based on ego-centered falsehoods atheists are intrinsically incapable of recognizing the truth unless it jumps up and bites them on the butt with a "God Shock" moment. Atheists are trapped in their intellect, which although a remarkable tool, is a less than stellar guide to the truth. If you think you'll find spiritual truth via the intellect, think again. (That would be like trying to weigh something with a thermometer – that is, using the wrong tool for the job).

Spiritual truth is forever relegated to the realm of direct experience and is inextricably tied in with one's state of consciousness, or state of being. The atheist's search for ultimate truths in the physical realm and the intellect is doomed to failure from the start. Their state-of-being/consciousness is almost universally ignored by atheists, and they therefore search for answers "for what ails them" in the environment outside of themselves — whether in the physical realm, or in the immediate environment of their intellect.

Liberals looking for "social justice" (as unspecific multi-purpose term as you are likely to see) forever ignore the root cause of their "angst and ennui" — i.e. themselves. God forbid their ego should ever feel threatened by shining a light of honest inquiry on it. Their egos would scurry like roaches.

Although the bulk of honest Christians (as opposed to nominal Christians) make haltingly slow work of their spiritual evolution, they are at least on a viable track to truth, and however haltingly, are making progress in the right direction (unless they're off the track altogether, as sometimes happens).

Atheists, who are by the nature of the beast, diametrically opposed to spirituality, truth, and freedom, are on the track to nihilism, arrogance, and gulags — check out their history if you doubt me (no wonder they are so big on historical revisionism). I lump liberal "Christian" teachings such as Liberation Theology in with the atheists.

(Sidebar: Why some of the more reprehensible of these "faiths" continue to enjoy tax exempt status is beyond me. A number of them actively preach the violent overthrow of America. Some idiots may think it a swell idea to have "we the people" pay to have our own throats cut but count me out).

Speaking of reprehensible faiths, Saul Alinsky (author of "Rules for Radicals") would be so proud of them all. After all, Alinsky championed an atheistic state of consciousness that glorified the ego, deified arrogance, and enshrined amoral nihilism. Obama, Clinton, and God alone knows how many others currently at America's helm follow Alinsky's reprehensible, atheistic, ego-driven insanity. It would be enough to keep me awake at nights if I didn't have deep, valid, spiritual roots.

Well time to be moving on to other things. I'll leave debating atheists in the capable hands of people like Dinesh D'Souza. Personally, I find debating them about as interesting and profitable as tuning an air guitar, but to each their own. No doubt *someone* needs to expose the vacuous, if Byzantine, rationalizations of these smug slaves to Ego.

"Better to reign in hell than serve in heaven," right atheists? Of course it is. Ta-ta for now — "*ex nihilo*" and all that. Enjoy your ego while you can — then again, why would you? You must believe that you and everyone else are valueless, motiveless, meaningless meat automatons — devoid of all dignity, purpose, or hope. That is, unless you have lied to yourself about the full ramifications of atheism — and surely you are much too smart, savvy, and honest to have deluded yourself like that — right?

Laus Deo.

23

Harvard, Homosexuals, and Far Left Fabians

January 6, 2011

I quote from "Keynes at Harvard" so extensively in this article that I would perhaps be guilty of plagiarism if I had not given credit where it is due throughout the piece. The book's chapter, "The Social Consequences of Moral Depravity," should be required reading in American colleges and universities. With the recent abomination at Penn State still unfolding, I can only hope that it will start unraveling the pervasive and powerful network of militant homosexual pederasts in America. Their insidious influence is much more widespread and influential than most heterosexual people understand — which is just the way the militant homosexuals like it.

"No matter what phase of left-wing infiltration we study, be it in government, in information media, in foundations, in labor unions...the tracks lead inevitably to Harvard University."

Zygmund Dobbs "Keynes at Harvard"

Zygmund Dobb writes in "Keynes at Harvard" that "Harvard didn't adopt the left-wingers, the left-wingers picked Harvard." A prestigious, hallowed center of learning — what better place to start spreading the poison that would first sicken and then kill a free United States?

In the late 1950s a group of conservative Harvard alumni, concerned and distressed over the increasingly leftist slant of their alma mater, started an investigation into the collectivist (Marxist, Fascist, Communist, Fabian...) infiltration of Harvard ("actually all these people are striving toward the same end — concentration of power in the hands of a few").

They quickly found that to research all of the teachers and departments was too big a job to handle in a timely manner. "After due deliberation it was decided to concentrate on the Economics Department...as the breeding ground of much of Harvard leftism." Even so, the research took around ten years to complete.

The alumni found that the primary economic system being taught at Harvard was the Keynesian system — named after John Maynard Keynes (1883-1946). They found that "'Keynesian economics' is a misnomer. It is not economics; it is a leftwing political theory."

Keynes (pronounced "canes") was a Fabian. Dobbs writes "The Fabians believe in 'easing' into absolute power by deceit. The Communists and Fascists believe in attaining power quickly by violence."

Keynes' genius, such as it was, lay in cleverly hiding his treacherous deceits behind a fog of arcane, verbose, obfuscating language (SOP for the Far Left).

"He clothed the clearest facts in the most complicated phraseology. In this way the clearest facts have been beclouded. Businessmen often confuse such verbiage for profundity and are led to believe that the Keynesians have exclusive knowledge of some magic formulas incapable of being grasped by the average man. This is exactly what Keynes and his followers wished. It gave them *carte blanche* to pursue their ends." (That quote, and all of the following ones unless otherwise indicated, are from "Keynes at Harvard").

Indeed, so successful has Keynes' legerdemain been that it long ago became difficult, if not impossible, to tell who is following Keynesian economics because they had been duped, and who was following Keynesism knowing full well it was a Far Left ploy to sicken and eventually ruin capitalism.

"Even sound economists do not realize that Keynes' obscurity is deliberate. ...They do not come to grips with the true state of affairs, namely, that Keynesism is not an economic theory. It is a weapon of political conspiracy."

If you wish a crash course in demystifying Keynesian economics and spotlighting its deceits, then I strongly recommend reading a copy of "Keynes at Harvard: Economic Deception as a Political Credo." Although it was first published over forty years ago, it is still remarkably fresh and relevant — perhaps of more importance today than when it was first published.

Dobbs continues, "In 1967 the world was startled by the publication of the letters between Lytton Strahey and Maynard Keynes. Undisputed correspondence shows that Keynes was a life-long sexual deviate. What was more shocking was that these practices extended to a large group [the Fabians and their coterie]."

"Homosexuality, sado-machochism, lesbianism, and the liberate policy of corrupting the young was the established practice of this large and influential group which eventually set the political and cultural tone for the British Empire."

What do you want to bet that America's "large and influential" group of Power Elites stands where Great Britain's stood fifty years ago? Any takers? Is it just me, or does there seem to be an inordinate amount of homosexuals, lesbians, and Keynesians in high government positions of power these days?

Dobbs describes an incestual orgy of love triangles, trysts, betrayals, drug use, and sex of such a bizarre and Byzantine nature that it would make a jaded TV soap-opera writer's head spin.

Dobbs observes that "deception and trickery coupled with acid criticism of everything moral...as 'reactionary' is standard fare among them. ...The fact that the Keynes-Strachey Fabian socialist coterie practiced sodomy, lecheurism [lecherousness], lesbianism, coprolagnia [sexual enjoyment of human excrement], scatophagy [eating human excrement], and uragnia [sexual enjoyment of human urine], is evidence of infantilism carried to the point of psychopathia."

One gets the feeling from Dobb's book that the list of depravities just named is only the tip of the iceberg ("...this writer struggled to keep the presentation within the bounds of good taste...").

Dobbs continues, "By persistent permeation of the centers of information, education, and government the deviates have been able to invest themselves with a 'Progressive' and 'Liberal' cover. ...They cultivated not only the deceptive devices of the covert pervert, but also inherited the massive arsenal of political tricks accumulated for generations in the socialist movement. The socialist perverts became in fact a living embodiment of continuous employment of falsification and practiced deceit."

Is it any wonder that Planned Abortion (sorry, Parenthood) should find such strong support among the Far Left judges, lawyers, and politicians who echo Keynes' strong "aversion to human conception, [and] marital fidelity," and his support for the "defeminization of women via state intervention, and the shattering of the family as a cohesive unit..."

"Keynes at Harvard" notes, "These organized perverts acted out a distorted 'Alice Through the Looking Glass' performance. Their bleatings for equal rights for homosexuality was promptly converted into general harassment of the normal population. The cry to be left alone hid covert moves to control and exploit the heterosexual majority."

Insofar as advancing that last bit, nothing has been so effective as Political Correctness — where we end up policing our own thoughts. The "Seinfeld" episode with the recurring "Not that there's anything wrong with that" line, is a classic case in point. (Self brainwashing made EZ — neat trick).

Dobbs continues with a quick psychological hip-shot. "Homosexual preoccupation with decreasing population and crusades for birth control has at its foundation their sense of revulsion against normal procreative sex." Speaking of psychology, Dobbs makes some eyebrow raising observations regarding the roots of psychiatry. At least *my* eyebrows were raised — maybe not yours.

"Havelock Ellis, a sexual deviant ['a masochistically feminine' Fabian who enjoyed the company of 'aggressive lesbians'], is hailed in our halls of learning as, 'The Father of social psychology' and is installed as one of the great progenitors of modern psychiatry. ...This might be analogous to investing the inmates of our mental hospitals with the right to set the guidelines for the sane population." Ellis was a co-founder of The Fabian Society in 1884.

To finish up with the less than stellar roots of psychiatry: After marrying fellow Fabian socialist Edith Lee, Ellis "drove her into lesbianism...plus drugs [which] caused Edith to lose her sanity. ...She [suffered] a complete mental collapse after Ellis wrote her that he was having a rather bizarre and abnormal relationship with Margaret Sanger..." ["sainted" founder of Planned Parenthood].

"Ellis antedated Freud when he declared, 'I regard *sex* as the *central* problem of life." [I'll just bet he did]. "Sigmund Freud was in close collaboration with Ellis...." In addition, "James Strachey, the brother of [Keynes' male lover], was addicted to a passion for young men, and his wife Alix was a consort of a notorious lesbian.

They both studied under Freud while adhering to militant atheism and Fabian socialism." (Told you this stuff is better (or worse, depending on your tastes) than any soap-opera).

All of this occurred after Freud (a rabid atheist) addicted a number of his patients to cocaine, and as Dr. Carl Jung recounts, seduced his wife's sister into a sexual relationship. No wonder Dobbs concludes, "A thorough scientific re-evaluation of the motivations and the distortions of the founders of psycho-analysis as a 'sick' movement is long overdue."

Great, just wonderful. Liberals hold up two twisted fruitcakes as paragons of mental health, and a one-time Harvard professor and homosexual/bisexual pervert *par excellence*, Alfred Kinsey, as the exemplar of proper sexual conduct — no wonder those people are so nuts.

To get back to Keynes, homosexuality, and the Fabians: I think that Fabian George Bernard Shaw (not "Mental Health Monthly" centerfold material either), is an ideal representative of Fabianism. Behind the genial avuncular look and demeanor of this liberal icon was the Machiavellian mind of a ruthless monster.

"Uncle George" informed us that "come the revolution" an Inquisition will be installed to decide who "can safely be allowed to live at large in a civilized community." Shaw goes on to say that "The convicted, knowing that the Inquisition was considering the case, could never go to bed with any certainty of being alive next morning. But this uncertainty would not concern the convicted only. It would concern everybody; for the question of fitness to live could be raised about anybody, whether any indictable crime had been committed or not." Lovely.

The hackneyed phrase "fiendish glee" springs to mind. Hackneyed or not, I can all too easily picture Shaw rubbing his hands together in "fiendish glee" as he imagines how his Fabian socialist "utopia" will be run. Modern day Fabians such as ex-British Prime Minister Tony Blair, or ex-Prime Minister Gordon Brown, would no doubt dismiss "Uncle George's" descriptions as "off the cuff idle blather," or some such. The thing is, G.B. Shaw spewed a *lot* of "off the cuff idle blather" — there was nothing "idle" about it.

Dobbs writes that "Shaw was a chief patron and sponsor of Keynes in Fabian socialist circles in England and the United States." Also of interest is the observation that "Henry Dexter White and Keynes were inseparable in the United States shortly before Keynes died. ..The facts are inconvertible that White served as a Soviet agent while doubling with Keynes as the architect of the World Bank and the International Monetary Fund [IMF]." (That should make us all feel better about where our hard-earned tax dollars are going).

In a recent issue of the purportedly conservative magazine "The Weekly Standard," Gary Schmitt and Cherl Miller wrote in an article about the repeal of DADT that, "Not everyone agrees with the decision to repeal Don't Ask, Don't Tell." (Yes, I suppose it *is* possible that there are a few heterosexual holdouts in the hinterlands of fly-over country).

Schmitt and Miller continue "But its repeal does provide an opening for repairing relations between some of the nation's top universities, and the military services..." Well we certainly can all be thankful for that! And here I am thinking that the vociferous campus rants against the military are fueled by a leftist hatred for America, capitalism, and America's military might. Silly me — just goes to show how wrong you can be.

In all seriousness, the "Weekly Standard" article underlines the vast chasm between Washington D.C.'s indoctrinated elite and "we the people." Remember that the "Weekly Standard" is a "conservative" Beltway insider magazine, and Republican Senators Susan Collins and Olympia Snowe of Maine, Scott Brown of Massachusetts, Lisa Murkowski of Alaska, George Voinovich of Ohio, and Mark Kirk of Illinois voted to repeal DADT — as well as 15 House Republicans.

I can tell you straight out that I am *not* all right with the repeal of DADT. I am so far from being "all right" with it that I can hardly begin to tell you how *not* "all right" I am.

I am sick and tired of keeping my peace as my rights, religion, country, and culture are debased, dismissed, dismantled, and destroyed. I have endured decades of this "death by a thousand cuts." No more.

There is absolutely no reason to turn our military upside-down and inside-out so that a small minority of sexual deviants can feel righteous. A century of Fabian/Communist/Fascist lies notwithstanding, they are *not* righteous.

No more "Mr. Nice Guy" — the Welcome Mat is officially withdrawn — now and forever.

Laus Deo.

24

In God We Trust?

January 24, 2011

I have written several articles that attempt to help assemble a unified Christian front to face the world-wide plague of atheism/secularism and the onslaught of Islam — this article is perhaps my best shot at it. Such an endeavor is no easy task, as the problems that must be tackled come from both within and outside of "the flock."

Jesus' message has been so intentionally perverted and watered down that schisms within some of the various Christian sects might be the best way to start "cleaning house." That may sound like a strange way to begin forming a united front, but it may well be necessary to prune away some unhealthy branches so that the tree of Christianity can again flourish in the West with vigor and power.

Right at the start of such a proposal we run into the problem of "what stays, and what goes; what is 'good' Christianity, and what is 'bad?'" To help keep things simple (but not so simple as to be ineffective) I would suggest that a possible guideline to follow for what constitutes a good Christian is belief in the Nicene Creed (technically the Niceno-Constantinopolitan) first written in 325 AD (modified in 381 AD). (Personally, I have no problem with considering the Apostle's Creed to be on a par with the Nicene Creed. I would also suggest that a belief in the Decalogue be included in any bare-bones description of Christianity, as well as acceptance of the Bible as our "text").

What about the Bible — which translation? What a can of worms we have there. To limit it to only one translation is not going to fly, but surely we can narrow the field down to around a half-dozen favored versions — e.g. the NIV, NAB, NKJV, KJ, and a few others.

Any Christianity worthy of the name must have historical roots and traditions, but it must also have room to grow in a healthy manner. Which brings up the issue of bad Christianity – what is it? Here again, I believe that the best way to go about things is to keep it simple. If a nominally "Christian" group promotes envy, lust, hatred, greed, etc. — in other words if it promotes teachings contrary to Jesus' teachings — then it is bad Christianity. It is "Christian" in name only and should be outed and shunned.

Of course not all bad "Christian" sects are blatantly evil. Some are much more subtle in spreading their insidious poison. The Marxist perversion of Liberation Theology springs readily to mind. Good, sincere people get enmeshed in these sorts of religious travesties and it is a shame — to put it lightly.

I could carry on with this introduction for some time and still barely scratch the surface of things. My longest article, "A Christmas Missive" (over 10,000 words) centered on spirituality, and I only managed to touch the tip of the tip of the "iceberg." There is only so much ground you can cover when your topic is infinity.

To create any sort of unified Christian front involves a balancing act of give and take. You cannot be so open-minded that your brains fall out, but you do not want to be so tradition-bound that you turn away many people who would otherwise swell the ranks. I suggest that we Christians leave the arcane theological wrangling for another day and agree on what we can for now. Christians must hold firm to their roots, but never be afraid to boldly go forward in search of the truth — we are told it will set us free.

"Because of Christ and our faith in Him, we can now come fearlessly into God's presence, assured of His glad welcome."

Ephesians 3:12

"You will keep him in perfect peace,
Whose mind is stayed on You,
Because he trusts in You.
Trust in the Lord forever,
For in Yah, the Lord, is everlasting strength."

Isaiah 26:3,4 NKJV

"Can the liberties of a nation be secure when we have removed a conviction that these liberties are of God?"

Thomas Jefferson (1743-1826)

In God we trust? Not hardly — not as a nation; not anymore. In my lifetime America's motto has gone from "In God We Trust," to "God Who?" I am here to tell you that is one hellacious cultural shift to go through in such a relatively short period of time. What happened?

First, a little back-story: The other day I was reading a well-written article on the various Far Left plots threatening America. After I finished reading the article I realized that among the several remedies offered to help extract ourselves from our present difficulties, turning to God was not one of them — prayer was not mentioned at all. In fact, God was not mentioned anywhere in the article. Sadly, that is to be expected.

It struck me that the absence of any mention of God was not re-markable in any way. That, in fact, I had come to take the absence of any mention of God in a "serious" discussion as a given. To see or hear any mention of God in a "credible" political/cultural discourse anymore is rare to the point of nonexistence.

I am not saying that God needs to be included in all, or even most, political discussions, but there should not be any reason to exclude God either. Can you imagine the wording of the Declaration of Independence — with its references to the Creator and Divine Providence — in a modern secularist document?

"In God We Trust" was adopted as the official motto of the United States in the 1950s, and it started to appear on our paper currency in 1957 (although it had appeared on our metal coinage since the 1860s). While it may have been the case as late as the early 1960s, American culture has not trusted in God for some time, and "we the people" need to return to our spiritual roots as soon as possible — with enthusiasm.

Because America was founded on Judeo/Christian principles that is where we should look — in particular, we need to re-examine and re-embrace Christianity, and it is there that this article will focus.

Why have we drifted so far from our spiritual heritage? Once you have taken a look at the centuries of caustic atheistic attacks on Christianity — both from within and without — the answer is obvious.

The ploys that the atheists (in particular Far Left atheists, and most obsessively, Far Left homosexual atheists) have used to undermine, ridicule, and diminish the influence of Christianity are manifold, clever, and ruthless — they run the gamut from the sublime to the ridiculous.

A favorite gambit of theirs is to ridicule, misinterpret, and downplay the Bible — including writing their own versions of it. For example, the following "scripture" is from a recent bible whose writers endorse "peace, justice, dignity, and rights for all" (social justice) — and, of course, sustainable development:

"Meanwhile Rocky was still sitting in the courtyard. A woman came up to him and said: 'Haven't I seen you with Jesus, the hero from Galilee?' Rocky shook his head and said: 'I don't know what the hell you're talking about!'" Matthew 26:69-70

Rocky? Jesus wept.

Moving on. Another favorite ploy is to spread myths and lies about Christianity. The number of myths/lies is so vast that it would take a sizable book just to enumerate them, let alone dispel them.

For starters I might mention that Galileo (1564-1642) was not persecuted by stupid Christian "flat-earthers," because he was so logical, scientific and all.

The book that got Galileo Galilei into trouble was his "Dialogue Concerning the Two Chief World Systems" — a book that championed the heliocentric (i.e. sun-centered) theories of Nicolaus Copernicus, (who had been urged to publish his theories by Catholic Bishop Guise and Cardinal Schonberg). The prevailing scientific model of the day held that the earth was the center of the universe, not the sun. This was not because of some Christian anthropocentric prejudice, but because of the almost universally accepted (in Europe) theories of Ptolemy (circa 90-168 AD).

The whole Galileo hoopla was in essence an academic disagreement dressed in the ecclesiastical clothes of the *intelligentsia* of the day. Although many Christians held to the commonly accepted views of Ptolemy, many others backed the newfangled heliocentric theories of Copernicus. The charged atmosphere surrounding heliocentrism at the time was caused by rancorous academic debate, not unscientific superstition. Christianity is largely responsible — a good case can be made that it is *exclusively* responsible, for the fact that science exists at all.

Christianity is always emitting various questing, growing, hopeful seeds of promise. As Thomas Cahill observes, the Christian view of the world "as a healing mystery, fraught with divine messages — could never have risen out of Greco-Roman civilization, threaded with the profound pessimism of the ancients and their Platonic suspicion of the body as unholy and the world devoid of meaning."

As opposed to the contractive, bleak, self-centered inanity of atheism, Christianity offers a life-affirming, expansive, God-centered world-view.

One example of the contractive influence of atheism — one could say a stellar example — can be found in America's space program, or lack thereof. NASA under Progressive control has gone from a "To boldly go where no one has gone before" attitude, to their new motto of "There's No Place Like Home." Go get 'em Dorothy.

Unlike atheists, who are limited (contracted) to a merely scientific viewpoint, Christians have the elevated vantage point of a more inclusive world-view — one that is not nearly so provincial and limited as the material reductionist one. The Christian view allows for, indeed encourages, an expansive, pro-active outlook.

As Dinesh D'Souza puts it, "Christians believe that reality is much bigger, and that there are ways of apprehending reality that go beyond rational syllogisms and scientific experiments. What looks like anti-intellectualism on the part of Christians is actually a protest against reductive materialism's truncated view of reality."

(Sidebar: This is as good a time as any to mention that the concept of "separation of church and state" is often misrepresented as being in the US Constitution, when nothing of the sort exists. The phrase comes from a letter Thomas Jefferson wrote, and was in reference to his refusal to let one particular Christian denomination become the officially sanctioned "state religion" of America. Perhaps, like Jefferson, we too should take an oath before God to bear "eternal hostility to every form of tyranny over the mind of man" — including atheistic secular humanism).

D'Souza also observes that, "This is not a time for Christians to turn the other cheek. Rather it is a time to drive the money changers out of the Temple. The atheists no longer want to be tolerated. They want to monopolize the public square and to expel Christians from it. ...They want to discredit the factual claims of religion, and they want to convince the rest of society that Christianity is not only mistaken but also evil."

Other whoppers that the Far Left have foisted onto "we the people" (and the world at large), is that Hitler was a Christian, the Holocaust was Christian inspired, and that Pope Pius XII aided and abetted the Nazis. All of those "facts" are lies, made up out of whole cloth.

Recently Rep. Steve Cohen (D-TN) compared Republicans to the Nazis; which seeing as the Nazis were a Far *Left* phenomena (Socialist Worker's Party? Hello?), is tantamount to the Left saying that the Right isn't right because they are more to the left than the Left. This no doubt makes sense to liberals, although I have given up trying to figure out their Byzantine mental constructs.

Leaving aside the question of atheistic attacks from *without* for now, let's take a quick look at the insidious influence of the atheist's attacks on Christianity from *within*. As damaging as the Far Left attacks on Christianity from the outside have been, they have not been as damaging as the attacks from the inside.

Perhaps the most damaging attack on the Roman Catholic Church, the world's largest Christian denomination, has been the infiltration of its ecclesiastical hierarchy by homosexuals. The fact that homosexual priests have been preying on young men and boys who have come to them for spiritual guidance and advice is an abomination that surely warrants hell for those responsible.

(Sidebar: Although I believe in hell, I do not believe in eternal damnation. I do not believe that a God that is Love metes out eternal punishment to His immortal "children" for being mentally and spiritually sick and like the Prodigal Son, gone astray in a "far country." I believe that such people in fact punish themselves, via a sort of karmic magnetism. That is, those who live rotten lives in this realm automatically condemn themselves to "punishment" in the next go-round. Although it may not be *eternal* damnation, it no doubt it can *seem* like an eternity.

The Bible warns us of the "what goes around comes around" nature of things: "As you have done, it shall be done to you;" "Your deeds shall return on your own head;" "God cannot be mocked;" "A man reaps what he sows." I am not proselytizing here — I am merely sharing my viewpoint in case it may be of interest to someone. I am *not* saying that my position in this regard is the correct one for me or anyone else — only that it works for me, for now).

My heart goes out to the vast majority of Catholic priests who are good, decent people — indeed sometimes saintly — who have been tarred with the same brush as their despicable brethren.

Paul Likoudis, a devout Catholic reporter, writes in his book "Amchurch Comes Out" that "the evidence is now irrefutable that an influential and very powerful coterie within the Catholic Church — well embedded and well protected by the Roman Catholic hierarchy

and their peers in the police, the courts, legislatures and the media —
is successfully advancing a sexual liberation agenda that will not end
until every social stigma attached to any sexual activity, no matter how
bizarre, has been erased."

By "Amchurch" Likoudis means the American Catholic Church. Putting aside the subject of homosexuals in the priesthood for the moment, it is worth noting how the Far Left's agenda jives with a
homosexual/lesbian agenda. I believe that "we the people" would be
shocked to learn of the pervasive extent of homosexuality/lesbianism
in America's "halls of power."

Likoudis concludes that the homosexual cabal within the Catholic
Church "will [in the end] be on the losing side of history, but the
damage they will have wrought will be enormous."

What about the various Protestant denominations, how are they
faring? They too have their own difficulties with homosexuals and
lesbians, of course, but the Protestants have other issues as well. One of
them is called the National Council of Churches (NCC).

"Front Page" editor Jacob Laskin writes, "Founded in 1950, [the]
NCC has...remained faithful to the legacy of its forerunner, the Communist front-group known as the Federal Council of Churches.
..Adhering to what is described as 'liberation theology' — that is,
Marxist ideology disguised as Christianity — the NCC lays claim to a
membership of 36 Protestant, Anglican, and Orthodox Christian
denominations, and some 50 million members in over 140,000 congre-
gations."

You should also be cognizant of the NCC's Geneva-based parent
group, the leftist World Council of Churches (WCC). All in all — whatever the Christian denomination — I think that it is safe to say that "the
fox is in the hen-house." Bruce Walker labels the collection of various
"foxes," under the umbrella term "Sinisterism."

(Sidebar: The word "sinister" springs from the Latin root word for
"left." I like the term "Sinisterism," as it is much more descriptive than
the bland word "collectivism," (which is rather tame sounding – as if
you were discussing a Rotary Club get-together, or a farmer's co-op.

Also, it allows one to avoid unwieldy verbal constructs such as "Islamofascist/communist").

The problems that Christianity has faced, and is facing, are of course much greater than the few examples that I have mentioned in this article. Like America itself, Christianity in America is in desperate need of "the divine hand of Providence."

The Far Left atheists have greatly shaken the "tree of faith" — which may turn out to be not such a bad thing. By shaking the tree of faith, hopefully much of the "rotten fruit" will drop out.

I have no desire to "turn back the clock" — such a thing is undesirable, even if it were possible. But surely we can work toward eliminating the worst excesses of atheistic secular humanism and rediscovering and reinvigorating the many blessings to be found in Christianity.

The teachings of the iconoclast Jesus were, and are, *revolutionary*. He was no lover of the status quo. Jesus *did* things; *changed* things; He was extremely pro-active. He shook up the establishment, ridiculed the Power Elites of His day, and yes, performed miracles. Are "we the people" just going to let it all slip through our fingers and forfeit our children's birthright for "a mess of potage?"

Laus Deo

25

Atheism 101: Trickle-down Poison

February 6, 2011

My life sometimes seems to me as if it has been nothing so much as one long (if often lackadaisical) search for spiritual truth. Consequently, it came as a bit of a surprise to realize what great inroads atheism has made in America. I recently read a magazine article in which the author praised, in all seriousness, Henry Potter – the avaricious, amoral scumbag from Frank Capra's movie "It's a Wonderful Life."

Such devious claptrap bespeaks an atheistic mindset, any disclaimers to the contrary notwithstanding. The message of the article was essentially that Potter had it right, and that George Bailey (Jimmy Stewart's character) was a sophomoric if not dangerous buffoon. Just the sort of ruthless self-justification one would expect from an erudite barbarian.

Compare that to Frank Capra's position regarding film making (he considered "It's a Wonderful Life" to be the best of the fifty-four films he directed). "[The purpose of making films is] first, to exalt the worth of the individual. Second, to champion man – plead his causes, protest any degradation of his dignity, spirit, or divinity. ...There is a radiance and glory in the darkness, could we but see. ...I beseech you to look."

The mindset that denies the divine spark in man and worships at the feet of mammon is at its core a thug's mindset, an atheistic mindset that sees charity and compassion as traps for losers and chumps. The elite's thugocracy that has replaced America's rule of law in Washington DC is reason enough to fight against the inroads made by the insidious spread of atheism throughout our land.

The fool has said in his heart, "There is no God."

Psalms 14:1 NKJV

"The propitious smiles of Heaven can never be expected on a nation that disregards the eternal rules of order and right, which Heaven itself has ordained."

George Washington: First President of the United States

Atheism is an intellectually shallow, morally stunted, and socially regressive blight on humanity. Its deleterious effects upon society can be seen all around us — from the self-serving arrogance of political elites, to the rampant greed and corruption in banking/business, to America's flagrant moral decay.

We live in an atheistic or "secular" society, one that worships at the altar of scientific positivism/secular humanism. Those are code words for a type of Godless barbarism dressed in the costume of sophistication and intellectual hubris.

Winston Churchill once said of Islam that "No stronger retrograde force exists in the world." I beg to differ — as a regressive, debilitating, socially destructive force atheism has no equal (although granted, it is a close contest).

I should mention up front that I do not dislike atheists *per se* — only their despicable philosophy, such as it is. I have friends that are atheists, and I treat them with the same respect and courtesy as I would anyone with a serious disease. (Perhaps "we the people" should start focusing more on the *disease* and not so much the *symptoms*).

Atheism and anti-Christian teachings/attitudes has been vigorously promoted by the Far Left since at least as far back as the French Revolution, and the history of its advance is an interesting one, but I'll leave that for another time. For now I will concentrate on why atheism *is* such a vile doctrine, and why it must be fought at every turn if humanity is to survive and thrive. (I will address the subset of "conservative," or right-wing, atheists later in the article).

Dinesh D'Souza has pointed out that atheistic pundits are no longer content with being tolerated; they want to prove that their view of reality is the correct one, once and for all. I concur — bring it on. One side of the debate is correct, and the other side is insanely deluded. It is crucially important to see which side is on the side of truth.

To say that atheism denies the existence of God does not tell us much unless we define what we mean by the label "God." I would be happy to discuss the concept/reality of God, but the focus of this article is atheism not God, so I'll employ a simple yet usable definition for now. I will have to leave questions such as whether God is a white-bearded guy sitting on a cloud, or a reality "in which we live, and move, and have our being" and other ontological/theological concerns for another time.

For our purposes here, I'll simply define God as the intelligent power behind creation. Atheists deny the existence of such a God, and from their denial spring a plethora of absurd, puerile, and socially harmful concepts.

Because many of atheism's adherents in the *intelligentsia* are under the mistaken impression that atheism is intellectually superior to a belief in God, it is perhaps best to start any discussion of atheism by drawing attention to its paucity of intellectual weight or validity. Atheism is, at the end of the day, nothing but a house of cards — a negative, nihilistic, ego-inflating life-denying doctrine that is based on nothing but ignorance, faulty logic, and egocentric hubris.

Atheists are fond of ridiculing the story of Creation as recounted in the Book of Genesis, preferring their own oh-so-brilliant version which runs something like this:

"Yea, in the beginning there was Nothing, and Nothing begat nothing — not even darkness. Nothing be praised! Then hark, for no reason Nothing became All That Is; yea Stuff happened to happen (all praise Stuff). Then behold, the pointless fumbling of the Hand of Chance (praised be Its name) breathed Life unto Itself. Lo, and Dead Stuff begat

Live Monkeys! And it came to pass that the monkeys begat humans, such as Bill Maher — thanks for Nothing!

Verily I say to you this is bulls—t, but atheists buy into such nonsense. (There is, I might point out, a vast difference between metaphorically depicted ineffable wisdom and spurious self-serving claptrap). The atheist's Creation myth has all of the warped absurdity of Kipling's "Just So" stories with none of the charm.

Those who have pursued spiritual growth earnestly know that truth mostly resides in consciousness and experience, and seldom in words and the intellect. Nonetheless scholars in the field of Intelligent Design (ID) have made admirable advances on the materialist's home turf. The circumstantial scientific evidence for the existence of an Intelligent Designer is now quite impressive. (I should mention that the scientists involved in ID are adamant about separating their research from theology).

It does not make a bit of difference to atheists. They steadfastly refuse to hear the truth, and remain like little kids with fingers stuck in their ears, chanting "La, la, la, I CAN'T HEAR YOU!" It would be laughable if the results of such willful ignorance were not often so tragic — and make no mistake, the social results of widespread atheism are no laughing matter.

Atheists often point to the "bloody history" of religion, while conveniently ignoring their own much more violent and bloody past. They have managed to pull off their staggering blood-bath in much less time then say, Christianity, whose body-count compared to atheism's is admittedly amateurish.

From Robespierre's Reign of Terror, to Lenin, to Stalin, to Hitler, to Mao, to Pol Pot, et al. atheism and its adherents have cut a bloody swath through history that leaves other doctrines in the dust — and in such a relatively short time too! I admit it is impressive in its own sick way.

Atheism is a symptom of a stunted, immature spirituality, and is a "naïve, childish concept" dressed in grown-up clothing. The *intelligent-*

sia who flaunt the *chic cache* of atheism are in truth merely cases of arrested development coupled with a narcissistic myopia.

What might be called "classic" atheism stems from the teachings of the ancient Greek Epicurus (341-270 BC). Like any good atheist he started from a predetermined position, and then went out in search of "evidence" to support it, as opposed to arriving at his conclusions via an unbiased search for truth.

In Epicurus's case the presupposition that he started out with was that the universe was strictly materialistic with no divine purpose behind it, or influence upon it. He then searched for "data" to support this position. Modern atheism is essentially tweaked variations on Epicurus' teachings.

Given that this is a relatively short article I don't have the luxury of delving into Epicurus' teachings in any depth, but by discussing a few of his concepts I hope to at least give the reader unfamiliar with Epicurean teachings some idea of what they are. For a more in-depth analysis of Epicureanism (and its modern-day counterparts such as Darwinism), I recommend Benjamin Wiker's book "Moral Darwinism: How We Became Hedonists."

Two of the main supports for the Epicurean (atheist) world-view, are atomism ("borrowed" from Democritus), and an eternal universe. It is worth noting that neither of these two major supports for Epicurean-ism/atheism was empirically verifiable by the science of his day. Therefore both of Epicurus' "proofs" were fallacies of the *Argumentum ad Ignorantiam* (appeal to ignorance) variety.

Epicurus described atoms as featureless, sterile, meaningless bits of matter. Epicurus knew that a sense of wonder about the universe might lead his followers astray. That is, they might start to believe in divinity and God knows what. As the Bible points out "The fear of the LORD is the beginning of wisdom" ("fear" in this case meaning a sense of profound awe).

Epicurus nipped any sense of awe in the bud by claiming that any apparent complexity and design in Nature was, at its root, merely the result of the chance arrangement of meaningless and pugnaciously undivine atoms. His followers could then say "Oh, is that all." Today we have a society filled with people saying "Oh, is that all." This despite the fact that we know today that atoms, as Epicurus described them, do not exist.

As Fritjof Capra observed in "The Tao of Physics," "Gradually, physicists began to realise [sic] that nature, at the atomic level, does not appear as a mechanical universe composed of fundamental building blocks, but rather as a network of relations, and that, ultimately, there are no parts at all in this interconnected web."

Indeed, it turns out that atoms are mostly space, containing swirling sub-atomic particle/patterns of data-energy. So mathematically elegant, precise, and complex are these bundles of data-energy that we call atoms, that it is reasonable to conclude that they are designed. They are most emphatically *not* teeny dead BBs of inert stuff.

(Sidebar: In any discussion of spirituality, or its antithesis atheism, it is worth recalling that words are merely metaphors. For example, if I tell you "I poured a glass of water on a rose." You cannot hold the "glass," drink the "water," or smell the "rose" because, quite obviously, words are not the things that they describe. Words are no more or less than a type of code for an ineffable reality.

Typically "we see through a glass, darkly" because of the veiling effect of layer upon layer of words. Whereas spirituality attempts to dissolve these verbal/mental veils, atheism uses them to obfuscate the divine).

Epicurus' description of atoms as "teeny dead BBs" is absurd. So what about his other main support for atheism — eternity? I should start by giving a brief description of why the concept of eternity is important to Epicurus' atheism.

On the face of it, the idea that inert mindless bits of matter (atoms as envisioned by Epicurus) should by chance arrange themselves into the undeniably complex universe we experience, seems a laughably jejune concept. But give those atoms eternity and infinity to bump around in, and anything is possible — so claim atheists.

This is a variant of the Monkey Theorem, which in essence states that a monkey hitting a keyboard for a long enough amount of time will eventually type out a given set of books, such as the works of Shakespeare. Research done with the help of computers has shown that the chances of such an outcome actually happening are slim to none. Take away eternity, and the odds of a monkey typing Shakespeare (or the universe arranging itself as it is by chance) drop to zero, or so close as to make no difference.

Many people believe that it was primarily Christians who opposed the Big Bang theory, because it disagreed with the Bible's Creation story, but that is simply not true. In fact it was a Christian, the Catholic priest Georges Lemaître, who came up with the theory, (with the Pope's enthusiastic support). Wikipedia observes that today "the [Big Bang] theory is the most comprehensive and accurate explanation [for the creation of the universe] supported by scientific evidence and observations."

It was primarily atheists who passionately opposed Lemaître's theory. They opposed it because it demolished the crucial atheistic crutch of eternity. If the universe had a beginning (even if billions of years ago), then the time needed for the Monkey Theorem to be at all viable just wasn't there.

For centuries atheists used science as their stalking horse, especially once the theories of Darwinian evolution came on the scene. But in the 20th century science "turned" on them via such discoveries as the Big Bang and quantum physics, and in the end pulled the rug out from under atheism, so to speak. So the Far Left attacked science.

And it is not just science that the Far Left attacked, but logic and reason itself. The ultimate atheistic position is anti-science, anti-logic, and anti-reason — all of which fits in nicely with their anti-life nihilism. The atheistic pursuit of truth extends only so far as it serves to further atheism's rationalizations, justifications, and lame excuses.

Any excuse that will serve as a crutch for their vapid doctrine will do. When science, logic, and reason failed to support atheism it was to be expected that the egocentric self-interest at the core of atheism would lash out — and so it has, and so it does, and so it will.

(Sidebar: Before diving [briefly!] into the murky depths of relativism, I should mention that all too many scientists remain atheists *not* because scientific research proves the nonexistence of God, but because of their *blind faith* in the religion of secularism. Their dogged adherence to secularism is nothing but a stubborn insistence on clinging to outdated paradigms of the past — i.e. propaganda foisted onto science by atheists over the centuries).

The Far Left turned on science a few decades ago because it was getting uncomfortably close to looking into things that did not jive with the atheistic world-view. So Far Left word-meisters got to work at deconstructing science.

The resulting gobbledygook was famously "outed" by Sokal's Hoax, which high-lighted the fact that the atheistic Left will tend to accept any sort of garbage thrown their way if you toss in the right buzz-words and phrase it in impressive sounding (if nonsensical) academic jargon.

Moral pluralism is a cultural sickness on a par with, and often connected to, atheism. As Stefan Jetchick observes "It is 'moral pluralism' that is at the heart of chronic hunger, environmental destruction, and third world debt, because 'moral pluralism' only begets moral indifference." Relativism — yeah, there's the ticket.

"When I use a word,' Humpty Dumpty said, in rather a scornful tone, 'it means just what I choose it to mean — neither more nor less.'" When Lewis Carroll penned those words for "Through the Looking Glass" he was ridiculing the absurdity of such thinking, but relativists admire this type of lazy empty-headed "reasoning."

In essence relativism says "It is true because I *say* it is — so there." *Au contraire mon frère*, if the convoluted linguistic knot of relativism were based on reason it might be true, but "as it isn't, it ain't. That's logic."

In the more refined language of Dr. David R. Hawkins: "The appeal of relativism...is to imbalance and excess rather than to truth, wisdom, or caution. ...To the prideful, narcissistic ("sensitive") ego, responsibility is "uncomfortable," as are certain facts of reality that impinge on social image. Thus, to protect itself, the ego welcomes the concept of [relativism] to dispense with unwanted realities. ...A serious downside to the pseudo-intellectualism of relativism is that it is a trap for academia, which confused intellectualism with erudition or intelligence."

Relativism is a sort of Nietzschesque anti-reason reasoning. The website "Atheism Analyzed" does an admirable job of showing just how lame some of the various relativistic/atheistic doctrines are.

For example, Bertrand Russell's dictum "We must require evidence for a thing if it is to be believed" (from his atheistic essay "Why I am Not A Christian"), is shown to be thoroughly faulty logic.

Russell's dictum is "commonly used as a law for materialism." Yet as "Atheism Analyzed" points out, Russell's statement is self-refuting — logically speaking it is rubbish. Does the fact that we don't (can't) have empirical "evidence" for love, truth, and faith mean that they are figments of our imagination? That is, does the fact that we cannot weigh and measure them mean that they do not exist? Does the lack of material evidence for awareness mean we are not aware?

Russell's looking for the wrong thing, with the wrong motives, in the wrong place, with the wrong tools. He reminds me of the proverbial fish swimming in the ocean derisively demanding "Show me the water!" If you add the extra fillip that the fish is also made of water, then his statement's foolishness is especially evident.

There is nothing intrinsically unscientific about spirituality — in fact it can assimilate science quite easily. Spirituality is much more open and inclusive than the limited framework of science, which has no methodology for dealing with life's most vital concerns such as values, morals, and meaning. Spirituality has no axe to grind with science.

In David Bodanis' book "E = mc2" he explains that the "E" stands for energy, the equals sign means "is the same as," and the mc2 refers to what we label "matter." In essence Einstein's famous equation is a way of saying that energy is matter, and matter is energy. Matter is simply a sort of congealed energy — which is why matter has such an explosive effect when its bound energy is rapidly released.

As Bodanis points out, if you were to abruptly release the pent-up energy in a common pencil the resultant blast would destroy a city block.

We use matter that is already unstable such as plutonium or uranium to make atomic bombs, but in truth *any* matter could theoretically be used. (Also noteworthy are the "new" forms of energy such as zero-point energy and dark energy which research suggests fill "empty" space. Is energy everywhere)?

The First Law of Thermodynamics states: *Energy can neither be created nor destroyed, only altered in form.* (Without using words, try to "describe" what energy really is — "For the kingdom of God is not a matter of talk but of power"). Is it not a valid scientific pursuit to inquire into possible connections between an Intelligent Designer and indestructible energy?

Such things as the scientific field of ecology and the Butterfly Effect point toward the unity of everything — a universe made of one interconnected reality, one energy, in all its various shapes and forms. Is this not similar to a God who is everything, or the One? Perhaps God is not energy, but that which created energy — or both; creator and creation? I am just asking in an open-minded way — as science should properly be doing, as opposed to its current one-sided gathering of "excuses" for atheism.

Is it not possible that aided by divine wisdom the mystics of old intuited truths only now being discovered by science?" Of course it is possible, even probable, as the new scientific field of consciousness research implies. It is only the fearful, arrogant, and foolish grasping onto provincial doctrines of anthropocentric atheism that prevent the obvious from shining forth.

The various Christian sects and their followers for all their faults and foibles are largely pointed in the right direction — toward truth and life, ("I am come that they might have life, and that they might have it more abundantly"). Atheism, which aggressively celebrates egocentricity, leads society inexorably towards destruction, nihilism, and death. Why would anyone in their right mind ever choose atheism/relativism of their own free will?

Oh I forgot, there is no such thing as free will in a Godless universe. Nor, say atheist pundits, are there such things as love, compassion, integrity, hope — in fact any emotion, or virtue (or vice). Atheism posits that these are all just the result of randomly created biological processes which produce the *illusion* of compassion, gratitude, hope, et al.

As Francis Crick, (atheist and co-discoverer of the structure of DNA), wrote in "The Astonishing Hypothesis," "You, your joys and your sorrows, your memories and your ambitions, your sense of personal identity and free will, are in fact no more than the behavior of a vast assembly of nerve cells and their associated molecules"

Atheism posits the belief that we are all just valueless, meaningless, emotionless, automatons adrift in a valueless, meaningless universe. Trust me, this is not the philosophy you want driving the people in charge of businesses, banks, and a bloated government bureaucracy. Ready for some sex and soma, Bernard — or shall we join Winston in Room 101?

Do most atheists even care about the full implications of atheism? Not hardly. Atheists are for the most part simply interested in protecting their self-serving life-style, and marching in lock-step with others who share in their smug delusion. Atheism means win, win, win all around for the ego — only society and culture lose. As Dr. Hawkins succinctly puts it, "In truth, we exist and survive, not *because* of the ego, but in *spite* of it" (Italics added)

The secularization of America started in earnest with the infiltration of Harvard by Fabian aficionados of Keynesian economics in the early part of the last century (the homosexual Keynes and his cohorts were against Christianity for the obvious reason that the Bible condemns their life-style — at least it did in those days).

American academic atheism received a further surge with an influx of communist professors from the "Frankfurt School" in the 1930s, and so the atheistic/anti-Christian message was passed down to generation after generation of students, and then passed on to "we the people" through a thousand-and-one subtle and not so subtle innuendos, hints, and nudges, coupled with constant "lawfare" waged by the ACLU and their ilk.

You could call it "trickle-down poison." The next, and last, major "surge" occurred in the 1960s.

No professional area (except possibly law) has been more complicit in the subtle spreading of atheistic/anti-Christian attitudes than the mass media. To take one of countless examples, the way that the media covered Jim Jones and the Jonestown tragedy is a classic case in point.

The "reverend" Jim Jones was a rabid Far Left ideologue who preached Marxism, sent church donations to communist Russia, and led his congregation in singing the Russian Soviet anthem as they all committed suicide under gun point by drinking cyanide-laced Kool-Aid. In addition, some of Jones' followers killed several people connected with a fact-finding mission to Jonestown — including Congressman Leo Ryan.

Far Left insanity all the way — and nary a peep from our stalwart media "watchdogs" about any of it. Instead they spread the lie that Jones was a religious nut; a *Christian* religious nut. How many other lies do you think "we the people" have been spoon-fed by the various media venues (magazines, newspapers, TV, movies, et al.)?

Given our country's Judeo/Christian roots, and the deplorable state of our culture, perhaps now would be a good point to retrench and then move forward with Christian values — and I don't mean any of the various watered-down and perverted Far Left versions of *faux* "Christianity" with their talk of social justice, collective salvation, and moral relativism.

Perhaps now would be an opportune time to reinvigorate, rethink, and rediscover Christianity — to have a sort of "spring cleaning." God, the "Ancient of Days," is after all also the "Wonder Child" — ever new, fresh, and bursting with inspiration and power. The word "God" is more a verb than a noun.

Although Jesus certainly promoted doing good deeds for others — His main emphasis was on changing oneself. He told the Power Elites of His day ("blind guides who strain out a gnat, but swallow a camel") that they should stop focusing on what was *outside* of them, and start focusing on, and improving, what was *inside*. In addition, as Paul wrote, "the letter kills, but the Spirit gives life." Atheists know nothing of the Spirit, hence the vast burden of laws and regulations Progressives have imposed on "we the people."

Atheists, who have no stable internal moral compass, always tend toward wanting to fix what they perceive as being wrong with *you*, and because their own spirits are stunted and atrophied, they generally have scant comprehension of personal responsibility and therefore believe that they must regulate everything (and everyone) from the outside.

I have become convinced that the Far Left, and even moderate liberals to a lesser extent, suffer from a mental pathology — one of the symptoms being projection/transference — where they project onto those that they disagree with the very qualities that they themselves possess; such as intolerance, elitism, and arrogance (or its marginally less annoying cousin — smugness).

Also, no doubt some are simply using transference as a ploy to prevent honest self-examination. In any event, attributing to others their own faults is an irritating and widespread trait among the left-wing. It ties in with the atheistic credo of protecting the ego (and its positionalities) at all costs.

Because atheism's bedrock foundation is senseless amoral nihilism, the best that they can do for a code of conduct is to ape Christian ethics and morals in order to cloak their barbaric core with a semblance of civility. Atheism cares only about atheism. When history does not suit atheists they rewrite history; when logic fails them they deconstruct logic; when science fails them they ridicule science, and when reason fails them they savage reason.

Atheists attempt to destroy anything and everything that gets in their way, and at the end of the day stand revealed as deluded slaves of ego. I for one am way past being sick and tired of their willful destruction of America's morality, ethics, and honor. They can go live in whatever benighted, vile, godless pit they want — but leave America alone!

In any event, I trust that those of you with open minds will hopefully see the truth in what I have written. Those whose minds have been sealed shut by atheism generally need a catastrophic occurrence in their personal lives for them to leave the comfortable, if stagnant, confines of their egoic prison.

To "conservative" atheists I say "get with the program people." You are either part of the solution, or part of the problem, and if you believe in the Godless nihilism of materialistic atheism then you are definitely part of the problem. I am not saying that you need to be born again or join a religion — simply conceding the point that there just may be a God, and you are not it, would be a start.

Laus Deo.

26

Power to the People!

April 2, 2011

The discussion about Beck, O'Reilly and the "birthers" really dates this article — as does my largely still dewy-eyed attitude toward "Fox News." I went on to essentially let Beck slide for his faux pas, because (1) he never repeated it, and (2) he brought so much important information to America's attention (trust me, I am aware that many of you have never let him off the hook for dissing the "birthers").

I still think that "Fox News" is the best (least detestable?) major TV channel that is currently available to "we the people" — I just take it with a much larger grain of salt these days. In any event, I watch very little television anymore, and I do not read newspapers or popular magazines. Almost all of the news I receive comes to me via the Internet.I am delighted to report that Geert Wilders was found innocent of all charges.

"Singing power to the people, power to the people, power to the people, power to the people right on!"

John Lennon (1940-1980) "Power to the People"

"Meet the new boss, same as the old boss. ...I'll get on my knees and pray, we don't get fooled again!"

The Who "Won't Get Fooled Again"

"The proper study of political mankind is the study of power elites, without which nothing that happens [can] be understood."

G.K. Chesterton (1874-1936)

When the Left says that they are giving power to the people — they lie. When governments say that they want to return power to the people — they lie. When politicians say they are *for* the people — they lie.

There is only one source of power to the people, and that *is* the people — "we the people" ourselves. "We the people" are our own strength, hope, power, and deliverer — with God's grace and guidance. It is time to take our power back.

One of the Left's historic ploys is to drag out the hoary old slogan "Power to the people!" The sentiment is all fine and good. The problem is that the Left has absolutely no interest in giving power to the people — they want to give power to a tyrannical government with themselves in control.

Look at any left-wing government and you will find a massive government bureaucracy run by a dictator and/or an oligarchy. How much power do the people actually have under such "people's utopias?" Little to none. Let us check out a few of these "people's utopias."

Because of Lenin's relatively early death, his body count only reached about 2 million. Stalin reached the more significant figure of around 30 million deaths. Hitler's "Socialist Workers Party," resulted in an equally impressive number — when you add those killed fighting fascism to those exterminated in his death camps.

China's communist dictator Mao, raised the bar for all left-wing dictators when he implemented government policies that resulted in the deaths of upwards of 80 million people. Pol Pot's Cambodian "Killing Fields" saw the murder of a notable one-and-a-half million people (which, considering the percentage of the total Cambodian population this represents, is actually a *very* impressive number indeed). Wikipedia observes of Cambodia's Khmer Rouge, that they are "remembered primarily for [their] policy of *social engineering* and the *genocide* this caused," can be applied to all Far Left efforts to give "power to the people" (Italics added).

"Social engineering" — a term near and dear to every Progressive's heart. "Power to the people," yeah right. And it is not just the left-wing, of course — there are a multitude of New World Order (NWO) types in the right-wing as well.

I grant that many conspiracy theories are bogus, and some are just downright silly.

But look into a valid history of the Club of Rome, Agenda 21, the Trilateral Commission, the CFR (Council on Foreign Relations,) the Rockefellers, the Nazi/Islam connection, Soros and the Open Society Institute, the Fabians, the Tide Foundation, the...

Well, just look into those for starters, and if you do not see the collusion, the international connections, the *conspiracy*, then you are simply choosing to remain willfully ignorant of the truth. The NWO means One World Government, which means the USA has to go down — in order to level the playing field and ensure social justice for all.

We are talking about a global nightmare. "Social justice" will mean equal misery for all, under a Draconian totalitarian regime run by a mega wealthy political/corporate/banking elite whose motto will not be "Power to the People," but "Screw the People, Screw Them All!"

And believe me, they will. How did you enjoy 2009, when you realized that your government "representatives" did not represent you, and there was not a d—n thing you could do about it? Never forget it, because that was only a tiny taste of what is in store for "we the people" if we lose this fight. So who to trust? Good question.

As far as the major news sources go, Fox News is the obvious choice, but even they have some areas where their honesty is suspect. I'm referring specifically to their treatment of Islam, and the "birthers."

The other night I watched Bill O'Reilly ask Sarah Palin about the "birthers." He had this pained "say it ain't so" expression on his face, as he asked her if she backed the "birthers" (Palin basically said that she thought that the "birthers" had the right to ask questions).

Glenn Beck has come down especially hard on the "birthers" — comparing them to some lunatic fringe group, akin to "flat earthers" — as if asking for proof of Obama's eligibility to be POTUS, is like claiming he is from mars. The other day (shortly before switching off my TV) I watched Beck lump "birthers" together with "right-wing nazis." (He should be aware by now that the Nazis were a left-wing phenomena).

Methinks Beck and O'Reilly doth protest too much. After all, what is wrong with wanting some solid evidence that our President is eligible to be POTUS? There is a larger, much more important concern here though — i.e. who *is* this guy? Who is Barack Hussein Obama? Why is all of his past history under lock and key?

Why was Obama's Selective Service document retro-written during the presidential campaign of 2008? Where are his college records — from Occidental, Columbia, and Harvard? What sort of passport did he use when he traveled to Pakistan? When did he legally change his name from Barry Soetoro? Did he *ever* legally change it? Was he adopted by Lolo Soetoro (Lolo Sutoro Mangunharjo) and still a citizen of Indonesia?

Those are not crazy questions, they are legitimate concerns and you had better believe that the liberal media would have vociferously demanded answers *long* ago if the person in question had been a conservative.

It is unconscionable that the President of the United States is being allowed to hide his past from "we the people." That Fox News is dismissing legitimate concerns regarding Obama's eligibility is disturbing. I repeat, who *is* this guy? That is not some "lunatic fringe" question — that a sane and valid *demand* to know who is at America's helm.

"We the people" need to ask ourselves, "why are Beck and O'Reilly isolating, minimizing, and ridiculing the "birthers" à *la* Saul Alinsky's rules for radicals?" More to the point, why are they focusing on the birth certificate issue, and *ignoring* the *larger* question of who Obama really is? We have every right to ask these questions; in fact it's our *duty* as an informed electorate to ask these questions.

A subject of perhaps greater concern is that the Fox News network is in bed with the Muslims. As Dr. Laurie Roth, Jerry McConnell, and a others have noted, Saudi Arabian Prince Ahwaleed bin Talal is the second largest owner of stock in Rupert Murdoch's, News Corp — the parent company of Fox News.

If you don't think that is alarming, then I suggest you read "Muslim Mafia," which is an excellent expose of CAIR (Council on American Islamic Relations). At least read Rep. Sue Myrick's (R-NC) short fore-word to the book, which is posted online.

The other week O'Reilly spoke with CAIR spokesman Ibrahim Hooper, and afterwards called him a "stand up guy." Not hardly. I'll show you a stand up guy — Geert Wilders. Wilders, a Dutch politician, is currently on trial in his native country for speaking the truth about Islam. You are not allowed to speak the truth in Eurabia these days. I'll take *my* "stand up guy" over O'Reilly's any day of the week.

For a taste of what's coming to America you might check out how Muslims shouted down free speech during a recent event at the University of California-Irvine. Shades of things to come – it is only going to get worse folks, trust me. (A great example of what liberals mean by "free speech" – you *are* free to say anything you want, as long as it is in *agreement* with the left-wing's group-think as disseminated by such propaganda outlets as the "New York Times" and NPR).

Does all this mean that I will not watch Beck or O'Reilly anymore? No, it doesn't mean that at all. They often provide helpful and insightful commentary. But it does mean that I take what they report with a grain of salt, and I don't assume that what they say is graven in stone.

As individuals we need to think for ourselves and think on our feet. As new facts become known to us we need to be able to shift gears, shift allegiances, and shift our minds. We must be rock-solid in our faith, determination, and vision, but supple and quick in our ability to learn and respond to changing conditions and data.

"We the people" have been on one heck of a steep learning curve this past year. For example: let's see a show of hands from people who did not know who Saul Alinsky was this time last year. That's what I thought — you can all put your hands down now, thanks. "We the people" are quick learners when we put our minds to it.

"We the people" don't need "leaders," we need representatives. And if our representatives show signs that they are *not* representing us then we must be prepared to drop them like a hot potato.

Back to the question, "who to trust." Now that the lame stream media and most politicians have lost "street cred," where do you turn for the truth? There are a number of good options and venues and the number keeps increasing daily.

Fox News, although it is certainly not without faults, is still the best major TV news outlet by far — just be sure to take your grain of salt first. The Wall Street Journal (another Murdoch enterprise) is similarly often a reliable source of news. Radio has become a vital link for trustworthy news. Then there is the internet — there are a plethora of good informative websites out there. (Unfortunately, there are also a plethora of bogus, misguided, and misguiding websites out there. *Caveat emptor* — buyer beware).

Now that "we the people" are engaged and involved in the political process, we are making ever-smarter choices as we learn on the job — our "job" being that of becoming an informed, active, and powerful, electorate.

To paraphrase a line from *Treasure of the Sierra Madre*: "Leaders? We don't need no stinking leaders." Judi McLeod, editor of *Canada Free Press*, recently wrote, "Much heart can be taken in this truth: Tea Party members call no one leader, for their only leader is the American Constitution."

Founding Father John Adams "guesstimated" that only around one-third of the population actively supported the Revolutionary War (another third actively opposed it, and the last third changed sides depending on which way the wind blew). "We the people" currently have much more than a third of the people with us. We can take back our power — we must. It will be both a revolution and a restoration.

When you get down to it, "we the people" ourselves are the ones we can trust. America's true patriots have always been the backbone of this country and we know what must be done. The only questions are how and when.

Power to the people? You bet.

Laus Deo.

P.S. Anyone with their hand still raised can consider themselves an honorary Progressive.

27

So Long, See Ya, Sayonara, and Slán Agat Bill O'Reilly

April 13, 2011

Sure and is this not the only article of mine to be having Irish Gaelic in it?
Tis. Well there you go then — no more need be said.

Bill O'Reilly's show last night calls for a response. I doubt his viewership will start running for the hills post-haste, but I do believe his ratings will take a hit in the weeks and months ahead.

O'Reilly's duplicitous smoke-and-mirrors act regarding Obama's eligibility is not playing in Peoria these days; at least it isn't playing well. "We the people" can see all too clearly that, at best, Obama is in over his head, and at worst deliberately nose-diving the US economy into the ground. Perhaps we are witness to a combination of both ineptitude, and treason.

Given what little we do know of Obama's past, and considering the type of people he has surrounded himself with, both before and during his Presidency, you would have to be extraordinarily dense and/or deluded not to be deeply concerned about Obama's credentials. Officer O'Reilly can say "Nothing to see here folks, move along" all he wants, but "we the people" know d—n well there *is* something here to see, and we are not going anywhere.

One of the first "important" myths that O'Reilly attacked Tuesday night concerned the First Lady's staff. "Mrs. Obama has more aides than any other First Lady. *False.*" Well thank you Bill O'Reilly for putting that frivolous and Constitutionally irrelevant rumor to rest, and lumping it in with the other, critically important questions that are crying out for legitimate, rigorous, and remorseless investigation.

O'Reilly's supercilious dismissal of the vitally important issue of Obama's eligibility to be POTUS is no longer amusing, if it ever was. This is a very different America than the one of just three years ago.

"We the people" are ever more aware of just how badly we have been lied to, ripped-off, and duped by the arrogant political elites, and just how leftist the slant of our media and entertainment venues has been. Media pundits who believe that we are still dependent on the pabulum and propaganda dished out by the various television talking heads are in for a rude awakening.

O'Reilly did not set anything straight on his show last night, except how in the tank he is for the Progressive agenda. That, or he is the most thick-headed Mick on the planet.

America increasingly goes to the Internet for its news. Among conservative websites the coin of the realm is truth and honesty — if you do not deal faithfully in that coinage you will soon lose street cred, and your audience. It appears that TV's talking heads have yet to learn that lesson. O'Reilly is trying to pass off counterfeit currency, and it will catch up to him sooner or later. So goodbye Bill O'Reilly, or as they say in Ireland "Slán agat."

In a recent article in "Canada Free Press" Phil Brennan signed-off by trying to bestir O'Reilly's patriotism with the ancient Irish war cry "Faugh 'a ballagh!" (Clear the way!). I have yet another old Irish war cry to sign-off with: Hey O'Reilly — "Téigh trasna ort féin!"

Laus Deo.

28

The Homosexual Agenda
and the US Military

May 14, 2011

What in the world are the Pentagon and Congress thinking? Have they all gone crazy?

Researching and writing about homosexuality is not something I relish, but the absurd notion that America's sexual orientation should cater to a miniscule minority of the population demands explanation. Why my sudden interest in the subject? The repeal of DADT, simple as that.

"At least in the beginning, we are seeking public desensitization and nothing more. We do not need and cannot expect a full 'appreciation' or 'understanding' of homosexuality from the average American. You can forget about trying to persuade the masses that homosexuality is a good thing. But if only you can get them to think that it is just another thing...then your battle for legal and social rights is virtually won."

From "The Overhauling of Straight America" November, 1987

"During times of universal deceit, telling the truth becomes a revolutionary act."

George Orwell (1903-1950)

Grab your thinking cap Poindexter, as we are going to cover some territory on this one. The subjects in this article lend themselves to straying off on strange tangents but I'll do my best to keep on message.

At the end of its lame-duck session last year the historically inept, treasonous, and corrupt 111th US Congress repealed DADT (Don't Ask Don't Tell). The acronym DADT is a misleading construct coined by a GLBT (Gay, Lesbian, Bisexual, Transgender) friendly media.

DADT was not merely about not asking and not telling, it was a law that prohibited homosexuals from openly serving in the US armed forces.

The marginally less despicable 112th US Congress has carried on from where the 111th left off and is moving ahead with the process of openly integrating homosexuals into the US military. Marines are already going through "gay sensitivity training" and it was announced recently that Navy chaplains would wed gay couples (jumping the gun it appears — the decision was later reversed).

Why the rush? Why this extremely expensive and disruptive campaign to make the US military homosexually compliant during tough economic times and a world-wide war against Islamists? After all, homosexuals account for at most around 3% of the population.

It has been said that "the Left doesn't look back" — and with good reason. If you had the blood-stained track record of god-awful screw-ups that the Far Left has you wouldn't want to look back either. Best to just stay in a state of denial and delusion — and they do. That the Far left (and to a lesser extent, the liberal) mental state is a dysfunctional, warped, and pathological *weltanschauung* or world-view is a given.

Just because the Far Left insists on lying about, twisting, or ignoring their past history does not mean that "we the people" need to follow suit. On the contrary, we must become aware of the insidious path that the communists, fascists, and other Far Left collectivist regimes have followed if we are to stand any chance of defeating their onslaught.

For the better part of the first half of the 20th century the left-wing *intelligentsia* promoted the racist teachings of eugenics, which championed the notion that biology was all important in determining one's life. Margaret Sanger, the "sainted" founder of Planned Parenthood, endorsed eugenics, as did Adolf Hitler, who took notes on the subject from American Progressives.

After the Nazi atrocities of WWII became publicized, the Far Left decided that perhaps eugenics wasn't such a swell idea after all, and they chose to try another tack — i.e. humans are not controlled by their *biology*, but by their *environment*. In a Homer Simpsonesque "Doh!" moment of revelation they realized that such a stance was much more up their alley in the first place, as it ignores the "fallen" state of human nature, and posits an infinitely malleable human personality.

Just the thing for a Far Left collectivist agenda — be it communist, fascist, Nazi, or whatever. Radical feminists especially latched onto the "it's all caused by the environment" credo with a vengeance.

The Tabula Rasa

The idea that human beings are essentially blank slates (*tabula rasa*) upon which anything may be written, was perhaps most famously summarized by the words of psychologist John Watson, "Give me a dozen healthy infants...and my own specified world to bring them up in and I'll guarantee to take any one at random and train him to become any type of specialist I might select—doctor, lawyer, artist, merchant-chief and, yes, even beggar-man and thief, regardless of his talents, penchants, tendencies, abilities, vocations, and race of his ancestors."

Progressives from all sorts of different professions set out to prove that human personality was simply the product of their environment. Dr. Brown performed an experiment to prove his theory — with the trademark detached creepiness of his ilk. He and his partner found a nine-month-old little boy named Albert to perform their tests on.

First the baby was given various objects to play with, all of which he smiled at and enjoyed. Then Brown introduced a white rat, and at the same time made a loud bang behind Albert's head. The little boy was of course alarmed, and started crying. Brown and his partner kept repeating the process until eventually just the sight of a furry white rat would cause little Albert to cry.

Unfortunately, as the "New World Encyclopedia" reports, "[Little] Albert was taken from the hospital the day the last tests were made. Hence, the opportunity of developing an experimental technique for *removing* the conditioned emotional response was denied" (Italics added). Yes...well, these things happen.

Be that as it may, after switching from "It's all about biology!" (eugenics), to "It's all about the environment!" (behaviorism), it appears that liberals have at long last decided to embrace the concept that human nature is the result of a combination of *both* nature (biology), *and* nurture (environment). (They sure took their sweet time at arriving at a conclusion that common sense should have pointed them toward from the start).

That's great — liberals have finally discovered common sense, right? Well actually no, no they have not. What happened is this: while the bulk of the Far Left continues to promote their "it's all about the environment" behaviorism, there is one group that broke away from the herd and in a glaring exception to the liberal status quo declared that biology, *not* environment, was the all important factor in their special case. That group is the homosexual activists.

Their thinking is: if the environment causes human nature, then if you change the environment you might be able to change homosexual behavior, or at least minimize its effects. So it is crucial to homosexual activists that they "prove" that homosexuality is the result of a biological imperative. Say hello to the "gay gene."

Actually, before we say hello to the "gay gene," allow me to give you a little back story on how homosexuality became culturally acceptable in the US — I'll be brief.

There is no specific location or personage to designate as the one person or place that started the homosexual ball rolling in America — although John Maynard Keynes and the proliferation of Keynesian economics throughout academia, starting with Harvard in the early 20th century, is certainly one person and place to start with.

Concerning the pederast Keynes, Zygmund Dobbs writes in "Keynes at Harvard" that "his condition was permanently ingrained and his philosophy was structured to consider homosexuality as superior, and the regular habits of the majority [i.e. heterosexuality] a boorish moral deficiency."

Alfred Kinsey and the Queering of America

In any event, there is no doubt that the homosexual agenda got its first great boost from Dr. Alfred Kinsey — one time Harvard professor, homosexual pedophile, and all around sexual psychopath *extraordinaire*. You had best hide the women, children, men, and sheep when Dr. Kinsey came to town. What a demented, dishonest, detestable waste of space.

Kinsey, of course, wrote the famous (infamous) "Kinsey Report" ("Sexual Behavior in the Human Male"), released in 1948. Dressed in his trademark white lab coat he bamboozled America into taking as gospel his often slanted and questionable findings. For example, some of his data about "the normal American male" came from questionnaires filled out by men in prison for sexually deviant crimes — you think that might have skewed his findings a bit?

In a nutshell, Kinsey promoted the idea that homosexuality was natural, as was pedophilia and bestiality. According to Kinsey most American males were polymorphously perverse (a term first coined by Freud, and popularized by Herbert Marcuse in his 1955 book "Eros and Civilization").

Polymorphous perversity is the "if it feels good do it" lifestyle and doctrine taken to the nth degree. Ultimately there are no sexual taboos whatsoever for the polymorphously perverse. To follow such a hedonistic doctrine (an atheistic doctrine need I add) is to be willingly led by the nose (or some other appendage) by an unconstrained libido. F—k everything.

Many homosexuals are polymorphously perverse, and we live in an increasingly perverse culture. Dr. Jeffrey Satinover observes that,

"What we call the 'gay life-style' is in large measure a way of life constructed around unconstrained sexuality."

Albert Mohler notes that "civilization cannot survive the triumph of the age of polymorphous perversity, because the idea of polymorphous sex is hopelessly incompatible with the very notion of civilization itself. Civilization is based upon order, respect, habit, custom, and institution — all of which are rejected outright by the age of polymorphous perversity."

Yet here is the US military, a mainstay of American society, openly embracing the homosexual lifestyle. And lest you think that polymorphous perversity is hip, slick, and cool beyond words, permit me point out that psychopaths are often polymorphously perverse. Also, like many homosexuals, psychopaths often indulge in anal intercourse (as do many Muslim men with their wife, or wives — more about that shortly).

Kinsey lied and schmoozed his way across America using his oh-so-professional demeanor, white lab coat, and book full of fraudulent "science" to hoodwink a gullible populace into relaxing its attitudes and laws regarding sexuality in general, and homosexuality in particular. (The white lab coat doesn't carry quite the panache it once did, do in no small part to frauds like Kinsey).

Homosexual Attacks on Psychology and Psychiatry

Another major victory for homosexuals was their successful 1973 attack on the American *Psychiatric* Association, or APA (although the American *Psychological* Assoc. has the same initials, I'll be using them only in reference to the psychiatric association). By staging what was essentially a coup, a relatively small sub-set of homosexual activists within the APA managed to ensure that homosexuality was "normalized" by the association — against the wishes of almost 70% of its members.

As Dr. Jeffery Satinover writes in his book "Homosexuality and the Politics of Truth," "How much the 1973 APA decision was motivated by politics is only becoming clear even now" — so much for empirical science. This was followed two years later by the American Psychological Association (at the time over three times as large a group as the APA) following suit. The "normalizing" of homosexuality within the professions of psychology and psychiatry has had far-reaching and deleterious effects on American culture.

Prior to 1973 homosexuality had been classified as a mental illness. It is not by happenstance that before homosexuality was normalized by the APA, *narcissism* was normalized. Homosexuality is by its very nature narcissistic. Satinover writes, "Narcissists were once deemed untreatable and unsuitable as analysts; now entire institutes of narcissists treat and train other narcissists."

In a little over twenty years (1948-1973) homosexuality went from being an illegal mental illness to being classified as a normal sexual activity and a perfectly acceptable mental state. Not everyone has bought into the smoke and mirrors deception, however. Dr. Joseph Nicolosi, writing for NARTH (National Association for Research and Therapy of Homosexuality) writes, "The dark side of gay life — characterized by sexual addictions and fixations — keeps stubbornly emerging, in spite of public-relations efforts to submerge it. ...How long can psychologists be in denial about the significance of the dark side, and ignore what it implies about the homosexual condition?"

Another important year for homosexual activists was 1988. As David Kupelian documents in his book "The Marketing of Evil," "In February 1988 some 175 leading activists representing homosexual groups from across the nation held a war conference in Warrenton, Virginia, to map out their movement's future."

Shortly afterward two attendees, a "Harvard educated researcher," and another "with a doctorate in politics from Harvard," wrote a book called "After the Ball" — a blueprint for a "long-term marketing campaign to sell 'gay rights' to straight America." Kupelian observes that "'After the Ball' became the public-relations 'Bible' of the movement."

The "push-back" against the militant homosexual agenda by NARTH and other groups or individuals is still a relatively small affair

— but they are rapidly growing in influence and numbers. Perhaps, as Zygmund Dobbs writes, "a thorough scientific re-evaluation of the motivations and the distortions of the founders of psycho-analysis as a 'sick' movement is long overdue" — along with a re-evaluation of the pathology surrounding homosexuality. In any event, now that we have a bit of background to set the scene, let us fast forward a bit to 1993, and the introduction of The Gay Gene.

The Gay Gene

As recounted by Dr. Satinover, the first "news" venue to announce the gay gene was NPR (National Public Radio). On July 15th, 1993 they announced the findings contained in an article to be published the next day in "Science" magazine. Satinover writes, "most laymen would have turned off the radio thinking that homosexuality is caused by a gene" — which, of course, was the intent.

The next day the "Wall Street Journal" (of all places) jumped on the story like a duck on a June-bug and published an article titled "Research Points Toward a Gay Gene" — which was a gross misrepresentation of the truth, if not an outright lie.

The "New York Times" (of all places), was much more precise in its recounting of the story and cautioned readers not to assume that the report might "mean anything as simplistic as that the 'gay gene' had been found."

The brouhaha surrounding the "gay gene" was caused by research done by Dr. Dean Hamer (a homosexual geneticist). Dr. Satinover writes that Hamer's study was "seriously flawed." In fairness to Dr. Hamer, I should mention that as far as I know he never himself claimed to have found a "gay gene" — which, however, did not stop homosexual activists from taking the ball and running with it. Quite successfully I might add, as many Americans today believe that the "gay gene" is a reality, and that homosexuals are "born that way."

The best that geneticists looking for a biological imperative behind homosexuality have been able to come up with is the hypothesis that homosexuals are predisposed to homosexuality because of certain innate biological traits — in much the same way that a tall person may be predisposed to play basketball, or someone with an ear for music may be predisposed to become a musician. Even this hypothesis is far from being considered proven. In any event, there is no such thing as a gay gene.

Homosexuality and Politics

Homosexuality is opposed to natural law, the way things are intended to be. If the idea of males and females being made for each other seems befuddling to you, then I suggest that you go grab yourself a nut and bolt and go play with them for awhile. Perhaps a light will dawn for you — perhaps not. The United States of America was founded on the principles of "the laws of nature and of nature's God," and that is the nation I will fight to defend – and no other.

Homosexuals generally have little or no interest in children (aside from the pederasts who regard them as sexual toys), and therefore are naturally aligned with the Far Left's death cult. The economic suicide run America is currently on is emblematic of their narcissistic lack of concern for future generations.

Not for nothing did "National Review" senior editor Ramesh Ponnuru name his book about abortion and the Democrats "The Party of Death." Here is a catchy political slogan for you: "Democrats — the Party of Debt, Death, and Destruction."

I must not forget to mention the anemic and rootless Republican Party, which is hardly as pure as the driven snow. Both the Democratic and Republican parties are infested with corruption, greed, and anti-American one-world globalists of one persuasion or another — Beltway Bubble boys and girls doing their best to get while the gettin's good and the golden goose of the United States still has some meat left on her bones.

Islam and Misogyny

The misogynistic nature of the Far Left, in fact their entire mental pathology, is perhaps nowhere better explained in layman's terms than in Dr. Jamie Glazov's book "United in Hate: The Left's Romance With Tyranny and Terror." Since misogyny and homosexuality often go hand in hand, it is important to understand the misogynistic nature of various Islamic cultures if we are to grasp some of the dynamics involved between Progressive homosexuals and radical Islam.

As America has been actively fighting Islamists for some time now, and the US military is in the process of queering the armed forces, this topic is of some importance. There are any number of examples of how various Islamic cultures keep women psychologically shackled and marginalized — from full body burkas, to beatings, to whippings, to genital mutilation, to acid attacks, to "honor killings" and rape. For the sake of simplicity I'll limit my discussion to FGM (Female Genital Mutilation) — a so called "female circumcision," in which part of a young girl's female genitals are cut off.

Dr. Glazov informs us that "how much is amputated varies among cultures. In Egypt only the clitoris is amputated; in countries like Sudan the woman haters are not so kind. In a savagery known as infibulation, the girl's external genital organs are completely removed..." I will spare you the specifics.

In more "civilized" Egypt, where the US recently backed a "pro-democracy movement" (in truth a ploy to aid the radical Muslim Brotherhood) close to 100% of the women are circumcised.

Glazov continues, "More than 130 million women living today [billions dead and gone] have suffered through this horrifying practice, and more than two million girls face assault by it each year.... Many girls lose their lives during FGM, which is often done with broken glass. Most victims suffer from chronic infection and pain for the rest of their lives."

The fact that a number of girls die while being forced to undergo this barbaric procedure is of little concern to most Muslim men, as in many places women are considered "less worthy than cows and sheep."

It is indeed puzzling that the same feminazis who go into a frothing hissy fit over such things as Madison Avenue's "objectifying" of women, seem to be perfectly okay with genital mutilation being performed on approximately 5,000 Muslim girls every day. Odd — makes you wonder.

I suppose that they simply do not deem little girls as being something worthy of attention. That, or the fact that the insidious, idiotic concepts of moral and cultural relativism dictate that they hold no opinion at all regarding the relative benefits, value, and desirability of various cultures over one another — excepting the liberal *leit motif* that Western civilization is *always* very, very bad.

If American women understood, *really* understood, just how debased and hard life is for many Muslim women, there would be a lot more Ann Barnhardts in this country, and a lot fewer Joy Behars.

(Sidebar: Pastor Terry Jones would also have a lot more supporters. He has been painted as a right-wing loon by the various propaganda outlets (i.e. "news" media), but he is one courageous fellow who has taken his pro-Christian/anti-Muslim message right into the heart of America's "enemy territory" (Dearbornistan , Michigan). Although I would not take the comparison very far, he brings to mind John Brown in the time prior to the Civil War. Will Dearbornistan turn out to be the new Harpers Ferry?)

Islam and Homosexuality

Dr. Peter Raddatz observes of Islam that "Being legitimized religiously, male dominance...condemns not only women to an animal-like existence, but also their sexual organ as a despicable opening.... Therefore the anus is preferred to the vagina to an extent that has raised the attention of UN institutions and secular Muslim scientists. Anal intercourse appears as an unusually common practice, and corresponding hospital reports often indicate brutal extremes in which terrible injuries have been inflicted in this area. This puts more light, clearly, on the alleged rejection of homosexuality in Islam."

"The *alleged* rejection of homosexuality in Islam..." Dr. Raddatz says "alleged," because homosexuality, while being publicly condemned, is privately rampant in certain Islamic cultures. How could it be otherwise given such misogynistic traditions?

Glazov notes that "A deafening silence surrounds this mass cultural pathology." (Can you say "cognitive dissonance")? Glazov writes, "Indeed, the hatred of female sexuality is directly connected to the widespread practice of homosexuality in this culture, which...is simultaneously demonized and denied."

(Yes, I know sharia law forbids homosexuality, and metes out death sentences for homosexual behavior — nonetheless, homosexual polymorphous perversity is actively practiced in a number of Muslim cultures, with an emphasis on pedophilia and pederasty).

The peculiar spectacle of homosexuals supporting a religion that purportedly hates them is beyond bizarre. Whether such groups as QUIT (Queers Undermining Israeli Terrorism) are indicative of "yet another dark reflection of the suicidal impulse" at the heart of the Far Left, or stem from a "nod and a wink" acknowledgment of Islam's misogynistic tendencies is a matter for debate.

I realize that the PC police will not permit us to admit that the US is at war with radical Islam, but does opening the gates of our military to homosexuals while we are in a *de facto* war with an enemy rife with closet queers seem like a smart move to you?

Homosexuals as Power Elites

Why does the push to queer the US military find so little opposition and such vocal support in Washington? Is it that the Power Elites are so riddled with homosexuals? Is it that the higher levels of government have a disproportionate share of homosexuals; way out of line with the nation's norm? Is it that the various news media have a disproportionate share of homosexuals as well, and that they push the gay agenda for all it is worth?

I suspect that it is all of the above, and then some. Homosexuals have a sense of self-preservation after all, and when you are such a small percentage of the overall population it behooves you to have as many like-minded fellows move into positions of power as possible. It is a no-brainer really, and I am sure that it is a process that has been clandestinely going on for quite some time. Especially dangerous are the militant minority who are pederasts and child abusers.

Gay Health Risks

I am opposed to gays in the military because I have no doubt that they would comprise a huge security risk due to their affinity for left-wing causes, and because their presence would be highly disruptive and detrimental to unit cohesion, moral, and fighting effectiveness, and because their presence in our armed forces flies in the face of well over two hundred years of hallowed tradition, and because their lifestyle finds a harmonic echo in various Islamic cultures, and because their acceptance into the military would lead to a similar acceptance by society at large (I believe that such an acceptance would be so-cial/cultural suicide), and finally, because of the health risks homosex-uals pose.

Dr. Satinover reports "...the gay male life span, even apart from AIDS and with a long-term partner, is significantly shorter than that of married men in general by more than three decades. AIDS further shortens the life span of homosexual men by more than 7%."

A thirty to forty year shorter life span than average...hmm. Liberals go ballistic over the fact that tobacco use shortens a person's life by less than ten years on average, yet promote homosexuality, which is much more dangerous to your health, to our school children. Their actions are worse, much worse, than passing out cigarettes to elemen-tary school students in order to get them hooked – and now the US military wants to embrace this life-shortening lifestyle? In God's name why?

Homosexuality in Our Schools

Diane Schneider, representing the National Education Association (NEA) recently told a UN group that comprehensive sex education is "the only way to *combat heterosexism* and gender conformity, and we must make these issues a part of every middle and high-school student's agenda." Ms. Schneider also proclaimed that those opposed to homosexuality "are stuck in a binary box that religion and family create."

I have her "binary box" hanging. Unfortunately Schneider's attitude is all too common among America's teachers. As an article on the "Mission America" website points out, "If your son or daughter is learning standard sex education at school, chances are excellent that he or she has absorbed this idea: that HIV is "everyone's disease" and that just about anyone can get it. It's simply not true. ...In spite of what you may have heard, male homosexual sex has consistently been the single biggest "transmission mode" for HIV in the U.S. HIV attributed to male-to-male sexual contact rose from 50% of all the HIV cases in 2006, to 56% in 2009."

Kupelian writes, "In truth, there is something wrong with homosexuality. Simply put, it is unnatural and self-destructive — just as Western civilization has long understood it." He goes on to note that "gay rights; are...not about *rights*. It's about redefining truth and censoring all criticism so that militant homosexuals can be comfortable in their 'lifestyle' without having to be disturbed by reality."

Conclusion

Given the known affinity of homosexuals for the Far Left, the danger they pose as a health risk, the socially destructive effects of polymorphous perversity, and the collusion between the Far Left, Islam, and homosexuals; the idea of having the US military welcoming homosexuals with open arms is simply insane.

Why in the world is the US military rolling over and playing dead regarding the queering of the armed forces? Is the Pentagon that full of homosexuals, or are they simply too frightened of crossing swords with the PC police — or both? I researched this subject on my own and I had no trouble accessing pertinent data. Are we supposed to believe that the Pentagon is incapable of similar due diligence before turning over the reins of the armed forces to homosexuals?

Make no mistake; once homosexuals have their nose inside the tent the US military will become one of the most homo-friendly environments in the world — but that's the plan, is it not?

Laus Deo.

29

The Mad Marine of Matareva:
A Cautionary Tale

May 23, 2011

As James Michener explains, homosexuality was not something discussed openly in the military back in the day. Nonetheless the events he wrote about took place, even during such prohibitive times. Given the much more relaxed social climate these days I shudder to think of the manifold opportunities that militant "chickenhawks" will be given due to the recent decision by the Pentagon to embrace homosexuality.

The late James Michener spent two tours (four years) of duty as a US Naval officer in the Pacific theater during WW II. It was his experiences and the stories he heard during that period that formed the basis for his book "Tales of the South Pacific" — later turned into the musical play and movie "South Pacific."

During his second tour he was assigned the task of traveling around the Pacific and compiling information for the official US Naval history of the war in that region. He visited forty-nine different islands during his travels, but it is one island, and what occurred there that concerns us.

The legal officer who assigned Michener his job of unearthing information for the Navy's history project was especially interested in finding out what had happened on one particular island. "Michener, I want you to read this court-martial record, take no notes, and forget it when you're finished," the officer told him. "We want you to visit the island and let us know, top secret, what *really* happened." Writing of what happened decades afterwards, Michener used the *fictitous* name "Matareva" in order "to protect the privacy of those involved in the real-life military tragedy."

Michener read the court-martial record and found that the young Marine general in charge of it had inexplicably halted the proceedings, called an end to it, and announced: "The trial is over. The twenty-two accused will be dismissed from the service and shipped out this night on any available transport. And no one will speak...of what happened in this courtroom."

Admiral "Bull" Halsey had wanted the Marines involved in the court-martial to be "scorched," as Michener puts it, and Halsy was furious that the Marine general had let them "off the hook." "Get me that son-of-a-bitch now!" Halsy roared.

Michener's briefing officer had been there when the young general (General Anderson) was ushered into Halsey's presence. Halsey started in on a rant, but when he took a breath Gen. Anderson said "I knew you'd be furious, so I typed out what the next line of testimony would have [been]. Would you really want this displayed in the record?"

Halsey read what was on the paper and then told Anderson, "If you had permitted that trial to proceed, I'd have chewed your a— for allowing that sewage to get into the Navy record."

Michener's briefing officer told him, "We've never heard another word about Matareva. But rumors have filtered back to Washington and they want a coded report... Stop by the island and give me something I can forward — but clean it up."

Upon arriving in Matareva Michener's first stop was at the Marine base where he tried to find out what he could about the two main defendants in the court-martial: Captain Mark Dorn and Staff Sergeant Michael Hazen. Although everyone who had been on the island at the time of the court-martial was long gone by the time Michener arrived, he was able to gather some accurate scuttlebutt about Capt. Dorn — at least about his history before he arrived on Matareva.

Michner writes "and there the discussion [would end], because no Marine, especially no officer, was willing to speak in even the most guarded language about Dorn's experience on Matareva." As for Sergeant Hazen, "No one knew anything about him...and no one cared to know; he was a man who never existed, and my queries about him were not welcomed."

Michener was finally able to track down a native who would speak to him about Dorn at the local outlet of the ubiquitous "Burns Philp" chain of general stores. The man's name was Robert Weed, but the natives called him Ropati. It was Ropati who first started filling in the missing pieces of the puzzle; giving details of what led up to the court-martial — what Ropati described as "the long downward slide of Captain Dorn."

Ropati told Michener, "Never met a finer man than Dorn. A bit tense, but sane and sober and, above all, a man of the most severe attention to honor in all details."

"Too rigid for his own good?" Michener asked.

"Not at all."

"What went wrong?"

"Staff Sergeant Hazen."

Ropati informed Michener that Hazen, who had arrived on Matareva after the Captain, detested Dorn. Sergeant Hazen hated Dorn for his family background (FFV — First Family of Virginia), fine education, and other reasons. But what really galled Hazen was the fact that the other Marines respected Dorn for his honesty, integrity, and valor. "Hazen was determined to destroy him. He hated him," Ropati said.

At first Dorn saw none of this; he simply wouldn't, couldn't, believe that a fellow Marine could be so base and petty. By the time Dorn understood how bad things were it was too late. When Michener pressed Ropati for more details Ropati told him that he had better talk with the native woman Tetua.

Michener describes Tetua as "an island girl whose movements were like palm trees swaying in the wind. She was lovely, with...a serenity that seemed impervious to any storm, any disappointment." She and Captain Dorn had been lovers. She told Michener, "I realized early on that Hazen was a confirmed homosexual."

As Hazen began to slowly isolate Dorn from running the Marine detachment he was aided by the fact that Dorn lived off-base. Tetua recalled that "When Hazen had Dorn isolated...he began a systematic campaign to entice the younger Marines into his net." Tetua told Michener that Hazen's "malignant power" was "incredible."

Michener asked Ropati why he had not tried to stop Hazen. Ropati told him, "Lieutenant, he was running the base. He was in charge. ...When he failed three times to get me into bed with him, he calmly drafted a report to my superiors in London charging me with incompetence and theft of funds...and — I — was — fired!"

Michener asked, "So inside the fence was a homosexual riot?"

"Yes," replied Ropati.

"At least thirty Marines cooperating?"

"Maybe more."

Tetua added, "In the end...Hazen wouldn't even allow [Captain Dorn] to come onto the base. Locked the gate against him and jeered when he tried to break in."

Michener found out that Captain Dorn, Staff Sergeant Hazen, and a few dozen other Marines were shipped back to the states, "and quietly dismissed from the service."

Michener writes, "Like Admiral Halsey when he finished with the court-martial record, I had heard far more about the Matareva incident than I really cared to know: I was satisfied that a first-class Marine captain...had allowed a vicious enlisted man...to steal his command, corrupt it totally, and lead it into the swamp of a hideous court-martial. Something like that should never have been allowed to happen, but happen it did."

The United States of America was founded on the principles of "the laws of Nature and of Nature's God" — you know, the laws we no longer respect, and the God we no longer believe in? Michener believed in the laws of Nature, and he felt that it was because those laws were ignored that the tragedy on Matavera happened. After looking at the strands of barbed wire surrounding the base, he thought to himself, "They wired themselves in and prevented the therapy of nature from helping."

Michener felt that the fact that Matareva was located in the Melanesian region of the Pacific contributed to the situation. He could not imagine something similar occurring in the Polynesian sector. "If the mad Staff Sergeant of Matareva" had started his operations on one of the Polynesian islands, Michener believed, the women would have gently, but firmly, nipped such nonsense in the bud, "and the poison would have been neutralized."

There are a number of morals to Michener's story, but perhaps the most important one is the danger posed by "chicken-hawks" in a military atmosphere, ("chicken-hawk" being slang for an older homosexual who preys on young males). Chicken-hawk senior NCOs and officers will have a field-day in a gay-compliant military — and don't tell me it will not happen. As Michener said of the breakdown of military discipline on Matareva, "something like that should never have been allowed to happen, but happen it did."

The "military tragedy" that occurred on Matareva happened back when homosexuality was much more stigmatized than it is today, so the odds of something similar to what occurred on that island happening today are that much greater.

In closing, it is worth noting that homosexuals serving in the military are nothing new. In fact, it is a throwback to pre-Christian paganism. The Spartans, for example, "used homosexual attachments to build solidarity among soldiers in war." Homosexuality and pederasty were *de rigueur.*

As Dinesh D'Souza observes, "when we rhapsodize about 'the glory that was Greece and the grandeur that was Rome,' we should keep in mind that the sexual practices of these civilizations live on today only in prisons and in the ideology of marginal groups like the North American Man/Boy Love Association."

There is nothing progressive about allowing homosexuals into the military; it is the "same old, same old" of ancient polymorphous perversity. America is rushing backward toward the pagan past — thanks to some first-class marketing, massive financing, and bold clever lies.

While the US military is proceeding, *post haste* with the "gaying-up" of the armed forces, Michener's true tale of "the mad Staff Sergeant of Matareva" may serve as a cautionary warning to them — to slow down and think about what they are doing.

They also might want to look into the homosexual pursuits of "bug chasing" and "gift giving," and consider the effects of such practices on the health of their personnel. They should also consider the fact that the homosexual lifestyle is much more injurious to a man's health than smoking. Do they really want to endorse and encourage such dangerous and unhealthy behavior? Why?

Laus Deo.

30

Nazi Homosexuals and the Slow Steady Seduction of America

June 13, 2011

Some folks might think that I am being cold and heartless toward homosexuals but that is not true. Promoting a sexual orientation that takes decades off of one's life — that is cold and heartless. Besides, it is mainly the chicken-hawks and pederasts (who are a minority within the homosexual community) who I despise, not the homosexual community as a whole. The thing is, although pederasts may be a minority, they are a vocal, powerful, and militant minority.

"The American homosexual movement really only began in the 1940s after the Allied defeat of the Nazis. ...The center of international "gay" power in the world did in fact shift from Germany to the United States after the demise of the Third Reich. This represented a huge setback for the "gay" movement, requiring it to begin "from scratch" as it were, since America in the 1940s was at least as family-centered as Germany had been in the 1860s."

Scott Lively and Kevin Abrams "The Pink Swastika"

"They exchanged the truth of God for a lie, and revered and worshiped the creature rather than the Creator, who is blessed forever. Amen."

Romans 1:25 (NAB)

Only in his dreams could Hitler have imagined the blatant homosexualizing of the German military. What Hitler could only dream of the United States is making fact, a scant sixty-six years after fighting a costly and bloody war to defeat Hitler and the Nazis.

Before I get ahead of myself, let me point out that the title of this article, and the article itself, are meant to be attention getting but do not constitute a spurious *ad hominem* attack on homosexuality; they are designed to bring attention to historical facts that are of profound importance to the future of America (and the world).

To give credit where it is due I first became aware of much of the material presented here after reading "The Pink Swastika" (4th edition 2002), by Scott Lively and Kevin Abram. The entire book can be accessed for free online. My reaction to the information contained in the book was similar to Scott Lively's reaction, "When I initially learned the truths set forth in ["The Pink Swastika"] I was first astonished and then angered."

At the outset of this article let me reiterate that Communism and Fascism (of which Nazism is a subset) are both Far Left ideologies. That is not to say that they are "like peas in a pod;" they are not — nonetheless they are both left-wing, top-down, big-government social engineering doctrines.

Comparing the two is not like "apples and oranges," but rather like comparing "oranges and tangerines." Many of the left-wing's "rank and file" are unaware that fascism is a left-wing doctrine, but their puppetmasters are well aware of it, and work in collusion with other Far Left doctrines — "united in hate" as Dr. Jamie Glazov puts it.

The reporter/author Oriana Fallaci (1929-2006), who certainly knew the Left very well, wrote in her book "The Force of Reason" (2004), "...there are moments when I curse myself for not having understood it earlier: for having let myself be fooled by the two soccer-teams for so long. ...It is a long-term ruler this Left that gave birth to Mussolini then Hitler, and always maintained its bond with their disciples. This Left which has always given trouble with its excesses and ambiguities, its brutalities and duplicities..." Oriana knew full well that communists and fascists eat from the same trough.

An obvious place to start discussing the subject of homosexuality and the Nazis is with Hitler himself. Was the Nazi leader, or Fuehrer (Führer), a homosexual? Although Hitler and the Nazi leadership went to great lengths to hide and/or destroy any incriminating evidence, the evidence that remains strongly suggests that Hitler was indeed a homosexual. At the very least, he was an extreme case of sexual dysfunction.

As Lively and Abrams put it: "The weight of the evidence indicates that Hitler was deeply involved in a series of short and long-term homosexual relationships. Even more certain is that he knowingly and deliberately surrounded himself with practicing homosexuals from the time he was a teenager. His later public pronouncements against homosexuality were designed to hide the life-long intimacy — sexual and/or homoerotic — which he maintained with the various men he knew and accepted as homosexuals."

Before discussing the men that Hitler surrounded himself with, let us look into some of the roots of German Nazism. The historical sources of German fascism included an interest in Hellenic (Greek) history, and a fascination with the occult. Both of these interests were fueled by homosexuals and when they merged in the Nazi movement the homosexuals moved along with them. Before discussing Hellenism and the occult, however, it's important to have some understanding of the difference between "Butch" and "Fem" homosexuals.

Perhaps the two most distinct branches of homosexuality split along the lines of those who are effeminate (the minority) and those who are hyper-masculine (the majority). "The Pink Swastika" uses the terms Fem and Butch to describe them, and I will stay with their lead on this for the sake of consistency. The difference between Fem and Butch homosexuals is an important one, and something that most heterosexuals are unaware of.

Fems (Femmes) are homosexuals who are effeminate ("a woman trapped in a man's body"), whereas Butches are ultra-masculine homosexuals. Contrary to what most "straights" think, the vast majority of homosexuals are Butch — which means that unless they want you to know you can seldom tell that a Butch is homosexual as there are few, if any, tell-tale signs).

Corey and LeRoy's book "The Homosexual and His Society" estimates that Fems make up only 5% — 15% of the homosexual culture. A recent survey taken of personal ads in homosexual newspapers observed that only 2% of them had a Fem theme — whereas 40% had a Butch theme (the rest were inconclusive).

Most heterosexuals think "effeminate" when they hear the word "gay" or "homosexual," but that is a foolish, even dangerous, misconception. Most homosexuals are *not* effeminate at all. Regarding Nazi Butches "The Pink Swastika" says "In their view, heterosexuals might be tolerated for the purpose of continuing the species, but effeminate homosexuals were considered to be subhuman and thus intolerable. ...Often these men, who so hated femininity, maintained a facade of heterosexual respectability throughout their lives [in most cases marrying a woman]" (Obviously cloning would be their preferred way to procreate, but that is a side issue that I will leave for another day).

Lively and Abrams call the battle between the German Fem and Butch homosexuals a fight between "two irreconcilable philosophies linked by a common sexual dysfunction." Nazis persecuted homosexuals to a certain extent, but it was largely a case of the Nazi Butches persecuting the Fems, rather than the Nazis' persecuting homosexuals as a whole — more about that in a bit.

The "grandfather" of the world's "gay rights" movement is considered by many to be a German lawyer named Karl Heinrich Ulrichs (1825-1895). He advanced the theory that homosexuals were a *third* sex, which he called Uranians ("Uranians of the world unite!" was one of his slogans). Ulrichs picked the word "Uranian," because in ancient Greece homosexual activities were said to be under the protection of the Muse, Urania. Urania is also, of course, the source for the name Uranus, the seventh planet from the sun (no snide comments please, we are all adults here).

(Sidebar: Uranus is not the only astronomical body with homosexual connotations. Jupiter's moon Ganymede is named after the victim of a pederastic rape by the Greek god Zeus. It is possible that the origin of the word "gay," being used to denote a homosexual, comes from this source. The Roman word for Ganymede is *Catamitus*, which is the eponymous source of the English word "catamite," meaning the submissive partner in a homosexual relationship. The night sky has a number of such homosexual references).

Ulrichs' activities opened the way for an international homosexual movement, and Germany (especially Berlin and Munich) became the movement's decadent "Mecca" ("Come to the Cabaret, old chum"). After Ulrich's death he was succeeded by the homosexual Magnus Hirschfeld. Hirschfeld (who coined the term "transvestite"), started the ISR (Institute for Sexual Research), about which more will be said shortly. Both Ulrich and Hirschfeld were Fem homosexuals.

At the same time that Ulrich, and later Hirschfeld, were trying to legitimize homosexuality, two seemingly unrelated strains of cultural elements were getting underway that would eventually merge and profoundly impact the Nazis — a German revival of interest in all things Hellenic (Greek), and a fascination with paganism (or the occult). Butch homosexuals were very influential in both movements.

The interest in all things Hellenic was especially attractive to the Butch homosexual leaders in the Nazi party, who were drawn to the ideal of "an ultra-masculine, male supremacist, homoerotic warrior cult." It is of some importance to note that Greece was not the only culture to elevate the status of homosexuality, however.

Indeed, the German Butch homosexuals in the Nazi party were following an ages-long global tradition of militant homosexuality and pederasty. From Rome to Babylon, from China to Borneo, homosexuality was an accepted way of life in many ancient cultures — pagan cultures.

It is from these pagan cultures that the Nazis drew some of their more famous (infamous) symbols, e.g. the twin lightning bolt SS runes, the skull and crossbones (Totenkopf), and of course the swastika.

Two of the leading lights of the German pagan movement were Guido von List (1848-1919), and Jorg Lanz von Liebenfels (1874-1954). Both men worshipped Wotan (Odin), chief of the Norse gods, and both greatly influenced Adolf Hitler.

(Sidebar: It is interesting to note that we all still worship at least four Norse gods every week [albeit unknowingly]. That is: on every Wotan's Day [Wednesday], Thor's Day [Thursday], Teiws Day [Tuesday], and Frigga's Day [Friday]. Some folks believe that Sunday and Monday are named after Norse gods as well; while others feel that they are named for the sun and the moon. Saturday [named after Saturn] is the only day of the week that is free and clear of any Norse connection).

Lively and Abrams believe that Guido von List was a homosexual. He has been called "the Aleister Crowley ('The Beast') of Vienna." Jorg Lanz (Liebenfels) was a homosexual and misogynist of the first order, who was kicked out of the Catholic Cistercian Order "for carnal and worldly desires." He once wrote "Nature herself has ordained women to be our slaves." He flew a flag with a swastika on it over his castle, some years before Hitler grabbed the symbol for his own use. Personally, I agree with Colin Wilson that "interest in occultism often involves a certain immaturity."

I should also mention Friedrich Nietzsche (1844-1900) as being an influence on Hitler. Both Nietzsche and Frederick the Great (a great homosexual) were important icons to Hitler. Nietzsche's best known quote is "God is dead," although he came up with plenty of other zingers, including: "Become hard and show no mercy, for evil is man's best force "and" Nothing is true so everything is permitted!" (Similar to Aleister Crowley's axiom "Do what thou wilt shall be the whole of the Law"). No wonder liberals love these guys.

The Nazi fascination with paganism and the occult brings up one of the important themes of "The Pink Swastika," and debatably one of the most important notions to appear in a book about the Third Reich. Lively and Abrams feel that the animosity that the Nazis showed toward the Jews was fueled by not only their eugenics/occult based belief in racial purity, but also their hatred for Jewish and Christian morality in general, and the Judeo/Christian proscriptions against homosexuality in particular.

I think they make a good case for their hypothesis. It may sound strange at first, but think about it. Homosexuality was widespread in the ancient world, and pagan cultures hated Judeo/Christian ethics and morality. The Nazis were (and are) basically a technologically advanced neo-pagan cult, with visions of ruthlessly imposing a Neitzschian rule of the elite on everyone. (It seems obvious to me that George Soros and his cronies have something very much along those lines in mind for us right now — you will recall that Soros has said that the year he spent under the wing of the Nazis, plundering Jewish property was "probably the happiest year of my life").

The thing is, if you destroy the roots of Judeo/Christian culture, then you destroy Western civilization along with it. (Is that Henry Higgins I hear saying "By George, I think he's got it?")

That was Hitler's game plan, and that is the game plan for today: the regression of humanity to a pre-Judeo/Christian morality (or lack thereof), and the installation of a ruling elite to lord it over what is left of "we the people." Meanwhile our propaganda outlets entertain us with such weighty matters as the state of Weiner's weiner.

Be that as it may, let us return to the Third Reich. The Nazi movement really began when Hitler started to associate with Erich Roehm (Röhm) at a *Bierkeller* homosexual hangout in Munich. Author William Shirer in his classic "The Rise and Fall of the Third Reich" describes Roehm as "a stocky, bull-necked, piggish-eyed, scar-faced professional soldier...[and] like so many of the early Nazis, a homosexual." Roehm was in anybody's estimation a nasty, mean piece of work.

In 1923 Hitler, with the backing of Roehm's SA (*Stuermabteilung* — Storm Troopers), attempted a coup on the government in Bavaria, Germany (the Beer Hall *Putsch*). The coup failed, and Hitler ended up spending nine months in prison, where he wrote his "textbook" for the coming fascist revolution, "Mein Kampf."

Also jailed at the same prison were purportedly homosexual chauffeur Emile Maurice, and close friend and aide Rudolf Hess. Hess had nicknames among the Nazi inner circle such as *"Fraulein* Hess," "Fraulein Anna," *"Fraulein* Paula," and "Black Emma." Hess like many homosexuals of the day eventually married, but his wife complained that their love life was on a par with that of a "convent schoolgirl."

Hitler's infamous SA Brownshirt thugs which Roehm led to a position of great power, were largely the creation of homosexual Gerhard Rossbach. Lively and Abrams write, "In the SA, the Hellenic model of masculine homosexual supremacy and militarism had finally been realized."

Historian Louis Snyder observes that "what was needed, Roehm believed, was a proud and arrogant lot who could brawl, carouse, smash windows, kill and slaughter for the hell of it. Straights, in his eyes, were not as adept in such behavior as practicing homosexuals." WW II correspondent H.R. Knickerbocker wrote, "unless a Storm Troop officer was homosexual he had no chance of advancement."

The homosexual Ludwig Lenz, who was one of the Fem homosexuals in charge of the ISR mentioned earlier, said of the Nazis "...not 10% of the men who, in 1933, took the fate of Germany into their hands, were sexually normal." He would know, as many of the Nazi leaders had been under treatment at his clinic.

After Hitler became Chancellor of Germany in January of 1933, the SA exploded from a force of around 300,000 men to about 3,000,000 in a year's time. This created some problems for Hitler, big problems. Certain powerful interests in Germany, including the *Wehrmacht*, told him in no uncertain terms that either Roehm went or they would withdraw their support from Hitler.

The result was "The Night of the Long Knives," or the "Roehm Purge," in which around 1,000 individuals, including Roehm, were murdered. Lively and Abrams note that "the Roehm Purge was not motivated by the homosexuality of its victims. The great majority of the victims were not homosexuals at all." Hitler used the opportunity to rid himself of a number of political enemies — some homosexual, but most not.

Waiting in the wings was Heinrich Himmler and the SS (*SchutzStaffel* — Protection Squadron) who now came into their own. Himmler was fascinated by the occult, and sent missions out around the world to track down various ancient artifacts (the inspiration behind the movie "Raiders of the Lost Ark").

On a much more serious note, Himmler was in charge of the extermination of the Jews. The Nazis built around 10,000 *work* camps, in which many died, but they only built six concentration camps, or *death* camps, in which millions were murdered. The six killing centers were: Auschwitz-Birkenau, Sobidor, Chelmno, Belzec, Maidenek, and Treblinka.

Gen. Dwight D. Eisenhower, Supreme Commander of the Allied forces in Europe during WW II, had many photos and movies made of what the Allies found at the concentration camps. He knew human nature, and wanted records made because he believed that "the day will come when some son of a b—ch will say that this never happened." Good call Dwight.

Homosexuals have taken to claiming to be victims of the Holocaust (*Shoah*), alongside the Jews. This is despicable nonsense. Less than 1% of Europe's population of homosexuals were incarcerated by the Nazis (almost all of them Fems). The Jews, however, lost around 85% of their population, and they were almost invariably sent to one of the six extermination camps. The Nazi regime, for political reasons, put on a facade of firm anti-homosexuality, but behind the facade it was a different story. As is always the case with the Far Left, it is not what they *say* but what they *do* you need to pay attention to. That their rhetoric is for show, misdirection, and cover is a given.

In a "Washington Blade" article historian John Fouts reported that "about 50,000 men were imprisoned for homosexual 'offences' by the Nazis between 1933 and 1945. Most of them...were imprisoned for relatively short sentences and in regular German prisons, not concentration camps." According to Lively and Abrams, perhaps as little as a few dozen, or a few hundred homosexuals were actually sent to a death camp. It is estimated that over 4,000,000 of the 6 million+ Jews killed in WW II were killed in the concentration camps.

The mind-boggling cruelty and ruthlessness of the Nazi death camps has been covered extensively elsewhere, so I feel no need to delve into it here, though I would like to point out that the bizarre and depraved atmosphere of Nazi fascism seems to have set free (or attract) an especially virulent form of sadism.

In his book "The Nazi Extermination of Homosexuals," Frank Rector writes "As for the SS, their behavior was typical among those who engaged in sexual bestiality. An example is a film...that was secretly made for the pornographic enjoyment of a select coterie of Nazis showing a wild drunken orgy of beautiful boys and handsome young men being whipped, raped and murdered by the SS." Purportedly, copies of this film are still making the rounds in certain exclusive European circles.

Before we leave the subject of the concentration camps there is one special camp I want to discuss. Dr. Judith Reisman writes in her book "Kinsey: Crimes and Consequences" that the Nazi industrialist Alfried Krupp maintained a concentration camp for children called *Buschmannshof*. Dr. Reisman believes that *Buschmannshof* was one source for the child orgasm statistics cited in Alfred Kinsey's "Sexual Behavior in the Human Male," published in 1948.

Reisman writes that "infants and children under six years of age were torn from their Krupp enslaved mothers and interned in Buschmannshof for their brief lives. *Buschmannshof* children died at the rate of some 50 per day for years...." William Manchester dedicated his book "The Arms of Krupp" to the unnamed and unknown young children of Krupp's *Buschmannshof*.

If you graduated from high school before, say 1990, you are probably aware that the Nazis lost WW II. I do not imagine that they even mention WW II in school these days — or if they do, it is probably portrayed as an arrogant imperialist expansion by that bad old purveyor of capitalist greed the United States.

In any event, I would now like to briefly discuss the ongoing homo-sexualization of America. After WW II the militant Butch homosexuals wasted no time in regrouping and going at things from a different angle. The Nazis went underground, but they did not go away.

Communism and Fascism — Oriana Falacci's two "soccer teams" — played together as one team after WW II. At least the various puppet-masters did; the "rank and file" apparatchiks remained largely una-ware of the collusion. (They were later joined by the Islamist "team," with whom the Nazis especially had cultivated a relationship with both before and during WW II).

Although homosexual activists like to play the "victim role" like a Stradivarius, the truth is far different. Lively and Abrams write, "The "gay" movement in America (as contrasted with the German version) is different in style but not in substance. It remains characteristically selfish and hedonistic, but more importantly it continues to be defined by what it is *against*: Judeo-Christian family-based society. ...In their quest for power, Nazi homosexuals are no different from today's 'gays.' Then, as now, the strategy was one of deception, infiltration, and subversion."

In 1948, just three years after the defeat of the Nazis, Kinsey pub-lished "Sexual Behavior in the Human Male" (the "Kinsey Report"), which started off the "sexual revolution" in America (just weeks after the release of the "Kinsey Report," Harry Hay launched the "Mattachine Society" — America's first influential homosexual group).

Dr. Kinsey presented himself to the public as a lab-coated paragon of respectability, professionalism, and honesty. Under his influence most of America's laws criminalizing homosexual behavior were dispensed with. In truth, Kinsey was one sick SOB, but it wasn't until the publication in 1997 of James Jones' biography, "Alfred C. Kinsey: A Public/Private Life," that the lid came off an especially revolting can of worms.

Jones' book "exposed Alfred Kinsey as a sadomasochistic homosex-ual who skewed his studies to validate his behavior." That this pervert-ed, pathetic, putrid waste of space could so thoroughly dupe the

American public, professions, and legal system is almost beyond belief — but dupe them he did.

Kinsey's efforts were boosted by the fact that there was already an underground network of homosexuals and bi-sexuals extant across America. For instance, John Maynard Keynes and a coterie of homosexuals had infiltrated Harvard, and then spread throughout American academia earlier in the century (see the book "Keynes at Harvard" — available for free online).

In addition to Kinsey's influence, just as had happened in Germany the churches were attacked both from within and without. Lively and Abrams observe that "few have noted the long period of "Biblical deconstruction" that preceded the rise of Nazism, and fewer still have chronicled the systematic perversion of German religious culture by the Nazis themselves. While the neo-pagans were busy attacking from without, liberal theologians undermined Biblical authority from within the Christian church." Ring any bells?

The homosexual lifestyle is one that leads away from truth and sanity, in varying degrees. Dr. Brian Clowes brought to light the fact that eight of the top ten serial killers in the United States were homosexual "and that homosexuals were responsible for 68% of all mass murders."

I do not mean to suggest that most homosexuals are wont to bury their lovers/prey under their house like John Wayne Gacy, or save them as frozen left-overs à la Jeffery Dahlmer, but you have to admit, the fact that eight of the top ten mass murderers are homosexual gives one pause. Those are pretty impressive stats for such a small segment of the population.

Add to that the fact that the homosexual lifestyle is decidedly unhealthy and you have every reason in the world to oppose the spread of this dysfunctional way of life.

Don Hank suggested a few years ago that young men ensnared in the homosexual life-style ought to look into suing the "gay" activist groups. After all, the homosexual lifestyle is a *much* unhealthier and deadly practice than smoking, and a number of people have successfully sued the tobacco companies. Peter LaBarbera of AFTAH (Americans For Truth About Homosexuality) has also promoted this idea.

If America is ever to get back on its moral track, it appears that it will be up to "we the people" to do it — or as former BP chairman Carl-Henric Svanberg endearingly called us, "the *small* people." Yes Carl, we know, you "misspoke." You no doubt meant to say "the ignorant, gun toting, Bible clinging, *inconsequential* people." We understand – boy, do we ever.

We understand that we are witnessing *déjà vu* all over again — that we are already feeling the effects of Weimar Republic-style hyper-inflation. We understand that QE (Qualitative Easing) is a recipe for financial disaster. We understand that "we the people" have been royally screwed by banksters, Wall Street, mega-corporations, and our own government.

We understand that today's militant "gay rights" activists are merely Roehm's bully-boy brownshirts dressed in modern clothes. Lively observes that "the 'gay' movement I have seen and investigated is neither benign, nor are its members 'victims.' It is vicious, deceptive, and enormously powerful. Its philosophy is Machiavellian and its tactics are (literally) Hitlerian."

We understand that the lame stream media is in bed with, if not controlled by, Butch homosexuals. It is a propaganda machine that the Nazi Minister of Propaganda, Joseph Goebbels, would have given an arm for.

We understand that Obama is using the unions just as Hitler did, and that crony capitalism has replaced free enterprise, just as it did in Nazi Germany.

We understand that our government representatives do not represent us and that their thinly veiled arrogance is emblematic of certain elements of Butch homosexuals and other narcissists.

We understand that the anti-Zionist movement is the same old anti-Judeo/Christian paganism that the Nazis practiced, behind a facade of rhetoric about "democracy," "human rights," and "social justice."

We understand that the same Nazi system that America fought a long bloody war to defeat, is back wearing a different disguise, but *this* time the Fascists hold the reins of power in America. "We the people" understand all of this, and we will do our best to restore America to the "bright shining city on the hill" that she was meant to be — whatever it takes.

Laus Deo.

31

United in Hate vs. United We Stand

July 6, 2011

I was raised as a Christian but left Christianity as a young man and subsequently studied and practiced a number of different faiths during my life. I do not regret this, as it has allowed me to bring to the Christian "table" things that I probably would not have had otherwise – things that I believe help to make me a better Christian.

When I "returned to the fold," so to speak, a bit over a decade ago and decided to "take up my cross" again, I threw myself into my old/new religion with a will. But what has really set me on fire as regards Christianity is the recognition of how long the atheistic Far Left has been waging war against Christianity, and how devious, clever and patient they have been (not to mention effective).

"We the people" need to get ourselves and America back on track, spiritually speaking. Christianity is not simply my personal preference, it is the religious faith that our country was founded on and whose principles guided us during the first century-and-a-half of America's existence. There is no need to reinvent the wheel here; we simply need to renew our dedication to being Christians, in a Christian nation – but one that is a free republic and not a theocracy.

"In the language of the holy writ, there was a time for all things, a time to preach and a time to pray, but those times have passed away. There is a time to fight, and that time is now coming! ...I am called by my country to

its defense. The cause is just and noble. I am convinced it is my duty to obey that call, a duty I owe to my God and to my country."

Reverend Peter Muhlenberg, 1776

In his book "United in Hate" Dr. Jamie Glasov points out that various diverse and divergent groups are temporarily united by their hatred of Western civilization, America, Israel, and Judeo/Christian traditions. One does not need an epiphany in order to recognize that American Christians as a whole need to regroup, retrench, and refocus in order to present a united front against this very real and dire threat.

The forces arrayed against "we the people" include Communists, Fascists (neo-Nazis), Old World aristocracy, banking cabals, globalist corporations, and Islamists. As a historically Christian nation founded on Christian principles it is of paramount importance that American Christians get their ducks in a row — quickly. Christians are facing brutal widespread persecution across the globe. It is time to "gird our loins."

The foes we fight are clever, vicious, dedicated, and nuts — a formidable combination. They have been ceaselessly undermining and subverting Christianity from both within and without. At present, American Christianity is diluted, confused, and divided. It includes such non-Christian "Christian" cults as the execrable Westboro group and Jeremiah "God D—n America" Wright's racist, envy ridden, rage filled "ministry."

Not only has Christianity been under unremitting attack for decades (centuries actually) but in addition to atheism the Far Left has been successfully promoting pagan-style belief systems such as Gaia (Mother Earth) worship and other anti-Judeo/Christian beliefs and practices.

No group is more of a threat to the Judeo/Christian culture than Islam. The Far Left and Islam are cynically using each other to attain diametrically opposed ends — the one wants an atheistic NWO, while the Islamists want a world-wide caliphate under Allah's rule. The

Islamists are being used as "shock troops" to help topple the West, while the Far Left atheists are being used by the Islamists for the same reason, but with a much different end game in mind.

America's Christians need to present a united front against our enemies. Now is not the time for ontological nitpicking and epistemological debate. Now is the time for dedicated focused action. Despite the numerous issues that have divided America's Christians there are certain core beliefs that mainstream Christians as a whole need to rededicate themselves to. We need a list of fundamental core beliefs — bedrocks of our faith.

Although I certainly do not consider the following list to be either exhaustive or graven in stone, I do believe it may be helpful in clarifying things and separating the wheat from the chaff. I offer it as a suggested guideline that others better qualified than I might use as a starting template. As Christians we believe that:

Jesus is The Lord.

Jesus is The Way.

Jesus performed miracles — not stunts, not tricks, not magic, but *real* miracles.

We rejoice in our hearts — we spread the "good news."

The Bible is a holy book – for us *the* holy book.

The Judeo/Christian tradition — Western civilization — is worth defending; worth fighting for and if need be, worth dying for. We are not rug-mats.

In addition, we believe in:

The Crucifixion and the Resurrection.

Divine reward and punishment (heaven and hell).

The Ten Commandments.

Permit me to briefly elaborate on some of the elements in the above list. Jesus changed things, changed reality, shook up the status quo and stood it on its head. I cannot overemphasize how important that is.

It is one of the main reasons why Christianity has been such a powerful force for constructive change in this world. Jesus was not a *"que sera, sera"* fatalist. Nor was He just some swell guy that helped people and came to a sticky end.

Call Him by the Hebrew name "Joshua," or the Aramaic "Yahshua," or the Greek "Iesous," or the English "Jesus," He is the world's preeminent spiritual teacher. No other religious figure comes close to having had the global impact of Jesus Christ.

Some Christians may identify with "Christ Consciousness" — fine, whatever floats your boat. But Jesus is our teacher, our exemplar, and our Lord. For Christians, Jesus and God are synonymous. Any of you who are deeply involved in a religious journey can rest assured that should you ever attain the spiritual heights and perfection of Jesus we will let you know, okay? In the meantime, *Jesus* is our guide, our savior, and our Way.

When we say that Jesus performed miracles we mean that He did things that are normally outside the laws of nature as we understand them. This is not, contrary to what some may think, tantamount to believing in hocus-pocus voodoo magic It is a legitimate scientific hypothesis, in line with what we now know about quantum mechanics and the importance of consciousness in determining our reality.

Miracles — that is, occurrences that transcend natural law — are not only possible, they happen all the time. There has not been a time when they did *not* happen. The ongoing constant genesis of the universe is just one example. This is not to denigrate science, whose postulates are crucial to handling material existence, but to put it in its proper place as just one subset or paradigm of reality.

There is, of course, much more that I could write about regarding these things, but that's enough for now. I hope that it serves to initiate some fruitful dialogue and I apologize if I have inadvertently offended anyone, but the times are dire and Christianity — Western Christianity especially — needs to buckle down and get its game face on.

George Washington, a man of unwavering faith and rock-solid integrity, was spot on when he observed that "There is but one straight course, and that is to seek truth and pursue it steadily." Christianity should hold on to its core principles and beliefs, but at the same time, never be afraid to tread new ground in the pursuit of Truth/God.

Christianity is not some reactionary, stagnant, outdated creed with no relevance to the modern world. It is a vibrant, dynamic, exultant thrust at the diabolical heart of the atheistic, nihilistic, self-centered insanity of the Far Left — in all its various deceptive guises and variations.

To conclude this article I would like to briefly discuss two related issues. First, some people are concerned about the possibility of the United States becoming a theocracy. To me this is a non-issue. The Founding fathers were quite aware of the problems that would arise should any one Christian denomination gain exclusive control over the US government. They went to great pains to insure that such a thing would/could not happen.

The fact that the new nation would be a Christian one was a given, but the idea of one particular Christian denomination being the premier religion of the country was wisely subsumed into the more generic idea that God *per se* would be the nation's guiding light — in order to forestall internecine religious squabbles.

For example, Maryland (Mary's land) was founded as a Catholic colony, and Connecticut came under the control of Protestant Congregationalists. It was in a letter replying to the concerns of Connecticut Baptists that Thomas Jefferson wrote his now famous (infamous) phrase about the separation of church and state.

As is obvious from even a glancing familiarity with the subject, Jefferson was talking about the need for the federal government to keep its nose out of "we the people's" business — in particular, our religious business. The last thing he wanted was for the federal government to get itself involved in when and where "we the people" should or shouldn't pray and other religious concerns. Such private matters are none of the federal government's d—n business.

In closing I would like to discuss American Jews. Hardly a topic that I can do justice to in a few short paragraphs, but nonetheless I think it is worth mentioning some things in passing.

For instance, it is worth noting that, like Christianity, Judaism is made up of a number of various divisions or sects (Messianic Jews, Karaite Jews, Samaritan Jews, and so on), and these various "denominations" are further divided into sub-sects. Most Christians are not aware of this, or at best have some vague notion idea that Jews are divided into the Reformed and Orthodox branches. This ignorance can have dangerous consequences in that it can lead to having a skewed and incorrect picture of the Jews as some monolithic block of like-thinking clones. Nothing could be farther from the truth.

I say such a misperception is dangerous because it devalues the precious individuality that lies at the heart of Judaism (and also Christianity through shared Biblical teachings). Such thinking of course makes it easier for the Islamists and Far Left neo-Nazis to paint Jews with broad-brush caricature strokes.

Also of some import is the recognition that while it is true that a list of atheistic Jewish radicals reads like a "Who's Who" of Far Left schmucks, Godless Jews such as Karl Marx, Saul Alinsky, and George Soros are hardly representative of Judaism. In fact, a strong case can be made that they are not Jews at all. At most they are *culturally* Jewish.

The liberal leanings of America's JINOs (Jews In Name Only) is a more puzzling conundrum — are these people insane or simply suicidal masochists? In any event they are without a doubt *me-shugenah*. They had best get their heads out of their butts before they get them snapped off at the neck.

How deluded do they have to be in order to remain ignorant of the global neo-Nazism quickly forming into the Fourth Reich (call it what you will)? Even I can sense the ovens being fired up again. You would think that America's Jews would be much more sensitive to such things than I am, but from all indications they remain blissfully unaware that anything is amiss. America's Jews had best wake up and smell the roses — or rather, the Zyklon-B.

The Far Left's stock-in-trade strategy of "divide and conquer" seems to be working quite well in dividing two groups that should be supporting each other — the Jews and the Christians. Increasing numbers of Christians are becoming anti-Zionist (anti-Israel — which *ipso facto* means anti-Jewish, no matter what "smiley-face" definition you slap on it) — as are, surprisingly, an increasing number of JINOs.

In addition, the insidious Leftist drivel about Hitler being a Christian and the Pope aiding and abetting the Nazis has harmed Christianity's rep among the Jews. Just for the record, Hitler was about as devout a Christian as Attila the Hun (who, being a pagan tribal leader was left-wing all the way). He was an opportunistic, Machiavellian, power hungry sociopath who would have quoted *any* source — Christian or whatever — if he felt it would further his agenda. I suppose that the murderous Pol Pot was a devout Buddhist — or maybe he was a Christian too since he attended a Catholic school for awhile. Give me a frigging break.

As far as the Pope's purported fondness for the Nazis goes, I suggest reading "The Myth of Hitler's Pope: How Pope Pius XII Rescued Jews From The Nazis" by Rabbi David G. Dalin before coming to any knee-jerk erroneous assumptions. Pope Pius XII once said "For centuries, Jews have been unjustly treated and despised. It is time they were treated with justice and humanity. God wills it and the Church wills it. Saint Paul tells us that the Jews are our brothers. They should also be welcomed as our friends." Does that sound like something a Hitler-appeasing anti-Semite would say?

Enough with the ill-informed and divisive finger-pointing. Israel is Western civilization's outlier fortress. If it falls, make no mistake, Western civilization itself will be next.

Israel is *our* Holy Land — the birthplace of Judeo/Christian spirituality, morality, and ethics. Israel was the Jewish homeland for millennia before Islam was even dreamt of, and is the seminal birthplace of Christianity. The Middle East was largely Christian for over six centuries before someone cherry-picked through our Holy Bible, added their own unique spin called it Islam and proceeded to wipe out any Judeo/Christian "competition."

No lie people — the time is upon us. We stand united, or "we the people" will surely fall. Time to hang tough. As an American patriot said in another dangerous, dire, and daunting time in our nation's history, "If we do not hang together, we shall surely hang separately."

Laus Deo.

32

Time to Reboot America

July 17, 2011

It would not be far off the mark to say that all of my prior writing for "Canada Free Press" culminated in this article, and that everything that I have written since has been something of a post-script to it. It is, obviously, past time to reboot America – by which I mean a return to the US Constitution as the law of the land and reinstating God to His righteous place of honor in our country's psyche.

"We have now sunk to a depth at which restatement of the obvious is the first duty of intelligent men."

George Orwell, author of "1984" (1903-1950)

I originally titled this article as a query, "Time To Reboot America?" but after a little thought realized that there is no question — it is *past* time to reboot America. By "reboot" I mean that it is time for "we the people" to avail ourselves of the instructions left to us by the Founders:

"We hold these truths to be self-evident, that all men are created equal, that they are endowed by their Creator with certain unalienable Rights, that among these are Life, Liberty and the pursuit of Happiness. — That to secure these rights, Governments are instituted among Men, deriving their just powers from the consent of the governed, — That **whenever any Form of Government becomes destructive of these ends, it is the Right of the People to alter or to abolish it, and to institute new Government.... Prudence, indeed, will dictate that**

Governments long established should not be changed for light and transient causes; and accordingly all experience hath shewn that mankind are more disposed to suffer, while evils are sufferable than to right themselves by abolishing the forms to which they are accustomed. But when a long train of abuses and usurpations, pursuing invariably the same Object evinces a design to reduce them under absolute Despotism, it is their right, it is their duty, to throw off such Government, and to provide new Guards for their future security."

There we have it; there it is, those are our marching orders. It is not only our right; it is our *duty* to fight a tyrannical, despotic government that holds sway over us, no matter under what label it hides — even when that government is wearing the garb of the United States of America. That we are indeed suffering under "a long train of abuses and usurpations" is no longer in doubt; no longer to be denied; no longer to be endured.

So the question becomes "What to do?" How best to effect the overthrow of a blatantly anti-American political/social cabal — as large, powerful, and entrenched as it is?

As our Declaration of Independence notes, such an important and monumental task is not to be undertaken for "light and transient causes," nor should "we the people" commit ourselves to a foolish or impatient course of action.

About six months after Obama usurped the Presidency readers started to email me asking "what can we do — what can *I* do?" "We the people" found various ways to get involved and I stopped receiving such emails well before the November 2010 elections. The emails started up again a few months back, but with a difference — now people are wanting to know where to *attack*, *when* to attack, *how* to attack. To say that "the natives are restless" would be a gross understatement.

In the relatively short time since I started to cover the political scene during the 2008 elections, I have watched "we the people" go from confused, to dismayed, to angry, to "locked and loaded." I suspect that the only reason that American Revolution II has remained on the back burner for as long as it has is only because of a lack of leadership and direction. Walt Kelly's statement that "we have met the enemy and he is us" was never more apropos than in regards to America today. Where do you point the gun without the risk of shooting yourself in the foot?

America has been so thoroughly infiltrated and infested with traitorous elements that it has become difficult to separate the wheat from the chaff, the patriot from the traitor. Nonetheless we must move to save America (and with it freedom), and we must move with some alacrity.

All well and good, but what sort of action, and in what direction? Aye, there's the rub. For in moving against the "establishment" which is now arrayed against "we the people" we must be very careful not to fall into carrying out a scenario they have planned for us. I do not believe that we can wait until the 2012 elections to take back America, but that does not mean that I advocate a violent revolution, or taking to the streets pell-mell and directionless.

In fact, it is my sincere wish that America can be spared such a thing. I would much prefer a "Velvet Revolution" comparable to the 1988 movement that overthrew the communist regime in Czechoslovakia.

When your house is on fire because of arson, finding out who the arsonist is and why they lit the fire should not top your "To Do" list. Putting out the d—n fire should be your number one priority. Nevertheless, "putting out the fire" in this case will involve jailing some of the lead "arsonists" as part of the process.

I am talking about pointing fingers and naming names. I am talking about jail time — serious jail time. I am talking about mass movements to unseat treasonous Americans across the country. I am talking about a "house cleaning" from top to bottom; side to side. I am talking about some very serious stuff folks. Things you would not dream of doing for "light and transient causes."

Freedom itself is at stake here. Future generations will live in freedom and light or darkness and shackles depending on what "we the people" do today. We did not want this fight, but it has fallen to us to be the torch-bearers, the Minute Men, the American patriots who once more take the fight to the enemy and make them rue the day they messed with America.

Most of you already know the score, so I will not bother going over the long list of "abuses and usurpations" — which go back for decades, even though they are coming to a head just now.

(Sidebar: There is no sense in asking "why us." It is what it is. Personally, I have often wondered how I ended up writing about politics ["Why couldn't I be churning out lucrative bodice-rippers about vampire love and lust, or some such. Why *this*?"]. Not wishing at this time to go into arcane minutia regarding karma, free-will, destiny, divine providence, and the like, I'll simply repeat — it is what it is).

Which means that it is up to "we the people" to put out the fire ("Once more unto the breech, dear friends, once more"). By the term "we the people" I mean that strong backbone of America that the country has always called upon in time of dire need, and who have always responded. It includes blue and white collar workers, high school dropouts and the highly educated, farmers and businessmen, soldiers and sailors...patriots all.

Our country needs us — once again. The stakes involved are as big and the outcome as uncertain as in any situation we have ever faced — including the Civil War, and the Revolutionary War. God willing, this revolution will not be as painful and bloody as those in our past. But if it is — what of it? It is *our* watch, *our* duty, and *our* time to stand tall behind the battlements of freedom — come hell or high water.

The time has come to reboot America. The time for talk is done. We should be about the business of forming patriotic cadres, groups and movements — from the national level down to splinter cells. The Oath Keepers, US Patriots Union, and Veteran Defenders of America are examples of what I am talking about. We should do this now. Some of you have no doubt been involved in such activities for some time. Now is the time to go into full battle mode — this is no drill.

We should keep on sending emails and letters, placing phone calls, knocking on doors, saying prayers, et al. — but there needs to be a new sense of urgency about it all. We need to ratchet things up — kick out the jams, pull out the stops, throw back the throttle. We need to broaden our scope, deepen our commitment, and fire up our righteous indignation.

I understand and respect the need for secrecy some of you must work under, but there is strength in numbers, and we should be about the business of openly organizing national as well as local NGOs to fight the enemy tooth and nail. Unseat them, impeach them, disgrace them, and otherwise use every legal means at our disposal to get rid of these parasitic leeches that have infested our country. Make sure that they understand just how much they are despised and how unwelcome their traitorous, arrogant, anti-American agendas are.

It is not a major concern that the bulk of Americans are still largely clueless about what is going on. It is to be expected after decades of intentional dumbing down and a steady diet of disinformation, propaganda, and frivolous distractions via America's various venues for "news" and entertainment. We do not need their participation. They are dead weight — but they are not the enemy.

If someone is a NWO, one-world-government globalist then *they* are the enemy — you know their catch phrases and lingo by now. If someone is a Muslim Islamist bent on world conquest through blatant or stealth jihad then *they* are our enemy. I won't go through the whole list — most of you know it by now anyway.

They are the enemies of liberty and "unalienable rights." They are the enemies of freedom and choice. They are the enemies of tradition and values. They are the enemies of family and marriage. They are the enemies of truth and honor. They are the enemies of the United States of America. They are the enemies of civilization itself. They are my enemy and they are your enemy.

It may appear that the enemy is vast and formidable, and I would certainly never underestimate them, but in fact they are only a relative handful of fanatics. The sheeple who swell their ranks will be the last ones to awaken to how they have been played — but awaken they will. Many of them are simply greedy, arrogant, self-centered twits, who wouldn't know patriotism if it came up and bit them on the butt. Their mind-sets are largely dysfunctional and self-absorbed (arrogance, angst, and ennui, oh my).

The dyed-in-the-wool fanatics are much fewer in number than "we the people," and they are much less impressive when stripped of their media propaganda "loud-speakers," and their political clout. That is, after all, why they went to such pains to subvert our media and government. It is the puppet-masters behind the fanatics, behind the sheeple, behind our corrupt politicians, who are dangerous — very dangerous indeed.

Speaking of corrupt politicians; it is a naive mistake to think that just getting rid of the politicians currently in Washington DC will solve our problems. A number of America's institutions are in desperate need of an over-haul. They should be included in the "house cleaning," and it will require some time and effort to set things right. One thing at a time (or everything-all-at-once — whatever works).

Some folks mistake the police for our enemy, due mainly to a few duplicitous and corrupt bad apples among them. It is well to keep in mind that, by and large, the police are patriotic conservative men and women who are dedicated to law and order, and preserving the peace. That means that the police should not, as a whole, ever be considered the enemy. For every Sheriff Dupnik there are many more true patriots like Sheriff Mack, Sheriff Joe Arpaio, and Sheriff Paul Babeu. Beware of the exceptions, but the vast majority of the police are on our side – constrained as they may be by rules and fulfilling their jobs.

Like the US government as a whole the US military is riddled with quislings, brain-washed dupes, and traitors of various sorts who will *not* uphold their oath to defend the US Constitution — but just as with the police, it would be a grave mistake to think of our armed forces as being the enemy — they are anything but.

Granted, some of the treasonous scum currently strutting their stuff in the Pentagon would turn on "we the people" in a heartbeat, but the vast majority of the junior grade officers and the rank and file will refuse to fire upon their fellow Americans — won't you, junior grade officers and rank and file? If they are unsure, they had better make up their minds in a hurry. The moment after receiving an order that they know in their heart is wrong is not the time to join the debating society.

They need to know beforehand where their allegiance lies — with America and the US Constitution, or with mega corporations, banks, and a temporary despotic regime. They need to make up their minds now. "I will support and defend the Constitution of the United States against all enemies, foreign and domestic...." Words are cheap — integrity and valor will cost you.

Patriotic organizations such as we currently have need to step things up a notch — make that several notches. At the same time we need to take as a given that any openly patriotic movement will attract enemy infiltrators like a magnet. Also, there are bound to be enemy sources of discord and disinformation masquerading as patriotic NGOs. These should be lumped together with other elements of controlled opposition and dealt with as time and opportunity allow.

If we wish to minimize disorder and bloodshed then acting now is our last chance to avoid major chaos and violence. If we act now riots worse than the ones in the 1960s may erupt, but if we do *not* act now the results will make the riots of the late sixties look like quaint schoolyard squabbles. There is a rapidly closing window of opportunity in which we have the luxury of doing things legally and non-violently. After that window closes all bets are off. *Après cette, le déluge.*

Although "we the people" no doubt have numerous patriots in our midst that would make the eco-terrorists look like rank amateurs, if the situation deteriorates to guerrilla warfare and sabotage, then we have lost America as a country, and it will devolve into a Byzantine network of splinter factions, regions, and enclaves. If that scenario should become a reality, then we will be well and truly screwed. That eventuality must be prepared for as well. May God grant we avoid it.

Lest you think that the views expressed in this article are extreme, I suggest that you find and read some *far* right blogs and websites. In comparison, I am the voice of moderation and prudence itself. My point here is that while the liberal propaganda outlets no doubt consider the views I express here to be extreme; the truth of the matter is that *they* are the ones who are extreme — extremely to the *left*. What is essentially a rather moderate conservative view becomes skewed under their warped perception into something rabidly far right.

At worst, they can accuse us of being what — anti-*globalists*? "We the people" are certainly not anti-*American*. America is what we are fighting for. *We* are not the ones leading our country into dark ruination through arrogant stupidity, avarice, and design. We are not the one's lauding one-world-government over America — disdaining America, reviling America, destroying America. That is their job, and they excel at it.

As I close, let me say that America needs to weave God back into our national fabric. This, more than anything, is what our country sorely lacks. We have lost our moral anchor, our guiding star, and only acceptance of God and His natural law can return us to our intended course. God either exists or He does not. If He does *not* exist then nothing ultimately matters and we are left with naught but the ash heap of atheistic nihilism.

But if God *does* exist then we would have to be insane to deny His existence, or more commonly, we would need to be in secret (often a secret hidden even from ourselves) rebellion against God — refusing to acknowledge anything higher, more important, or more worthy of devotion than our own sweet selves. Such an attitude is a soul sickness, and America is sick in her soul.

It is time to reboot America. May God guide, bless, and protect us in our endeavors to keep the torch of freedom lit. "We the people" did not ask for or want this fight, but with God's grace we will d—n sure *win* this fight — for ourselves, for our children, for humanity, and for freedom.

Laus Deo.

33

Oslo and Profanity for Profane Times

July 31, 2011

This article's main focus (my use of profanity) was not written so much to defend my cussing as to explain it. I do not defend my occasional use of curse words in my articles, and I do not argue with those who find their use offensive — I respect their stance. If you find my occasional use of profanity off-putting then please feel free to not read my work — no problemo.

Normally I would avoid using profanity in my articles like the plague, but these are anything but normal times and the continuing egregious, outrageous, insane doublespeak and manipulations of the Progressives infuriates me.

As I point out in my article "we the people" have been lied to and played for suckers for a long, long time, and if that does not call for a cuss word or two then I don't know what does.

"Under certain circumstances, urgent circumstances, desperate circumstances, profanity provides a relief denied even to prayer."
Mark Twain (1835-1910)

"If you can't say f—k; you can't say 'f—k the government.'"
Lenny Bruce (1925-1966)

"I've been accused of vulgarity. I say that's bulls—t."

Mel Brooks

Before getting into the meat of this article I would like to briefly discuss the recent acts of terrorism in Oslo, Norway. No sane person, and certainly no Christian worthy of the name, could possibly condone such horrific activity.

Yet our purveyors of leftist anti-American doublethink — the media — have been quick to promote the myth that the alleged perpetrator, Anders Breivik, is a "right-wing Christian fundamentalist."

That is a lie. Breivik's manifesto has much more in common with the rants of eco-nut Ted Kaczynski than the teachings of Jesus Christ. But I will let that pass for the moment and shortly direct attention to some other whoppers that the mass media have told us. These lies, or Sorelian myths if you prefer, are sometimes given as evidence of the media's hypocrisy and double-standards. I prefer to call the media bald-faced liars – it is more to the point.

The "New York Times" headlined one of its articles about the Oslo killings: "As Horrors Emerge, Norway Charges Christian Extremist." This is the same newspaper that forgot how to spell "Islam" after the Islamist Ft. Hood murders. The pro-Islamic/anti-Christian bias in the media is palpable.

In the chapter on the Decalogue (the Ten Commandments), in his book "What We Can't Not Know," J. Budziszewski states, "Even a liar's speech expresses something true; it may not tell us the state of the world, but it tells us the state of his heart."

The state of the media's heart is rotten, corrupt, and arrogant. They have become little more than an overt fifth column for the neo-Nazi NWO. Their anti-Judeo/Christian, anti-American agenda is now clearly visible through the tattered remnants of their ludicrous facade of "journalistic integrity."

(Sidebar: Although Communists and Islamists are, of course, important players in the ongoing war against Western Civilization

(Europe is crumbling and America on its way), I would say that the overall gestalt of the NWO is shaping up to be more of a neo-Nazi version of Far Left totalitarianism than anything else).

The Left lies, and the Far Left lies incessantly, as a matter of course. I have known people like that — pathological liars — who lie when the truth would serve them just as well, if not better. They do it just to stay in practice I suppose, or simply because it has become such an ingrained habit that they cannot help themselves.

Being for the most part atheists (in practice if not in name), the Left has no spur to goad them toward honesty. Atheism's whole Byzantine house of cards ultimately rests on a nihilistic foundation of — nothing. Thin air would be an improvement — at least thin air is *some* thing; at least thin air *exists*. Atheists have no reason *not* to lie. Anything that serves the human ego is on the table, while anything that serves the Creator is anathema.

Be that as it may, following are three examples of some of the numerous lies that the media has told "we the people" – the tip of the tip of the iceberg. These lies should be kept in mind as "news" about the Oslo atrocity continues to be fed to us in the coming weeks and months.

Media Lie: Hitler was a Christian fundamentalist. This statement is sometimes coupled with the accusation that Hitler's radical Christianity was the direct cause of the Holocaust.

The Truth: Hitler despised Christianity. The only religion that Hitler had any respect for was Islam, whose totalitarian methods and messages he admired.

Media Lie: Following the Jonestown mass suicide in 1978, the media implied that Reverend Jim Jones was a right-wing Christian wacko who used religion as a means to trap people inside his insane "Death Cult" agenda. Talk of his radical Marxism was uniformly swept under the rug.

The Truth: Jim Jones was a Far Left radical who used Christianity as a front for his Marxist agenda. One of his last acts was to send money to (then) communist Russia. He was as left-wing as they get. The Far Left and death fit together like a knife and sheath — check out some history (honest history).

Media Lie: Oklahoma City bomber Timothy McVeigh was a Far Right Christian militia nut.

The Truth: Timothy McVeigh was a Far Left agnostic with ties to radical Islam (via Terry Nichols) and neo-Nazism. As faithful readers well know, I have pointed out the reasons why Fascism (and its subset Nazism) is a Far Left collectivist doctrine numerous times. That the media and clueless liberals continue to call the Nazis "right-wing" is bad enough, but that patriotic conservatives continue to do so is beyond the pale. Here is a handy mnemonic that might help: "Nazis are *left*-wing, Nazis are *left*-wing — 'Socialist Workers Party,' hello? — Nazis are *left*-wing."

To call new or old Nazis "right-wing," is such a gross distortion of the truth that I have to rein myself in before I start spouting expletives whenever I hear the term "*right*-wing Nazi" — which brings me around to profanity.

When I get upset thinking about how thoroughly, blatantly, and ceaselessly "we the people" have been, and are being, lied to by our politicians and media I start rattling off the verbal equivalent of a string of firecrackers going off (with the occasional cherry bomb thrown in). In short, I vent.

This is why writing is my forte, and not radio or TV. Did you ever see that clip of Glenn Beck going ballistic on one of his radio callers? Well, that would be me on a daily, if not an hourly, basis. As for TV interviews; one "Yeah, well f—k you too!" out of me and I doubt Chris Matthews would ever ask me back.

If I did not have the luxury of editing my writing before submitting it for publication my profanities would melt computer screens. The extemporaneous world of live radio and TV is not for the likes of me — years of working in rough trades and frequenting waterfront bars where profanity-laced language was the *lingua franca* have left their mark. Hit one of my "hot buttons" and I regress to salty language hard won, long used, and deeply embedded.

That is not to say that I cannot be shown in public, or that I do not know how to restrain my language. I can bite my tongue with the best of them, but it slows down my speech and does my rep for quick *repartee* no favors. My inner censor automatically translates a thought such as "Screw that bulls—t!" into "Gee, I strongly disagree with that." When I am very upset about something my inner censor kicks into over-drive and my speech becomes halting and slow as a result.

I watched Laura Ingraham on "The O'Reilly Factor" the other night (I know, I know, but it was suggested that I watch a repeat of the show just for the segment with Laura). Ms. Ingraham's arguments — *sans* profanities — exhibited a self-control that I found admirable, although I have my doubts about wishing to emulate her in that regard.

I realize that by using profanity I no doubt annoy and/or offend a number of readers who would otherwise enjoy my articles and that I run the risk of appearing boorish and parochial, so I use invectives judiciously, if at all. Indeed, most of my articles are profanity free.

I use profanity for emphasis, color, and to express strong disdain or anger, but if that was all I used it for I would probably dispense with it altogether as being an unwarranted distraction. The main reason why I use profanity in some of my articles is to shake my PC cage a bit — to rattle my chains as it were. I have never been a big fan of being told what to think and how to speak.

Also, profanity serves as a reminder that the stakes we are playing for are extremely high, and that fair-play, good taste, and "hail fellow well met" attitudes are at times inappropriate for the down and dirty tactics we might sometimes have to use in order to fight effectively for America's survival.

This ain't play time kiddies and it is no time to be hobbled by the niceties of cultured society — not when the destruction of Western Civilization is at hand. The enemy deals in lies, low blows, and subterfuge, and it would be nothing short of suicidal to be afraid to get our hands dirty or worry overly much about the finer points of polite discourse while a knife is pressed to our throats.

In addition to using discretion regarding when and where I use profanity, I also make use of the em dash or symbol tropes to substitute for letters, feeling confident that readers will get the drift of such statements as "@#&% Congress!" The use of em dashes and symbols allows me to get my point across while at the same time allowing me to show some respect for my reader's sensibilities.

Is profanity for everyone? Should *every* author or commentator use profanity? No, of course not, but I believe that there is a place for writers such as myself who use expletives sparingly and with a certain, dare I say, decorum.

The main point that I wish to get across here is that I don't use cuss words just for grins. I give the various pros and cons surrounding expletives a fair bit of thought before deciding whether or not to include these words in any given article — and my articles *never* use the Lord's name in vain.

If you are not infuriated by the traitorous behavior of our government "representatives," media, and courts, then either you are a traitor yourself, or have chosen to remain willfully blind, or are popping some powerful "downers," or you are one blissed-out Obi-Wan. Personally, it p—ses me off no end.

The trick is to transmute that passion into coherent, focused, cool-headed action — which does *not* include the indiscriminate killing of innocent people or other forms of terrorism. We will leave that to the Far Left and other assorted nuts.

Laus Deo

34

Tea Party Hobbits vs. Sauron and His Minions

August 3, 2011

For the Shire! I noticed the TPTB stopped comparing patriots to hobbits rather quickly — perhaps they belatedly saw the folly in handing the "hobbits" a ready-made heroic myth to identify with.

Since writing this article I have had the pleasure of reading philosopher Peter J. Kreeft's book "The Philosophy of Tolkien: The Worldview Behind 'The Lord of the Rings.'" As a great fan of LOTR for some decades now, I found Kreeft's book to be an enlightening and entertaining read. I certainly would have quoted from it freely in this article if I had read his book at the time I wrote it. Instead, permit me to add a short excerpt from Kreeft's book as a sort of pre-addendum (offset in quote marks):

"The literary establishment in England was stunned, shocked, and scandalized...when a major bookstore innocently polled English-speaking readers, asking them to choose the greatest book of the twentieth century. By a large margin "The Lord of the Rings" won.

...The critics retched and kvetched, wailed and flailed, gasped and grasped for explanations. ..."Why bother teaching them to read if they're going to read that?"

The polls revealed one important thing about "The Lord of the Rings:" that it is a classic, that is, a book loved by humanity, by human nature, wherever it is found. And they revealed one important thing about the critics: that humanity isn't found in that arrogant oligarchy of utterly-out-of-touch elitists.

And they revealed one important thing about our culture, that our culture is not egalitarian at all, in fact...it is perhaps the least egalitarian culture in the history of the world. For in what other culture has the worldview and life view of the teachers differed so radically from that of the students?"

"[Gandalf said], 'Always after a defeat and a respite, the Shadow takes another shape and grows again.' 'I wish it need not have happened in my time,' said Frodo. 'So do I,' said Gandalf, 'and so do all who live to see such times. But that is not for them to decide. All we have to decide is what to do with the time that is given us. And already, Frodo, our time is beginning to look black. The enemy is fast becoming very strong.'"

J.R.R. Tolkien (1892-1973) "The Fellowship of the Ring"

"There are other forces at work in this world...besides the will of evil."

From the LOTR film trilogy "The Fellowship of the Ring"

John McCain, Maureen Dowd, "The Wall Street Journal" (WSJ), and others have taken to referring to the Tea Party and conservative members of Congress as "hobbits" — the wee folk from the "The Lord of the Rings" trilogy (LOTR). As Brian Wesbury notes, "This is not a term of endearment. What the WSJ editors [et al.] mean is that Tea Partiers live in a 'fantasy world.'"

Not only are conservatives being called hobbits but terrorists as well. Apparently the Progressive apparatchiks fear that terrorist hobbits will bring about the end of the Nanny State's entitlement culture. We should all be so lucky.

I believe that members of the Tea Party and patriots of all persuasions should consider the hobbit appellation an *honorable* one. After all, in the LOTR trilogy it was the hobbits who were dismissed as inconsequential by the evil overlord Sauron, yet who, against all odds, ultimately defeated Sauron and overturned his villainous plans for a Middle-earth NWO. ("Sauron sucks! He can kiss my little-bitty hobbit butt — friggin' wanker!")

That last bit is entirely mine. You will look in vain to find that quote in any of the LOTR books — more's the pity. In any event, the hobbit label can and should be worn with pride. The author of LOTR, J.R.R. Tolkein, was a conservative in the best sense of the word, and his trilogy is essentially a paean to the indomitable nature of the individual human (hobbit) spirit. For all of the heroic men and women, elves, Ents, and dwarves the most important heroes of the trilogy are the hobbits Sam and Frodo. Everything hinges on *their* success or failure, on *their* bravery and tenacity.

One of the books that make the list in Benjamin Wiker's "10 Books That Every Conservative Must Read," is the LOTR (Wiker "cheats" and counts the trilogy as one book). Wiker notes that "Sauron...presents the very essence of totalitarianism: the desire to override all the real wills of real persons...and reform all that is below him into one master plan. He imposes government from the top down, crushing everything in its path as of no consequence."

Seen in this light LOTR is indeed a must read for conservatives, no doubt. I wrote an article some time back where I compared Sauron to George Soros, but Dr. Wiker has the right of it, and Sauron is representative of totalitarianism as a whole — the doctrine that crushes freedom and individuality under the boot-heel of cookie-cutter conformity and brutally enforced Draconian laws.

In Tolkien's novels the hobbits want nothing so much as to be left in peace to live out their unspectacular lives in their beloved Shire, but mighty events beyond their understanding — in fact scarce to be believed — force the hobbits Frodo, Sam, Merry, and Pippin to leave home to face great hardship and danger. In the end, it is these hobbits, especially Sam and Frodo, who save the world from the doom of Sauron's rule.

"We the people" are indeed similar to hobbits in that we love our "Shire" — America — and will fight valiantly to defend it. We are generally peaceable and friendly, but when called upon to do so we can be stalwart, indefatigable, and implacable foes. For the Shire!

Laus Deo.

35

Go Green — Natural Law

September 11, 2011

I am sometimes asked "Why do you bring God into the equation? Is it not enough that we honor the Constitution and are fiscally responsible?" No, I would say that it is not enough, not nearly enough — hopefully this article helps to clarify why.

"...the separate and equal station to which the laws of nature and of nature's God entitle them...."
"Declaration of Independence" 1776

"As Jacob said, awakening from his dream, the world, this palpable world, which we were wont to treat with the boredom and disrespect with which we habitually regard places with no sacred association for us, is in truth a holy place, and we did not know it."
Pierre Teilhard de Chardin (1881-1955) "The Divine Milieu" 1927

The Obama Administration appears to be striving for a Goth look — if the DOJ's website and Obama's use of Darth Vader's "Back in Black" tour bus is any indication.

While "Empire Black" is no doubt an apropos color scheme for the nihilistic, destructive, Fascist/Marxist *mélange* of the Obama Administration, I propose that "we the people" counter with a more eco-friendly look — a "green" look, a natural look. And what is "greener" and more natural than natural law? Surely Mother Nature would approve — not to mention God.

Why is natural law important? Because without an emphasis on natural law all fiscal and political maneuvering is simply rearranging deck-chairs on the Titanic.

As John Adams so clearly saw, for America to remain a free republic under the rule of law (i.e. the Constitution) Americans must by and large be a morally upright people: "Our Constitution was made only for a moral and religious people. It is wholly inadequate to the government of any other."

The removal of God and natural law from America's psyche is not the result of happenstance or "enlightenment" — it is the result of the atheistic Left's long-term unrelenting agenda to destroy Western civilization's Judeo/Christian roots (and hence destroy Western civilization itself). A modicum of research will show that statement is not hyperbole.

It is not enough for America to get its fiscal house in order; we must refresh, rediscover, and reinvigorate our spiritual roots as well. Without God in our lives and culture we are directionless — sans compass and rudder. Our ethics become vapid, and our morality insipid and situational — we can see the results of such spiritual anemia all around us.

What is so *natural* about natural law? Long ago, back in the days when men were men and women weren't, people used to take for granted that there was a thing called "human nature." Broadly speaking the term "human nature" refers to the idea that people are interested in themselves, first and foremost. That is, it is *natural* for us to be selfish.

Instead of delving into a discussion on the whole Malthusian/Hobbesian/Darwinian "survival of the fittest" scenario, suffice it to say that when left to our own devices we tend to be selfish SOBs. Fortunately, our Creator endowed us with an intuitive knowledge of right and wrong which, if we pay attention to it, keeps us from reverting to barbarism, and when cultivated leads us toward bettering both ourselves and society as a whole. This "intuitive knowledge" is what is known as natural law.

Natural law was a concept familiar to the ancient Greeks but it was most famously outlined and encapsulated in the Decalogue, or Ten Commandments. One could say that the Ten Commandments are not true because they are in the Bible so much as they are in the Bible because they are true. (The Decalogue should not be confused with Mosaic Law, which covers much more ground than just the Ten Commandments).

The Ten Commandments are sometimes separated into the First and Second Tablets — the First Tablet consisting of those Commandments dealing with God, and the Second Tablet referring to those Commandments dealing with human relationships. There has been an ongoing effort to keep the Second Tablet while jettisoning the First.

Perhaps the main problem with removing all reference to a Creator from the Commandments is that minus God, "shalts" become "shoulds," and "oughts" become mere suggestions. When God is taken out of the equation the Commandments no longer have any strong moral authority or gravitas and hence are weakened to the point of being ineffectual — situational integrity becomes the norm. We need *all* of the Commandments.

A sophisticated understanding of atheism shows its bleak insanity clearly, but most atheists have no idea about any of that and simply use it as a convenient crutch to help justify and rationalize their natural self-centered proclivities. A society built on such a nihilistic foundation cannot last and must collapse as the result of overwhelming hubris crushing its spindly supports.

Conservation and conservatism fit together hand in glove. The Judeo/Christian ethos tells us that "we are stewards of God's earth, ruling over that which is not ours." Despite the lies vociferously spouted by radicals using environmentalism as a front, "we the people" are the true stewards of America's natural abundance, and always have been. It is natural for us to "go green" *but* we must be careful to separate the wheat from the chaff, the false from the true.

For example, the Sorelian myth of Global Warming, the insidious effects of Agenda 21, and other purportedly eco-friendly agendas must be seen for the anti-American freedom-stealing manipulations that they are. There are plenty of legitimate worthy environmental causes "we the people" can address (such as putting an end to the dolphin killings in Taiji, Japan), without getting waylaid by duplicitous harmful nonsense.

The EPA should be the first federal department put on the chopping block in a government-reducing economy-saving belt tightening (followed quickly by the Department of Energy). That the EPA has designated carbon dioxide (one of the world's most important and life-enhancing gases) a dangerous pollutant is at best ignorant, and at worst diabolical. "We the people" need to put a stop to such harmful ideologically driven pseudo-science.

In any event, let us return natural law back to its rightful place of honor as the keystone of America's foundation – it is only natural.

Laus Deo.

36

America's Slow Turning from Freedomphobia

October 4, 2011

"We the people" have been in thrall to big government for so long that we no longer recognize freedom when we see it. "Liberty – what's that?"

"It's a slow learning — from the inside out A slow turning — but you come about"

John Hiatt "Slow Turning"

In the tradition of the left-wing's penchant for coining new words (such as "homophobia" and "Islamophobia"), I feel that "we the people" ought to have a word to describe the Progressive's fear or phobia of freedom — "freedomphobia."

The core fear of Freedomphobes (freephobes) is the dread of taking personal responsibility for *anything*. They love the "blame game" and blame anything and everyone but themselves for all of their woes — real or imagined. The more controlled and regulated their environment the better, to their thinking — makes it easier to know who and what to point their finger at. Freedom scares them.

Freedomphobes mistake licentiousness and chaos for liberty and freedom. They call indentured servitude to the government a patriotic duty (*your* duty — not theirs), and they equate *their* spending *your* money with charity and largesse. The more that their unbridled greed and corruption bother their conscience (those that have one) the more "charitable" they become with *our* money.

Freedomphobes are by their very nature unpatriotic not to mention un-American. They *fear* freedom so how could it be otherwise? They fear America's greatness, promise, and freedom hence they seek to tear down and belittle America however, and whenever, they can.

Freephobes hate freedom. They want to rein it in, trample on it, and destroy it — all while singing its praises with studied hypocrisy (the better to lure the unwary into their freedom-destroying web). They look down their noses at the "we the people," while comfortably ensconced in lucrative taxpayer-funded jobs (government), cushy NGOs (foundations), or other *intelligentsia* approved vocations (e.g. law, media, teaching, etc.).

Freedomphobes come in all stripes and persuasions — both Democrat and Republican. Unfortunately, much of the Republican ruling-class is as thoroughly freedomphobic as their Democratic counterparts and must be systematically deloused from our political system as well. They both want to smother "we the people" under a mountain of rules and regulations designed to eradicate freedom and replace it with socially engineered servitude.

At this point it is worth spending a moment to address a particular conundrum — I'm speaking of left-wing "anarchists." How can a nanny-state-loving freedomphobe be *against* big government? The answer is, they cannot. The "anarchists" currently protesting Wall Street are a cynical canard.

Unlike true anarchists of the extreme right, the left-wing *faux*-anarchists are not against governments *per se;* they merely wish to replace limited government with a monolithic nanny state of one sort or another. Mega-wealthy freephobe parasites such as George Soros fund much of their activities (granted, calling a freephobe a parasite it somewhat redundant — *à la* "freeloading freephobes" — or if you'll permit me to run the alliteration into the ground, "frigging freeloading freephobes"). To get back to the core theme of this article, how did freedomphobia take root so perniciously in a freedom-loving country like America?

The short answer is through the stealthy long-term spread of secularism, political correctness, polymorphous perversity, relativism, and various Marxist/Fascist teachings — aided and abetted by a leftist media, and an American populace that was largely asleep at the wheel.

As far as the "asleep at the wheel" thing goes, I stand guilty as charged. Like millions of Americans I was blissfully unaware that the federal government had turned into Frankenstein's monster and was about to run amok in the village.

It was not until a couple of months into Obama's term as POTUS that faint alarm bells started going off in the distance — soon to be replaced by a deafening foghorn next to my head — WAKE UP! Like many of you, I started to research into what was going on, and thought to myself "Holy-moly, things are *way* worse than I realized" (my thinking comes out grammatically unedited).

"Way worse" indeed — and things rapidly got uglier and/or my appreciation for how bad things were rapidly grew. The unrelenting litany of bad news, shocking discoveries, and disheartening revelations was (is) depressing, to say the least. But it is what it is, and it is best to know the truth come what may.

After all, "we the people" need to know what we are up against if we are to have any chance of retaking America from the freedomphobes who have cleverly used their social-engineering ploys to steal our freedoms, one by one.

Any freephobe is *ipso facto* an enemy of freedom and America. They are a traitor to their country and a pox on mankind. They are morally stunted, spiritually barren, and shamelessly self-centered and avaricious — and that is some of their less distasteful qualities.

As I hope I made clear in my article "Time to Reboot America," I consider revolution to be the only viable solution to our current predicament — peaceful if possible, otherwise if not.

Like Jesus in the Temple we will need to go through Congress as an avenging angel. The anti-American freedomphobes must be eliminated from our government, churches, courts, and schools. The New Media outlets of truth must replace the Old Media propaganda outlets, and the regressive Progressives, Socialists, Communists, Fascists, and their ilk shown the door.

The Fed and FFB (Federal Financing Bank) must be disciplined and the unholy collusion between big government and big business squashed. The players gaming the system by switching back and forth between Wall Street and Washington should start serving time instead of serving themselves. The Department of Education, Department of Energy, and EPA should be abolished, or at least greatly reduced in size. The spurious "science" behind global warming must be exposed for the fraud that it is. Agenda 21 must be jettisoned *post haste*. The insidious spread of FTZs (Foreign Trade Zones) must be stopped, and then dissolved. Insane radical environmental regulations must be abolished and real conservation take their place. And on and on it goes — so much to do and so little time.

Most importantly, "we the people" must see to it that God, the Constitution, and natural law are restored to their proper places of honor in our society and culture. The days of no accountability, *carte blanche* morality, and glorified decadence must come to an end.

On a positive note, It has been extremely heartening to see the rapid growth of the New Media (the quality of which keeps improving by leaps and bounds) and the amazing number of ways that freedom-loving patriots ("we the people") have found to defend America and start taking it back.

I am sure that for those who have been awake to America's peril for decades, the change in direction "we the people" are taking must seem like a molasses-slow turn, but considering that most of us were still asleep three years ago, we have become pretty darn savvy in such a relatively short time.

At long last the tide is turning against the freedomphobes, and back toward the freedom-lovers. Victory or death.

Laus Deo.

37

The Mob, We the People, and Arrogant Aristocrats

October 10, 2011

It took me some time to finally remove the blinders placed on us by the MSM and Progressives from both political parties, but once I had removed them it became very clear that that they were doing nothing but protecting their places at the food trough and the people be damned.

"You and I are told we must choose between a left or right, but I suggest there is no such thing as a left or right. There is only an up or down — up to man's age-old dream of the maximum of individual freedom consistent with order, or down to the ant heap of totalitarianism."

Ronald Reagan (1911-2004)

Following in the asinine tradition of the liberal credo "you must *spend* in order to *save*," the US government has been *selling* people guns in order to stop people from *buying* guns. Operation Fast and Furious (one of the more jaw-droppingly insane gambits undertaken by the Obama Regime) was a devious ploy designed to take away our right to bear arms by blaming gun stores and gun owners for an influx of weapons funneled to the drug cartels in Mexico by the US government. RIP Brian Terry and 200-plus Mexicans (and counting).

The media (well, CBS) has by some strange fluke actually been covering this newsworthy story that throws the Obama Administration into a bad light. Sharyl Attkisson, a CBS journalist (*mirabile dictu,* doing *real* journalism) was recently yelled at by some high level government staffers for her tenacious investigation of Operation Fast and Furious. According to a report by Fox News "Judging from the White House's reaction to her investigation, it seems officials there know they are in deep, hot water."

Imagine that — the Obama Regime being concerned about what the ignorant masses think — who'd have thought? But this article's main concern is not with nefarious attempts to take away our 2nd Amendment right — I merely wanted to give "Holder's Noose" some air-time. What I mainly wish to discuss here is the difference between the liberal mob, "we the people," and America's "aristocrats."

Ann Coulter in her book "Demonic" painstakingly describes the mob mentality that fuels the left-wing's behavior — a mentality that is sometimes menacing, often irrational, and always self-righteous. In what must be considered a serendipitous turn of events for book sales, Coulter no sooner published her book on the Left's mob mentality then they furnished her with live demos, as if on cue — first in Wisconsin, and then with the OWS crowds.

Be that as it may, if you have been doing your homework you now know that the left-wing mob pretty much owns the store when it comes to hate, violence, and bigotry: Nazis, KKK, Black Panther Party, Killing Fields, Concentration camps, Gulags, et al. — they *all* have their roots in the Far Left.

So now that "we the people" know who *really* lays and hatches these eggs of poison we can just put all of the eggs into one basket and *watch that basket* — right? Well not quite, there is still at least one other element that "we the people" need to keep an eye on — the "aristocrats."

Coulter does an admirable job of describing the left-wing mob during the French Revolution. But as well researched as "Demonic" is, there is one factor that is conspicuously absent from the book — i.e. a discussion of the nobility, the aristocracy, the Right.

Our use of the terms "Left" and "Right" originated in the days of the French Revolution "when members of the National Assembly divided into supporters of the king to the president's right and supporters of the revolution to his left."

While it is indisputably true that the French left-wing was responsible for horrific bloodshed and terror, it would be a grave mistake to think that the right-wing was free of faults. There would have *been* no French Revolution had the French aristocracy not largely been arrogant a—holes. They were certainly, by and large, no friend to the people.

The reason I bring this up is because it would be dangerous for us to assume that just because someone opposes the Far Left it automatically means that they are on the side of the angels. America has its ruling class, its "aristocracy," and they are interested in acquiring and keeping power, not in protecting the rights of "we the people." They come in a right-wing version as well as a left, and "we the people" had best take them into account.

In order to join the aristocracy you must above all things be a conformist. As S. T. Karnick noted in his article "The Productive Class and the American Aristocracy," "the ruling class is by no means a meritocracy. On the contrary, what is required is conformity, and it is enforced without pity."

The subject deserves its own article so I'll not pursue it here, but simply say that it is important that we start recognizing some of the differences between, for example, a true constitutional conservative, a *faux* conservative, a reactionary, and an "aristocrat." True conservatism is always moving forward, evolving, improving — there is nothing reactionary in it, and most certainly there is nothing aristocratic about it.

As Ronald Reagan knew, in truth the political spectrum is really more of an Up versus Down, than a Left versus Right. Down toward tyranny, greed, violence, contraction, despair, stagnation, and Godlessness; or Up toward freedom, peace, logic, expansion, spirituality, hope, and God. Time to get active — to paraphrase Hillel "If not me who, if not now when?"

Laus Deo.

38

Breaking Apart the United States

November 17, 2011

I, of course, pray that America does not split apart, but nonetheless I believe that it would be wise to have plans in place so that if the bottom should fall out of things a new republic can quickly arise from the ashes.

"The truth is that there is no compromise possible between Liberty and Tyranny. We have irreconcilable differences with the Progressives, and every attempt to compromise with them, always results in an incremental loss of our Liberty, not to mention our income. Perhaps it is time for a divorce."

Dave Hunter "Why Live in a Salad Bowl"

A little over two years ago I wrote an article in which I discussed the idea of letting the liberal elements in America go their way and conservatives go theirs. At the time I felt that it was not a good idea and that maintaining the union was the best way to go, all things considered.

Recently Dave Hunter sent me an article that he wrote on the topic, and after considering his proposals I found myself thinking "You know, this may be the way to go after all — sort of a Red-state/Blue-state separation — an amicable separation, instead of a civil war."

It is no news that the United States of America is a parody of the free republic that it was designed to be. Our Godless, rudderless Ship of

State has morphed into a ship of fools, mismanaged by a glib crew of brigands and cut-throats – barbarians in three-piece suits. American culture is a moral wasteland that has exchanged restraint and virtue for gluttony and greed.

The infiltration, infestation, and indoctrination of America's culture by elements inimical to decency, truth, and honor, has been going on for so long that a sizable percentage of the American public is, in effect, treasonous. I do not consider them to be my fellow countrymen or women.

I find listening to them a "fingernails across the chalkboard" experience and would just as soon live on a different planet, let alone in a different country. Compare the typical OWS mob to the people found at your average Tea Party rally and you will have an idea of the sort of ideological divide that I am talking about.

I cannot begin to tell you how sick I am of the duplicity, phoniness, greed, and incessant whining of the liberal element in America. I am more and more tempted every day to simply say "Fine — you can have *your* country to run, and we'll have *ours.*"

As the model of what such a liberal utopia might look like, what better place to pick than a place where the liberals have held the reins of power for decades, where the unions are king; and where multiculturalism is the law of the land. America has such a place — Detroit, Michigan. I suggest that you check into the housing market in Detroit; check out the crime rate, drug use, corruption, graft, and all around general destruction of that once fine city.

What the liberals have done to Detroit they do most everywhere that they go. The *only* reason that each and every liberal enclave has not imploded under the weight of liberal stupidity, greed, and cupidity is the constant influx of revenue from the more conservative and responsible (and yes, honest) citizens in America. These responsible citizens are not deemed forthright and upstanding by the liberals, they are considered fly-over-country rubes and suckers — chumps to be alternately stroked, flattered, used, and discarded as the situation warrants.

As I have mentioned before in my articles, either God exists or God does not exist. There is no half-way — God does not *sort of* exist," or sort of *not* exist. This being the case, *someone* is very, very far off track and deluded to the point of mental derangement. I should mention that the vast majority of atheists are liberal.

Seeing as how atheists are the ones who overwhelmingly tend to embrace such concepts and "realities" as relativism, chaos, nihilism, narcissism, polymorphous perversity, and moral ambiguity there will be no awards given for correctly guessing who the deranged ones are here. I do not honestly know if I have the stomach for any more "up close and personal" dealings with lunatic liberals anymore (there is no lunatic *"fringe"* — *all* liberals are deluded to one degree or another). Perhaps, as Dave Hunter says, a "divorce" would be best.

The patriots in the Revolutionary War at least had an ocean separating them from the main force of their enemy. "We the people" have no such luxury — our enemies are firmly entrenched among us and they will not miraculously become freed from their anti-American globalism and other liberal notions as the result of a conservative win in 2012 — should we be blessed with such an event.

The times call for bold and innovative reforms — thinking outside of the box. The threats and troubles facing "we the people" are so dangerous, so numerous, and so multi-directional that *radical* conceptualizing must be the order of the day. (Speaking of thinking outside of the box, parts of Canada might be interested in joining such a new republic — "we the people" could actually end up with more land mass than we started with).

Some folks may say, wouldn't it be less stressful to work within the system to change America? Not necessarily. In addition to a mass media, educational, and legal system that will need a massive attitude adjustment, there are any number of dug-in government bureaucrats, union leaders, and inside players who will fight tooth and nail to protect their various "kingdoms" and meal tickets. There are ideological zealots and indoctrinated crazies who will throw all manner of wrenches into the works and an army of establishment "legal eagles" who will practice unceasing lawfare against any attempted changes being made to the status quo.

James Francis Byrnes (1882-1972) knew a thing or two about power — he served as both a Representative and as a Senator in the US Congress, and was also an Associate Supreme Court Justice, the Secretary of State, and Governor of South Carolina. As one who knew the lure and attraction of temporal power well, his words regarding the subject carry substantial weight: "Power intoxicates men. It is *never* voluntarily surrendered. *It must be taken from them.*" (Italics added)

All things considered, it might be more practical and less cataclysmic to separate America into liberal and conservative regions, than to attempt to fix a perhaps irreparably broken system. Of course conservatives, who comprise a substantial majority of the population, would receive the vast bulk of the land in such an arrangement. The details and particulars of the separation (referendums, etc.) can be worked out as the process moves along — but if such an undertaking is to be implemented it should be undertaken soon. Time is not on our side.

Separating from a tyrannical US government is in truth no more radical than what the colonial revolutionaries did when they separated from the British government. Remember they too had an enemy firmly entrenched in their country — Tories and British soldiers. They, also had a populace that contained a sizable element that was clueless and/or apathetic to what was going on around them. I am not talking about covering totally new ground here. This sort of thing has happened before — right here in the good ol' US of A.

Of course there would be a plethora of problems surrounding a venture as drastic as cutting loose from Washington DC — but think of the benefits! We could tell the liberals "Here — here is your own area — call it a state, a country, a utopia — call it what you will. You can pay OPEC as much as you want for their oil. Oh that's right, you *hate* fossil fuels. Your Muslim buddies will not like that I suspect."

"Heck, who cares, the thing is you can let in as many illegal foreigners as you want; invite *all* of Mexico to come if you like – Chinese,

Muslims, whatever. The more the merrier I say. You can go back to nature and bang on drums to your heart's content. You can f—k your dog and marry a goat — it will be polymorphous bliss. You really should *go* — go *now*. Oh and leave any guns you might have with us – you will not have a need for such things anymore of course. Ta ta."

"We the people" on the other hand will set up a free republic under God that will promote personal freedom and free enterprise — capitalism will be respected and encouraged. Energy independence will be a given, with new forms of energy welcomed as they become practical. The environment will be conserved in a responsible manner, but humanity, not animals, will be the stewards of nature. Rules of law will be cut back, but the laws that remain will be honored — the Decalogue, or Ten Commandments, will hold pride of place.

We have the blueprints for such an undertaking — the Declaration of Independence, US Constitution, and Bill of Rights — as I said before, this is not exactly untrodden ground. The Founding Framers did it before us, and with God's grace we can do it again.

One thing that any new republic will have a special need for, however, is a well defended border. In short order people from the new liberal utopias will be clamoring at the gates for entrance — sure as the sun rises in the morning.

After mulling over the idea of separating America into conservative and liberal areas, what do I think? To be honest I don't know. Although I would not (yet) call myself a proponent of dividing up and remaking the United States, I no longer dismiss the notion out of hand. I'm thinking about it — seriously.

Laus Deo.

39

Salute Her While She Sinks

December 8, 2011

It is a good thing that I did hold off on writing this article or my words would have made Lenny Bruce blush. I neglected to mention that while the Holy Bible was considered to be politically incorrect, improper, and unwelcome at the Walter Reed hospital, the Islamic holy book, the Qur'an, was apparently deemed worthy of admittance — nary a peep about banning that book from the hospital.

"College professors have felt the heat of this repressive new order; researchers and scientists have encountered its ire; ministers have found themselves muzzled; teachers have been intimidated; employees have lost their jobs; even parents have been told that they cannot exercise their rights. Queer has become something to fear, and gay is beginning to rule the day."

> Dr. Michael L. Brown "A Queer Thing Happened to America"
> (from the chapter "Big Brother is Watching, and He Really is Gay")

I started to write an article about the banning of Bibles at the Walter Reed ("Wally World") military hospital the other day, but I was concerned that it would end up sounding like an off-the-leash rant by the late comedian Sam Kinison. Although righteous anger is certainly apropos given the nature of the insult, clear-eyed resolve will be more effective in the long run. (Note: the "old" Walter Reed has moved shop, and is now known as Walter Reed at Bethesda).

The news about the banning of the Bible at Walter Reed followed closely on the heels of the announcement that the US Senate had voted to repeal the ban on sodomy and bestiality in the US military.

Which left me to wonder exactly how traitorous *is* the US military High Command these days — are *most* of them quislings or is it still a minority? It is no secret that many of our bravest and best fighting men and women have left the service in frustration and disgust. What have they left behind — *who* have they left behind? Bureaucratic paper pushers, or something more sinister and dangerous? What kind of patriot warriors are our military academies turning out these days? Who is running the show, and what *sort* of show is it?

I recently had reason to send someone a copy of an old article of mine in which I wrote "when you're sworn to defend your country, and you see your country sliding down the tubes, what're you supposed to do — salute while it sinks?" The person that I sent the article to (a former Army SF operative) wrote back that he was afraid that the US military was indeed doing *exactly* that — saluting while America sinks. Nice send-off at least, right troops? I would say that "Taps" would be apropos.

As they are symbolic of the type of "heroes" we have leading our military these days let me briefly discuss two individuals: First, Gen. George Casey who was the Army Chief of Staff at the time of the Ft. Hood shootings, and was more concerned about the safety of *political correctness* than the safety of his *people*. You perhaps recall his words at the time: "As horrific as this tragedy was, if our diversity becomes a *casualty*, I think that's worse." That's *worse*.

First of all, it was not simply a tragedy. It was a vicious terrorist attack by a Muslim extremist who murdered 14 defenseless people in cold blood (if you count Francheska Velez's unborn child, as we should), and shot 30 others. The Muslim, Maj. Nidal Hasan, had no legitimate reason to be in the US Army after he had exhibited a plethora of warning signs indicating his disturbed mental state prior to the shooting — signs that were ignored because of the asinine politically correct rules instituted by morons like Casey in the first place. Second-ly, abstract doctrines like "diversity" do not become casualties — *people* do.

Casey can take his diversity and shove it where the sun doesn't shine. The US military needs *leaders* not arrogant idiots who do not know the difference between protecting the troops and politically correct butt-kissing.

Next let us turn to Adm. Mike Mullen, who as chairman of the Joint Chiefs of Staff was a driving force behind arm-twisting the US military into embracing homosexuality. He must have been positively ecstatic when the Senate repealed the ban on butt f—king, and screwing animals

Actually, forget Mullen, let's discuss homosexuality itself. Let me say up front that while some people might think that I hate homosexu-als that simply is not the case. I take people as they come, and if they are decent and respectful to me I generally treat them the same — the exception being people that I know are vile scumbags behind a veneer of polite sophistication. I do not hate homosexuals, but I detest having our military and culture force-fed homosexual behavior as being on a par with heterosexual behavior— it is not.

Rather than explain how unhealthy and life-shortening the homo-sexual lifestyle is, or how socially destructive it is, or going into how it has been slyly inserted into the American culture (talk about stealth jihad), I would like to take this opportunity to focus on two important issues — one I have written about before and the other I have not.

The first topic I'll discuss (the one I have written about previously) is the importance of being aware that the majority of homosexuals do not normally act gay — by which I mean *effeminate*. The "stealth jihad" waged by the militant homosexual clique has promoted the falsehood that homosexuals are by and large unmanly — such is not the case, not at all. Most homosexuals are, if anything *hyper*-masculine.

You would be making a grave mistake to remain unaware of the machismo and arrogant attitude at the core of many of the militant homosexuals. Far from being effeminate, soft, or weak; they are often arrogant, strong, and ruthless.

There are any number of homosexuals who would laugh at the idea of backing away from a fight — they would just as soon "tear your head off and s—t in the hole." An example would be the late Ernest Röhm, the scar-faced thug in charge of Hitler's brown shirts (although it is well to keep in mind that a number of militant homosexuals would consider such a man to be a déclassé Neanderthal).

So I would never accuse homosexuals as a whole of lacking strength, stamina, courage, or any of the other qualities one might look for in a military operative. They can and have served honorably in the past, and no doubt will in the future. My problem — and it is a *big* one — is with the military being forced to swallow the lie that homosexuality is essentially no different from heterosexuality and that embracing it will not hamper the military's effectiveness at all. Oh really? I would love to discuss the topic at length but it would unfortunately lead us too far afield at present — some other time, with pleasure.

There are a number of very serious issues that arise from such misguided, short-sighted, and ultimately destructive missteps by the Pentagon and Congress. A couple of the more obvious pitfalls were mentioned above. The mental and emotional quirks alone would fill volumes (it is not by happenstance that one of the first professional areas to be targeted, infiltrated, and subverted by militant homosexuals was the mental-health field). Due diligence was not performed before DADT (Don't Ask Don't Tell) was repealed during the lame-duck session of the 111th Congress — or if it was performed it was suppressed.

This leads me to the second topic that I wish to focus on: the minority within the minority — pedophiles and pederasts. A pederast is of course an adult homosexual who preys on young boys (a "chicken-hawk"), and pedophilia is an umbrella term that can signify sexual exploitation of either young boys or girls.

These practices are some of the few taboos left in our society, but their illegality and social stigma have been under long-term attack by their proponents. Thanks to homosexual/liberal icons such as John Maynard Keynes and Dr. Alfred Kinsey, America now has abominations like the pederasty at Penn State and the recent revelations about pandemic pedophilia in Hollyweird.

Why do I bring this up? It is not because in any way I accuse the homosexual community as a whole of practicing pederasty and/or pedophilia — they do not, and I do not wish to imply that they do. There is, however, a significant minority who *do* practice and promote pederasty and pedophilia (there is some confusion on the terminology here because homosexual pederasts are often classified as pedophiles), and this vile bunch has power and influence *way* out of proportion to their numbers. They have for many years (centuries in some cases) made it their business to infiltrate and take over positions of power and authority.

This powerful and influential cabal of perverts is at the heart of the subtle, slow, steady seduction of America's culture. You had better believe that there are some powerful "movers and shakers" involved. The "if it feels good do it" philosophy of polymorphous perversity is essentially a codification of the homosexual lifestyle, whose acceptance by American culture accelerated greatly under the auspices of child abuser Dr. Alfred Kinsey.

Where does such depravity end? It does not — there *is* no end to the debauched chaos of polymorphous perversity. There *is* no bottom to that particular pit. The perverted movers and shakers who saw to it that the US Senate repealed the ban on bestiality are the same ones who saw to it that DADT was repealed and who applaud the "strange beauty" of the movie "Zoo," which depicts the true story of a man in Oregon who was f—ked to death by a horse in 2005. Kenneth Turan of the "LA Times" called the movie "Elegantly made and eerily lyrical." Sure it is. (That is not to imply *any*thing about Mr. Turan. He may a man among men and the salt of the earth as far as I know — I know nothing about him).

It is nice to know that the US Senate gave such a big thumbs up to endorsing similar behavior for our men and women in uniform. Is this a great country or what? And we wonder why much of the Muslim world sees America as a degenerate, depraved and corrupt cesspool. It is a win/win situation for Far Left atheists — they destroy America's moral standards and then turn to their Islamist buddies and whisper "Look, look how bad America is."

Speaking of Far Left atheists; while researching the many troubles America faces and the history behind them, I came to the conclusion some time ago that the militant homosexual agenda and the Far Left agenda are virtually identical. (Again, I am not speaking of homosexuals as a whole, but the relatively small subset that is behind much of the cultural chaos we see around us. I am discussing a very specific *type* of homosexual — not homosexuals in general).

I have no time to do justice to the topic here and I hope that the reader will do some investigating of their own. I should underline the fact that I have been dealing with a general "rule of thumb" and that there are, of course, exceptions to the rule. In addition, it is of some importance to take note of the fact that the ranks of the militant homosexual pederasts are swelled by heterosexuals and bisexuals who have taken the same polymorphously perverse lifestyle to heart, and there are also those who are neither pedophiles, nor pederasts, nor polymorphously perverse but who simply share common interests in other areas. In any event, I would like to write a few words about atheism and homosexuality before closing.

The authors of "The Pink Swastika" believe that Hitler's genocide against the Jews was in large part fueled by his distaste for, and disgust with, the Judeo/Christian ethos. According to the authors, Hitler's animosity toward the Judeo/Christian tradition traces its roots to the Bible's condemnation of homosexuality. Before you scoff, read the book with an open mind, and I believe you will see that they make a good case for their hypothesis.

By the by, being the well read and knowledgeable reader that you are, you are no doubt aware by now that the Nazis were (are) a Far *Left* phenomena and not a *right*-wing outfit. That opens a whole other avenue to explore that unfortunately we will have to leave for another day.

If you can see your way past all of the leftist nonsense about Hitler being a staunch Christian (bulls—t), then the atheist/pagan/occult nature of Nazism becomes quite evident (you might want to throw in a strong dash of ancient Hellenic homosexuality as well). The militant homosexual subset that I have been discussing follows much the same formula as the Far Left Nazis of WW II did. In short, they despise the Judeo/Christian tradition and have been working with a will to suppress it and drive it out of America's culture — quite successfully I might add.

Although the *type* of homosexual that I have been discussing (arrogant, vain, predatory) infests our government and military from the lowest levels to the highest, they are probably not America's chief problem at this time — but they *are* a problem, and a *big* one. It is because of men like them (and the collusion of like-minded women) that the Senate repealed the ban on sodomy and bestiality in the armed forces. It is because of men like them and the insidious poison they have spread that things like the banning of Bibles at Walter Reed happen.

So what can "we the people" do — anything? I suggested to a friend the other day that we should turn the pitiless searchlight of Critical Theory upon them. Shine its bright glare upon the demented Marxist/Fascist drivel that they peddle and see how long *their* vaunted ideologies stand up to the remorseless pick, pick, picking of constant fault finding. My friend replied that he felt that would be beneath us and bring us down to *their* level.

I answered that "we the people" *used* to understand that sometimes it is necessary to fight fire with fire — not because we wish to; not because we *want* to, but simply because we *must*.

Allowing that which is good, decent, virtuous, and holy to be trampled into the mud is not *Christian*; it is not *civilized*, and by God it is not *American*. It is ignorance, sloth, and cowardice dressed up to look like something admirable. When push comes to shove sometimes the only thing that will beat back evil is *physical* resistance, and your life becomes forfeit for a cause more important than *you*. Liberty was once such a cause in America.

From what I have seen of the Pentagon these days let me say that after refusing to honor their oath to defend the Constitution; choosing to ignore America *in extremis*, and turning their backs on Lady Liberty as she is scuttled — the *least* they can do is salute her while she sinks.

Laus Deo.

40

Ron Paul in a Landslide?

December 16, 2011

After I wrote this article I did look into what Dr. Paul has to say about various issues — sans the MSM filter — and I found that I liked what he had to say for the most part — liked it a lot. He is perhaps the last true statesman (as opposed to politician) that America has. The lies, smears, and disinformation surrounding the man are a wonder to behold.

(I should underline the fact that my support for Ron Paul is a personal choice and is in no way meant to imply an endorsement of him by "Canada Free Press").

Before anyone gets their knickers in a knot, let me hasten to say that the headline for this article is in reference to a "USA Today" poll that I took recently — and yes, Ron Paul did indeed win *my* poll in a landslide. The results took me by surprise.

The online poll weighed your answers to various questions against the answers given by the different 2012 Presidential candidates and tabulated the results. The results of my poll looked something like this:

1. Paul (just under 70% agreement)
2. Bachmann (just under 50%)
3. Gingrich (just under 49%)
4, 5, and 6. Santorum, Perry, Huntsman — in that order (all close - around 45%)

7. Romney

8. Obama

As you can see Ron Paul did not win my poll in a "squeaker" — he won it walking away. This left me to wonder if I should take a more in-depth look at the Ron Paul candidacy – nay-saying pundits notwithstanding.

I will do just that. I will perform due diligence checking out Ron Paul's credentials. Up front I can say that there has been one thing especially that has bothered me about Paul, and that is his strict Libertarian stance regarding religion — but I may come to terms with that depending on what a more substantial analysis of his views comes up with. After cursory research it appears that Paul opposes any *national* policy regarding God — pro or con — simply because he believes that such questions are best left up to the individual states to decide.

Personally, I can live with his position on that for the time being, if it means that the many other issues crying out to be addressed will be taken care of — and Paul seems like he may just be the one to take care of a number of them.

Regarding downsizing the federal government and with it our mind-boggling debt, Ron Paul has a long track record of being just what the doctor ordered. He has been warning us about the dangers of a bloated government, the Federal Reserve, lobbyists and banksters for years.

As far as the other candidates go I do not have much to say at this point — except that I am disgusted with the blatant manner in which TPTB are trying to force conservatives to "choose" between Romney and Gingrich. It is not that I especially dislike either one, but I do not see either of them as representing the radical change that America so desperately needs at this point in time.

In addition, Mitt Romney has this little matter of his standing as a Natural Born Citizen (NBC) as required by Article II, Section I of the US Constitution. Through either ignorance or cupidity the media and most political hacks have ignored the fact that Romney may well be ineligible to run for POTUS (or VP for that matter).

First McCain and now Romney — if I did not know any better I would think that the political elites were purposefully muddying the waters by presenting us with candidates to run against Obama who have suspect NBC credentials.

If not being Natural Born disqualifies Obama from being POTUS ("Once a Brit, never legit") then "what's good for the goose is good for the gander" and I'm afraid that Romney's eligibility must be examined as well. To hear the political pundits tell it, heck darn near *anybody* can run for POTUS. The pundits are wrong though.

"We the people" need at least one state to have the *cojones* to stand up to the establishment and declare Obama ineligible to run for POTUS in 2012. New Hampshire recently failed to uphold its laws in this regard; next up in the batter's box is Georgia. Those who oppose knowing the truth about Obama's eligibility, those who mock and chase after birthers — the afterbirthers — can mock and ridicule all they want but the truth will out.

Obama — the Campaigner in Chief — is not a Natural Born citizen as the US Constitution requires the POTUS to be. According to what little we "know" about him Obama *is* a US citizen (barring his having been adopted by Lolo Soetoro), and even a *native born* citizen (born on US soil with at least one parent American), but as his father was a British subject at the time of Obama's birth he *cannot* be a Natural Born citizen (born on American soil to *two* US citizens). The subject has been covered well, and in depth *ad nauseum*, so I will not discuss it any more just now. Suffice it to say that Obama is not eligible to be POTUS, and everyone knows it but the clueless afterbirthers.

Be that as it may, for all of my talk about the 2012 elections I have serious doubts about whether free elections will be held at all. The fact that Draconian laws recently breezed through Congress; that Homeland Security feels that *patriots* are the *real* threat to America, and that the current administration cannot bring itself to put the words "Islam" and "terrorist" together leads me to believe that things are looking very grim indeed for freedom in America these days.

Have I decided which candidate I would like to see receive the Republican nomination? No I have not, but due to the results of my "USA Today" poll I will certainly be taking Ron Paul more seriously. Granted at first blush his image is not all that "presidential," and perhaps he doesn't send thrills up your leg, but we have seen what getting suckered into buying a stylishly packaged, hip, slick, and cool candidate got us the last go-round.

There are Republican candidates that I like, and some that I am not so fond of, but I would take *any* of them over Obama. May we be so blessed as to have a chance to vote for them next November.

Laus Deo.

About the Author

Jim O'Neill was born June 4, 1951 in Philadelphia, Pennsylvania. He served in the US Navy from 1970-1974 in both UDT-21 (Underwater Demolition Team) and SEAL-2. He worked as a commercial diver in the waters off of Scotland, India, and the United States. While attending the University of South Florida as a journalism student in 1998 he was presented with the "Carol Burnett/University of Hawaii AEJMC Research in Journalism Ethics Award," undergraduate division. (An annual contest set up by Carol Burnett with money she won from successfully suing a national newspaper for libel). He has earned US Army, US Navy, South African, and Russian jump wings, and is a member of Mensa and lifetime member the UDT/SEAL Association.